GROWING CH AND EMOTIO

Growing Children's Social and Emotional Skills examines how parent–educator partnerships can be achieved to enhance the development of children's social and emotional skills.

The book presents the TOGETHER programme, a training programme that emphasises the importance of the relationship between caregivers and teachers with the children in their care, as well as deepening the collaborative partnerships between teachers, educators and caregivers. Using a case study approach, the book explores the application of the TOGETHER programme across various home and early childhood education contexts through the unique voices of those involved.

The TOGETHER programme presented in this book is:

- Easy to implement and adaptable, requiring minimal training time for parents, teachers and educators
- Designed to emphasise the importance of relationships in developing children's social and emotional skills
- Supported by photocopiable resources and a downloadable e-manual that can be used to implement the training

With the vision to empower caregivers to take an active role in building children's social and emotional competence, this book is written in a way that will appeal to academic researchers and tertiary students, early childhood educators and other caregivers. It will assist in recognising children's strengths and deepening collaborative partnerships between families, educators and other caregivers.

Joanna Grace Phillips holds a PhD from Swinburne University of Technology and is a registered early childhood teacher. Joanna has extensive experience as an early childhood teacher and early intervention and behaviour specialist, and has taught for several years in the university setting. Joanna has been a contributor to chapters in three books published with Routledge: *Early Childhood Education and Care in the 21st Century*, Vol I (2018), Vol II (2019), Vol III (2020).

Sivanes Phillipson is Dean International and Professor of Education at Swinburne University of Technology. She is the Routledge Editor for the Evolving Families Series, which focuses on issues, challenges and empirical best practices surrounding evolving families that impact upon their survival, development and outcomes. Sivanes has over 100 publications to her name including books, peer-reviewed papers and book chapters. She has written eight published books focusing on teacher education and parent engagement with the latest four books published with Routledge. The latest books are *Early Childhood Education and Care in the 21st Century*, Vol I (2018), Vol II (2019), Vol III (2020), with the newest being *The Power of Expert Teaching: Lessons for Modern Education* (2020).

Gaye Tyler-Merrick is a Senior Lecturer at Nottingham Trent University, where she leads the National Award for Special Educational Needs Co-Ordination. Gaye has worked in all sectors of education. She initially trained as a kindergarten teacher and then specialized in special education. She worked as a Resource Teacher: Learning and Behaviour in primary and secondary schools before moving to tertiary education, first, as a lecturer in early childhood education and then in special education. Gaye initiated, developed and taught the Post Graduate Certificate in Positive Behaviour Support at the University of Canterbury in New Zealand before moving to the UK in 2017. Gaye's teaching and research interests are in early intervention, behaviour screening, positive behaviour support/classroom management and developing family/teacher partnerships. Gaye led the team that wrote the New Zealand-based chapters for three books published with Routledge: *Early Childhood Education and Care in the 21st Century*, Vol I (2018), Vol II (2019), Vol III (2020).

EVOLVING FAMILIES

Series Editor: Sivanes Phillipson

This series focuses on issues, challenges and empirical best practices surrounding evolving families that impact upon their survival, development and outcomes. The aim of this series is twofold: (1) to showcase the diversity of evolving families and the multiple factors that make up the function of families and their evolution across time, systems and cultures; (2) to build on preventative, interventionist, engagement and recovery methods for the promotion of healthy and successful evolving families across generations, social and political contexts and cultures.

International Perspectives on Early Childhood Education and Care
Early Childhood Education in the 21st Century Vol I
Susanne Garvis, Sivanes Phillipson and Heidi Harju-Luukkainen

Teachers' and Families' Perspectives in Early Childhood Education and Care
Early Childhood Education in the 21st Century Vol II
Sivanes Phillipson and Susanne Garvis

Policification of Early Childhood Education and Care
Early Childhood Education in the 21st Century Vol III
Edited by Sivanes Phillipson and Susanne Garvis

Growing Children's Social and Emotional Skills
Using the TOGETHER Programme
Joanna Grace Phillips, Sivanes Phillipson and Gaye Tyler-Merrick

For more information about this series, please visit:
www.routledge.com/Evolving-Families/book-series/EF

GROWING CHILDREN'S SOCIAL AND EMOTIONAL SKILLS

Using the TOGETHER Programme

Joanna Grace Phillips, Sivanes Phillipson and Gaye Tyler-Merrick

Routledge
Taylor & Francis Group
LONDON AND NEW YORK

First published 2022
by Routledge
2 Park Square, Milton Park, Abingdon, Oxon OX14 4RN

and by Routledge
605 Third Avenue, New York, NY 10158

Routledge is an imprint of the Taylor & Francis Group, an informa business

British Library Cataloguing-in-Publication Data
A catalogue record for this book is available from the British Library

Library of Congress Cataloging-in-Publication Data
Names: Phillips, Joanna Grace, author. | Phillipson, Sivanes, author. |
Tyler-Merrick, Gaye, author.
Title: Growing children's social and emotional skills: using the TOGETHER programme / Joanna Grace Phillips, Sivanes Phillipson and Gaye Tyler-Merrick.
Description: Abingdon, Oxon; New York, NY: Routledge, 2021. |
Series: Evolving families | Includes bibliographical references and index.
Identifiers: LCCN 2021007179 (print) | LCCN 2021007180 (ebook) |
ISBN 9780367439187 (hardback) | ISBN 9781032045979 (paperback) |
ISBN 9781003006466 (ebook)
Subjects: LCSH: Affective education. | Early childhood education. |
Social learning. | Emotional intelligence. | Parent-teacher relationships.
Classification: LCC LB1072 .P45 2021 (print) |
LCC LB1072 (ebook) | DDC 372.21–dc23
LC record available at https://lccn.loc.gov/2021007179
LC ebook record available at https://lccn.loc.gov/2021007180

ISBN: 978-0-367-43918-7 (hbk)
ISBN: 978-1-032-04597-9 (pbk)
ISBN: 978-1-003-00646-6 (ebk)

DOI: 10.4324/9781003006466

Typeset in Bembo
by Newgen Publishing UK

Access the Support Material: www.routledge.com/9780367439187

Nāku te rourou nāu te rourou
ka ora ai te iwi
With your basket and my basket
The people will thrive

For my son Jonty, who continues to teach me so much as a parent and teacher.
Joanna Phillips

CONTENTS

Find the complete TOGETHER Training Manual Online for teachers, educators, and parents to use at *www.routledge.com/9780367439187*

FIGURES

PREFACE

More than ever the development of children's strong social and emotional skills in the early years has become a pressing matter. While the development of this book has occurred over the past few years, with the impact of Covid-19 recently, children have been missing out on opportunities to practise their social and emotional skills. Across the world, early childhood settings and schools have been closed for months and families have become more isolated. While the impact of the virus is still unknown, we are beginning to see the impact on children's development through our own work. With Joanna working directly with children and families daily throughout the pandemic, she has been hearing about their struggles in guiding their children's development. Repeatedly the lack of opportunities for children's social and emotional development is being voiced by the parents she works with. They are concerned about children being isolated from their peers and not being able to practise their social and emotional skills out of their home. In turn, parents are voicing their feelings of isolation and lack of support. Essentially, over the past year many children, parents, teachers and educators have been missing out on opportunities to develop strong relationships with each other. These missing opportunities have demonstrated the importance of relationships in children's social and emotional development even more.

Therefore, the programme presented in this book, TOGETHER: Growing Children's Social and Emotional Competence has the potential to help parents, teachers and educators to navigate the challenges they have faced over the past year. TOGETHER emphasises the importance of strong parent–child and teacher–child relationships. It also places importance on strong collaborative partnerships between parents, teachers and educators. Through such relationships and partnerships children are provided with opportunities to understand and practise social and emotional skills.

In addition, TOGETHER places value on being responsive to the contexts in which a child is raised. At this very moment, contexts are constantly shifting for many families. Being responsive to a child's context is vital in early intervention to facilitate family and educator partnership in mutually beneficial activities for children's development. TOGETHER is developed as a contextually responsive and collaborative programme for parents, early childhood teachers and educators to build their skills in developing children's social and emotional competence. TOGETHER relies heavily on the trust early childhood teachers and educators form with children, their parents/caregivers and extended family as a way of responding to contextual needs and variance.

Furthermore, TOGETHER is informed by other established programmes in its collaborative and contextually responsive approach. However, the key difference is that it is designed to be easily and quickly learned for a sustained delivery. TOGETHER is developed to help reduce contextual barriers which may prevent participation, such as being time poor. TOGETHER is the first programme that requires a minimal training time for parents, teachers and educators. It is designed to be easy to follow and adaptable across contexts.

This book introduces TOGETHER as a viable parent, teacher and educator training programme for developing children's social and emotional skills. The book explores its application across various home and early childhood education contexts. To illustrate TOGETHER in action this book presents three stories from case studies of three early childhood settings that participated in the TOGETHER programme. Each story represents diverse early childhood education and home contexts in Melbourne, Australia. Each story demonstrates how TOGETHER, a universal tier programme, can be adapted to be contextually responsive to child, family, teacher and educator needs. The stories also demonstrate how TOGETHER encourages parents, teachers and educators to collaborate on children's social and emotional development.

The aim of the story approach of this book is to engage readers in the experiences of children, parents, teachers and educators. Through their stories we hope readers develop an understanding of how the TOGETHER programme is applied practically in the home and early childhood settings. We hope readers will find inspiration from the unique experiences of the participants of the programme. Finally, we hope that the simple, easy-to-follow strategies of TOGETHER will empower parents, teachers and educators with a tool that is easy to use and fits into their complex and busy lives.

Considering the vision of this book is to empower our readers, we also present our own individual journeys as authors which has led to the formation of TOGETHER.

Joanna's story

The journey that saw the eventual conception of this book began back in 2008, when I became a mother and began my journey as an early childhood teacher.

I recognised that as both a mother and a teacher there was much to learn about ensuring a positive developmental trajectory not only for my own child, but all children. As a mother, I understood that my approach to parenting is highly influenced by previous generations before me. I have been truly blessed to have had parents who recognise the importance of providing positive guidance and encouragement. Despite this, there were still questions about how I would approach my own parenting.

Firstly, as a pre-service early childhood teacher, I started to question the most effective way to build children's social and emotional skills. So often I felt ill equipped to be working with children who presented with social and emotional delays. I found that the pre-service early childhood teacher course on which I was enrolled did not address my questions. I found myself going back to my psychology papers from my Bachelor of Science to better understand ways in which I could encourage the growth of children's social and emotional skills.

Once I became an early childhood teacher the journey continued. I worked with an amazing group of teachers and educators across various settings. Yet, I continued to feel that I lacked understanding and needed to improve my practice. The teachers and educators who I worked with also felt the same way. We were constantly embarking on professional development programmes that focused on working with children with challenging behaviours and exploring ways to grow their social and emotional skills. One such programme was the Incredible Years Programme for teachers – a course that ran over a six-month period. Here the passion for growing children's social and emotional skill through positive interactions grew.

Through the training and a change in my own practice I was beginning to see positive changes with the children I worked with. Such changes were visible with children who were experiencing substantial social and emotional delays. One child comes to my mind, whom I shall call Caleb (pseudonym). He had been to several preschools, and sadly, was not made to feel included at either of them. We were his third preschool. He was only three years old. Caleb would always arrive at our preschool with the biggest smile and eagerness to play. He had a strong connection with music and showed an amazing talent for playing the drums. However, he had limited verbal language and was struggling to play safely alongside his peers. He found the concept of turn-taking hard. He would often hit or kick other children in order to play with the object they had. Caleb also found it very distressing when other children played too close to him and would often push them away. His social and emotional delays were causing considerable stress for the teaching team. The preschool was also receiving numerous parent complaints. It became clear that many of the aggressive outbursts were a result of him not having the words to communicate with his peers, struggling to understand social cues, and having sensory needs relating to crowds. He was also finding it difficult to regulate his emotions when he became frustrated. The good news was I was able to use my new-found knowledge from the Incredible Years (IY) teacher training in guiding children's behaviour to focus on building his social and emotional skills.

Once I understood the function behind his behaviours, I was able to work with my teaching colleagues to come up with a positive behaviour guidance plan which responded to his social and emotional needs. We discussed the prosocial behaviours we wanted Caleb to achieve. These behaviours included playing gently alongside his friends and developing his turn-taking skills. Our plan was to focus on the times when he was being gentle with his hands, when he was able to indicate when he would like a turn (either verbally or through soft gestures), and when he would let others play close to him. We made a point of giving him descriptive praise and encouragement when he engaged in such positive behaviours. We ensured he had spaces to regulate himself when he became overwhelmed and he was provided support when children were playing close to him. We put together an action plan for when he did hurt other children, including taking the time to sit and watch with a teacher to see how other children played gently. Above all else, we ensured that we gave him at least five instances of positive feedback over the negative. While the change was not instant his social and emotional skills improved substantially over the next two months. Previously Caleb would engage in aggressive behaviour almost every hour. Over time this reduced to less than once a week. The change in Caleb sparked my passion to ensure that children were provided with positive and supportive early childhood environments where their social and emotional skills could flourish.

Therefore I embarked on my Master of Education, which included child and family psychology papers. My thesis focused on the development of an early intervention programme to train early childhood teachers and educators in strategies to build children's social and emotional skills. I continued to work as a teacher throughout my master's journey. I soon discovered that while the training programme emphasised the importance of working with parents, there were barriers as to how they were involved. The same could be said for my own teaching practice and my experience as a mother. There were instances where the partnership I had with the families I worked with needed to be stronger and more responsive. The same feeling also extended to my role as a mum. There were also times as a mum where I felt on the outside of my own child's development at school. I recognised that more was needed in ensuring that parents, teachers and educators were provided with opportunities to work together to grow their children's social and emotional skills. Hence the drive behind me embarking on my doctorate, leading the creation of TOGETHER: Growing Children's Social and Emotional Competence and this book.

Through this journey I have recognised that the role we have as early childhood teachers is one of immense value to the children and the families we interact with. Children's development in the early years has a profound effect on the adults they will become. I do not take lightly my roles as a mum, teacher and researcher. The responsibility I have in each of these roles has the potential to influence the growth of children's social and emotional skills. My hope is that, you, the reader of this book, recognise the very important role you have in children's lives. In fact, you may be one of the most important people a child may come across in their lifetime.

Sivanes's story

When Joanna first approached me to be her doctorate supervisor, I was both intrigued and perplexed. Intrigued because her proposed study is what I have always wanted to add to my own work with parents. How wonderful it would be to get parents and teachers learning to work together in a collaborative manner to achieve one specific goal – to help children regulate their behaviours. Perplexed because I had doubts as to how we were going to get families and teachers and communities to work together when people have little time and patience to spare. I am glad my intrigue made me say yes to Joanna to embark on the TOGETHER journey. I not only found this journey gratifying as an academic and mother, but also made a discovery of a talented early interventionist in Joanna, and a lifelong friend and colleague in Gaye as we co-supervised Joanna's doctoral study to completion.

I firstly started my teaching career totally engrossed with behavioural patterns displayed by gifted children. These children showed obsessive tendency in completing a task of their interest. They also showed inclinations towards perfectionism. Most of all they tended to have profound memory but their memorisation was dominated by their tendency to repeat a task to perfection. This interest of mine translated into teaching autistic and behaviorally challenged children in mainstream schools. My career took me to parts of regional Australia and Hong Kong. In one of the schools where I was teaching in Hong Kong, I was faced with one of my biggest challenges in teaching in the form of a student in year 1, named CW. From his first day at school, I found CW intolerably loud, defiant and disruptive. He ran around the class all the time and despite my instructions, he rarely finished any set tasks in the classroom. The one important lesson I learned from my interactions with CW was that I needed to know all about him and especially what was going on at home. His mother, who took him to school, always rushed off before I could stop her for a chat. When I did call her, she was quite dismissive, saying that CW had his problems but I was his teacher and I should teach him. Frustrated with her behaviour, I decided to persist with trying ways to get through to CW. However, it took further weeks of disruptive behaviours for me to turn to CW's mother again. A few more phone calls but this time simply to touch base as to how she was and what I could do to help with some homework, got her talking about his behavioural challenges at home. Soon I was chatting about strategies with his mother, which helped her manage her own frustrations and dilemma of bringing up her son. This experience and the relationship I formed with families in my teaching positions played a big role in my own doctoral studies that investigated parents' role in children's achievement.

Fast forward, I have now written and published significantly around the importance of families in children's development. The fundamental premise in all my research has been that families cannot do the job of raising well-rounded children themselves – they need the help of and need to work with those who are around the children including educators, teachers and the wider community. With TOGETHER, this premise is workable and achievable, and I feel fortunate to have been part of this journey with Joanna and Gaye, to put TOGETHER forward to the world.

Gaye's story

Where do I start? As a young single mother in a small town in New Zealand in the mid-1970s, I was privileged to attend the local Play Centre (early childhood setting) with my young daughter. It was in this setting I was first introduced to the value of early childhood education and the importance of developing strong partnerships with parents. Of particular note was that the Play Centre movement (then and now) focused on parent education and this was where I first started to really understand how children develop their social-emotional competence skills. I was fascinated in the "why" children engage in challenging behaviour and "how" this could be stopped. I wanted to know more. Of course, at that time I never realised where this fascination would lead me. This very early experience led then to working in the special education field with young adults with complex needs, kindergarten teaching, working with teachers in primary and secondary schools with students with behaviour and learning needs and then onto lecturing, first in early childhood and then special education at the University of Canterbury, culminating in my own research and publishing journey based on the development of young children's social-emotional competence skills and behaviour and learning in general.

Along the way, I have been very fortunate to be mentored by friends and colleagues who have helped shape my career and gently push me to explore that "next step." Each step has been enriching as not only have I developed my knowledge and skills on how young (and older) children develop social-emotional competence skills, but, as time went on, I have got to share my knowledge and skills with the growing talent of students who will carry on this work well after I have gone. One such person is Joanna. I first met Joanna when she popped into my office with her son Jonty to discuss her master's thesis. We quickly realised we shared a common interest in developing children's social-emotional competence and fully concurred that teachers and parents needed to work together in order to achieve this. Thus was the start of her research journey and her project was born. It started small with her master's thesis and this in turn provided part of the backbone of the TOGETHER programme and then, with Sivanes, this blossomed into a parent/teacher programme in its own right.

Throughout my career, I have always been committed to working alongside and empowering parents and teachers to learn and feel confident and competent to use the best evidence-based practices to teach social-emotional skills to young children. Working alongside Joanna and Sivanes on the TOGETHER project has been a privilege as we have shared our knowledge and skills together and, of course, learned a lot more from the evidence-based literature. The TOGETHER programme has been our dream project and we hope you enjoy working on it as much as we have enjoyed developing it for you.

I finish with a Maori proverb (whakatauki) which embodies and underpins my journey with Joanna and Sivanes and the premise of the TOGETHER programme:

> *Mā te whiritahi, ka whaktutuki*
> *ai ngā pūmanawa ā tāngata*
> Together weaving the realization of potential

This book

This book is born out of Joanna's own doctoral thesis and is written to provide a guide as to how early childhood research can be applied practically to everyday contexts. It is presented over seven chapters and an e-manual. In Chapter 1, we begin with addressing the importance of growing children's social and emotional competence – a key theme of the TOGETHER programme. In Chapter 2, we provide an overview of the conceptual framework that forms the basis of TOGETHER, how the programme was developed, and how it is delivered. In our third chapter, we present our approach in investigating the effects of TOGETHER, with the hope that others will be inspired to begin their own research journey. Chapters 4, 5, and 6 present three stories from early childhood settings. Each story illustrates the thought-provoking and often complex journey experienced by researchers, parents, teachers and educators in the development and delivery of the TOGETHER programme. In Chapter 7, Lessons learned – It is not all puppies and rainbows, we present valuable and practical lessons for all readers in growing children's social and emotional skills. Finally, we provide in the Appendices some forms that will help you to begin using TOGETHER in your own home or early childhood setting.

As we have discussed, relationships and partnerships form the basis of TOGETHER. Such relationships and partnerships have also been pivotal in the formation of this book and the programme itself. Therefore we take great pride in acknowledging all those that have joined us on this journey. Firstly, the children, parents, teachers and educators reflected in each story have been essential partners in helping us understand the effects of TOGETHER. The time they have given to participate in the training and offer their voices has been immensely valuable. Secondly, the support from our research assistants Mye, Cat, and Sonja in collecting the data has ensured we have gathered a clear picture of what was happening in each setting. They also provided incredible interpreting services when needed. The same goes for Sarah and Zoe, who brought their exceptional teaching skills to help care for the children during the workshops. We would also like to acknowledge the financial assistance from the Faculty of Health, Arts and Design of Swinburne University of Technology in the preparation of this book.

Finally, I, Joanna, would like to acknowledge four very important people who have supported me throughout the rollercoaster journey that has led to the book you read today. Firstly, my heartfelt thanks are given to Professor Sivanes Phillipson and Dr Gaye Tyler-Merrick. Their wisdom and guidance have inspired me to pursue this important research. Their passion for family partnerships and children's social and emotional development has been passed on to me, and for this I am truly grateful. In addition, their ongoing encouragement to push through and persevere through the thick and thin has been incredible. Secondly, a huge shout-out needs to be extended to my husband Matt and son Jonty. For Matt, his ability to keep our household running and Jonty entertained when my head was buried in the computer screen does not go unnoticed. For Jonty, his late-night hugs were so valuable when he saw me working hard. He kept me going and reminded me why I do what I do. I have been so blessed to have a child who has taught me so much about how to be a mum and a teacher.

GLOSSARY

BPRQ	Beliefs, Practices, and Relationships Questionnaire
CBC	Conjoint Behaviour Consultation
CSD	Communication Styles and Demographics Questionnaire
Early childhood educator	Refers to a person who holds a diploma or certificate III in early childhood education and care
Early childhood teacher	Refers to a person who holds an approved early childhood teaching qualification, such as a three- or four-year bachelor degree or above
ECE	early childhood education
EYLF	Early Years Learning Framework
EYM	early years management
IY	Incredible Years
Parents	Refers to those who have the primary caregiving role for a child. Roles include biological parents, step-parents, nominated guardians or relatives.
Parent–educator	Refers to the relationship between families, early childhood teachers and educators
SDRS	Social Development Rating Scale
TOGETHER	TOGETHER: Growing Children's Social and Emotional Skills Programme
VEYLDF	Victorian Early Years Learning and Development Framework

1

INTRODUCTION

This book is written for some of the most important people in children's lives – parents, early childhood teachers and educators. It is also written for those who work directly with children in a professional capacity (such as educational psychologists, speech pathologists and occupational therapists) and those who undertake research in early childhood education (ECE) and junior schools. With your dedication to children's development, many children will experience valuable interactions that can enhance their social and emotional competence. The role you play in a child's life is vital for them to develop skills in forming friendships and participating positively in social settings. It is also vital as you assist children to manage their emotions and engage in meaningful play and learning. However, it is important to remember that your role in a child's social and emotional development is part of a bigger team that is working together in partnership.

Developing positive and effective partnerships between young children's parents, educators and other early childhood professionals is an essential element in the development of children's social and emotional competence (Park et al., 2016; Sheridan & Kratochwill, 2007), as is the understanding of the home, educational and community contexts surrounding the child. When we refer to context, we are not only referring to ethnically and culturally diverse contexts but also to diversity across generations, socioeconomic status, and family and educational settings. The contexts surrounding a child have a profound impact on how successful they are in developing strong social and emotional competency skills (Murray & Farrington, 2010; Webster-Stratton & Taylor, 2001). Children's social and emotional development is influenced by the relationships, communication patterns and environmental contexts to which children are exposed every day (Shonkoff et al., 2017).

In acknowledging the importance of partnerships and context in developing children's social and emotional competence, we introduce you to a new early intervention programme. The programme is called TOGETHER: Growing Children's

DOI: 10.4324/9781003006466-1

Social and Emotional Competence (Phillips et al., 2017). Through this book, and the TOGETHER programme, we show you how to develop and extend children's social and emotional competence in the early years. We also present ways to be more contextually responsive and deepen the parent–educator partnership.

TOGETHER is a contextually responsive and collaborative programme that has been specifically designed for parents and early childhood educators to build skills in developing children's social and emotional competence. The programme has been designed for use both at home and at preschool. The contextually responsive and collaborative elements of TOGETHER are supported by a conceptual framework that underpinned the development of the programme. The framework draws on the theoretical models of family-centred practice (Dunst, 1997, 2002; Dunst & Trivette, 1996), the ecological model (Bronfenbrenner, 1986), and the social learning theory (Bandura, 1977). The framework is introduced in more depth in Chapter 2.

As you read further, you will begin to understand what constitutes a successful early intervention programme in developing children's social and emotional skills. You will learn how TOGETHER can be used as a tool to build children's social and emotional skills through understanding the contexts in which parents live and educators work. You will understand how such knowledge helps build collaboration between the parents, teachers, and educators when discussing a child's social and emotional skills. Through the three contextually different stories, you will learn how parents, teachers, and educators worked together to develop a programme that suited their context. You will be able to apply these same principles to your own context.

We provide a narrative for you to begin your own journey in learning about, and then developing, strategies to improve children's social and emotional skills in your own contextual environment. Maybe you are a parent who is seeking new avenues to develop your child's social and emotional competence skills. You may be an early childhood teacher or educator who already has much experience in teaching children social and emotional competence skills. Maybe you are a recent graduate or teaching student who is looking for ways to improve your classroom practices. Or maybe you are an early childhood professional looking at new ways to build the capacity of children, parents, teachers, and educators. Whatever your situation, this book provides several lenses for you to learn, through the TOGETHER programme, the skills to do this successfully and appreciate the journey of the child, parent, or educator. Most importantly, the book aims to inspire you to develop stronger parent–educator partnerships, improve your own practice in this area, and take the TOGETHER practices (and lessons) and apply them to your own context.

The importance of growing children's social and emotional skills

First, what does the data tell us about the importance of growing children's social and emotional skills? In Australia, the country of origin for the TOGETHER programme, the importance is evident from the statistical data provided by the Australian Early Development Census (AEDC; Australian Government, Department of Education and Training, 2019). The census indicated that in Australia there is a significant number of children either at risk or vulnerable to developmental delays in their social and emotional skills. Children considered to be at risk of developmental delays experience some emotional and social challenges such as: cooperating with others, showing respect for property and others, following instructions, exhibiting self-control, and being kind and helping others. They may also experience problems with anxious behaviours, aggressive behaviours, and inattention/hyperactivity. Children considered vulnerable to developmental delay experience the above challenges on a more regular basis. Vulnerable children struggle to get along with others more regularly, are disrespectful of others and property, have low self-control, and find it difficult to manage aggressive behaviours. A total of 42,434 (14.4 per cent) are at risk of developing social delays, and 28,673 (9.8 per cent) are considered developmentally vulnerable to social delays. For emotional development 42,390 (14.5 per cent) are at risk of developing emotional delays and 24,3770 (8.4 per cent) are considered vulnerable in their emotional development. These statistics highlight the importance for parents, teachers, and educators to learn skills and strategies to strengthen children's social and emotional skill level, with the hope of reducing the number of at risk and vulnerable children.

Our response to such concerning statistics has been the development of TOGETHER. The key concept of TOGETHER is to train parents, teachers, and educators so that they can assist children in growing their social and emotional skills. The term "growing" is apt in this context because young children's social and emotional development and growth depends very much on the contexts of their environments (Bronfenbrenner, 1986; Fox et al., 2003).

When a child is provided with effective support from their parents, teachers, and educators in a consistent and collaborative manner, their social and emotional development improves. For example, Sheridan et al. (2012) found that positive changes in children's behaviours were stronger when there were improvements in the parent–educator relationship. Children who develop strong social and emotional skills in their early years are typically more successful in their schooling, more effective at connecting with others, and are able express their needs and feelings (Denham et al., 2013). Therefore, it is vital that parents, teachers, and educators work together to grow children's social and emotional competence.

When children are not provided with support from their parents, teachers, and educators, their social and emotional development is at risk. Children with persistent challenging behaviour are at risk of developing ongoing antisocial behavioural patterns (Bongers et al., 2004; Whitted, 2011). These patterns have the potential to reduce the development of their social and emotional skills, decrease their academic potential, and heighten their vulnerability to exclusion through isolation from their peers and teachers. A positive social and emotional developmental trajectory is more difficult to achieve for children with poor social and emotional skills. The risk is increased when the support in their environments, such as at home and in early childhood settings, is minimal (Lim et al., 2013).

Children who are considered either vulnerable or at risk in their social or emotional development find it difficult to express themselves and interpret social messages from others, as well as struggling academically (Wigelsworth et al., 2010). In addition, children who are struggling with their social and emotional skills have fewer positive social interactions and are often viewed as being socially incompetent by either their parents or educators (Bornstein et al., 2010; Wigelsworth et al., 2010). Such views can lead to the development of externalising and internalising psychological disorders. Thus, the importance of supporting young children to develop social and emotional skills early on is paramount, as is the development of strategies to teach these skills to parents, teachers, and educators. Addressing social and emotional delays early is considered a preventative measure to stop children from following an antisocial trajectory in later childhood, adolescence, or adulthood (Patterson et al., 2016). Therefore, over the decades, early intervention programmes have emerged that aim to alter that trajectory.

Such early intervention programmes that assist children in the development of strong social and emotional skills are available for parents, teachers, and educators. Successful programmes include Incredible Years (Webster-Stratton et al., 2001), the Teaching Pyramid Model (Fox & Hemmeter, 2009), and Conjoint Behavioural Consultation (Sheridan & Kratochwill, 2007). These programmes focus on enhancing the development of children's social and emotional skills earlier in life through either parent, teacher, or educator training. As a result of earlier intervention, such programmes have been effective in reducing delays in children's social and emotional development. Outcomes have included a reduction in children's challenging behaviours, an increase in parenting satisfaction, and a decrease in parental stress. Each programme provides many evidence-based practices that lead to effective early interventions, including the use of positive behaviour guidance to build children's social and emotional skills.

For example, Incredible Years offers separate programmes for either parents (Webster-Stratton, 1990) or teachers and educators (Webster-Stratton, 2000). Incredible Years focuses on helping parents, teachers, or educators establish skills so as they can guide children in the development of their social, emotional, and academic skills. Studies have found that Incredible Years programmes have led to consistent changes in parent, teacher, or educator practices. Changes have included an increase in the number of positive behaviour guidance strategies such as descriptive praise (Webster-Stratton et al., 2001). In turn, there has been a significant change in child behaviour, social competence, and family relationships, with improvements in all areas (Fergusson et al., 2009; Trillingsgaard et al., 2014).

The Teaching Pyramid Model, on the other hand, is an evidence-based intervention programme that has produced some promising results in the development of children's social and emotional skills. The programme has been established -on the principles of positive behaviour support with an early childhood focus (Sailor et al., 2009). Research has shown that children in the care of teachers/educators who have participated in the programme have demonstrated more socially appropriate behaviours. In addition, children identified as "at risk" show higher levels of positive social interaction skills (Hemmeter et al., 2016).

Finally, in Conjoint Behavioural Consultation (CBC) parents are viewed as essential partners in early intervention (Sheridan & Kratochwill, 2007). They are empowered to contribute when developing individualised interventions for children who have social and emotional delays. Parents, teachers, and educators work in collaboration with an educational consultant. They embrace strength-based principles to build the social, emotional, and academic wellbeing of children. In a study of three children experiencing social and emotional delays, it was found that CBC interventions were effective in increasing appropriate child behaviour, specifically compliance, in both educational and home settings (Bellinger et al., 2016). The interventions contained strategies for providing positive reinforcement (descriptive praise), clear expectations, the self-monitoring of practices, and visual supports.

Programmes such as Incredible Years, the Teaching Pyramid Model, and CBC illustrate the postive effects of early intervention on children's social-emotional trajectories. These three programmes have informed the development of TOGETHER. They have also informed the strategies being taught to parents, teachers, and educators in how they can contribute to the development of children's social and emotional skills.

The TOGETHER programme, however, takes into account the need to address children's social and emotional skills early in their lives through strength-based practices. The key difference is that TOGETHER aims to improve children's social and emotional skills with a minimum amount of training for parents, teachers, and educators in the same context. It recognises that this kind of programme can be implemented with minimum time and effort. These premises of TOGETHER assume a good understanding of the assumptions that sit behind the TOGETHER programme, including the definitions of social and emotional skills. The next section thus aims to provide a beginning to this understanding.

Social and emotional development

Both the words "social" and "emotional" are intertwined in the development of children's prosocial skills, and throughout this book they are used together. However, it is important to understand what we mean by each concept.

Social development

Successful social development involves the growth of skills that are linked to effective interaction with others. With children these skills include turn-taking, being cooperative with adults and peers, understanding others' feelings, and holding back from aggressive behaviour or social withdrawal (Bornstein et al., 2010; Denham et al., 2013). In programmes such as the Teaching Pyramid Model social competence is regarded as a child's ability to build positive relationships with others, solve common problems, and engage and persist with challenging tasks (Hemmeter et al., 2006). The development of such skills is an important aspect in children's development as they prepare for a successful transition from preschool to school.

As explained earlier, children who have developed strong social skills are more successful in forming friendships with peers and participating in group and community activities, and are able to engage in reciprocal interactions (Bornstein et al., 2010). The development of a child's social skills needs to also take into consideration the child's temperament, the home and early childhood settings, and the relationships the child forms in these environments (Murray & Farrington, 2010; Webster-Stratton & Taylor, 2001).

How one views social development is also influenced by a child's environment and context (such as the way of doing things at home and at the ECE setting, religious beliefs, diversity across generations, socioeconomic status). Therefore, it is especially important to recognise that individual differences contribute greatly to how a parent, teacher, or educator perceives what child social skills are. For example, one person may believe that maintaining eye contact is an important part of social connection, whereas for another, such contact may represent disrespect. A child voicing their opinions in a classroom may be viewed by some as a child who is confident in contributing their ideas and is celebrated for the contributions they make; others may view the child as disruptive and non-conforming. Therefore, understanding what is socially acceptable in each context, together with understanding the context of the family and their values and beliefs, is essential in helping a child develop their social skills.

Emotional development

Children's emotional skills are a precursor to, and connected with, the development of children's social skills (Campbell et al., 2016). Emotional development is the ability to articulate, understand, and regulate one's emotions, as well as recognise and understand the emotions of others (Denham, 2006; Hemmeter et al., 2006). Children's emotional skills involve children being able to express and regulate their emotions (Denham et al., 2012). The development of strong emotional skills is considered fundamental to the development of social skills. It is also strongly linked to the development of stronger prosocial relationships with peers and adults and higher levels of academic success.

As with social development, emotional development in children is also highly dependent on the environment that surrounds them (Allen & Steed, 2016). It is dependent on the social experiences of the child, their relationships with the parents/caregivers/relatives in their lives, and the systems of beliefs that influence their lives. For example, before children can verbalise, they come to understand that their own emotional responses can be used to communicate. An infant will smile to show joy and connect with those close to them. They will cry to communicate they are hungry, uncomfortable, or tired. How a child manages their emotional responses represents their developing emotional competencies. As previously mentioned, a child's emotional response is influenced by how their parents/caregivers respond to them. Children who interact with parents/caregivers and educators who are highly attuned to be responsive to a child's emotional communications are more successful in regulating their emotions (Housman, 2017). Conversely, children who experience unpredictable responses from parents/caregivers and educators find it exceedingly difficult to understand and regulate their own emotions. They often present with emotional delays such as heightened anxiety, fears, and aggressive behaviours (Denham et al., 2003). Therefore, it is vital that children experience consistent responses from both their parents and educators. So, you may ask, how do we develop consistency? The first step is developing an understanding of a child's context through *contextually responsive practice*.

Contextually responsive practice

We have learned what we mean by social and emotional development. We have also talked about the importance of knowing and understanding the context of where a child lives, learns, and interacts. Such understandings are especially important in the development of their social and emotional skills. Now, let us unpack what we mean by *contexts*. As mentioned earlier, context does not only refer to ethnically and culturally diverse contexts; it also refers to diversity across generations, socioeconomic status, and family and educational settings. The contexts surrounding a child have a profound impact on how successful they are in developing strong social and emotional skills (Murray & Farrington, 2010; Webster-Stratton & Taylor, 2001).

Given the impact of context on children's social and emotional development, it is important to acknowledge how context influences the participation in programmes that promote children's social and emotional skills. For instance, there are contextual barriers that prevent families and educators from seeking assistance with a child's social and emotional competence skills. For example, poverty, social isolation, and lack of access to resources can inhibit parents from requesting support for their children who have social and emotional competence needs (Stern et al., 2015). In addition, the demands of family life, challenges with childcare, transportation, and time constraints can create barriers to a family's ability to seek assistance. Such barriers may also reduce a family's ability to participate in any resulting early intervention programme.

The beliefs and practices that families hold are also greatly influenced by the context they live in and, in turn, impact on a child's social and emotional development (Barnett et al., 2010; Kazdin, 1996, 2000). Finally, differences in child-rearing beliefs and practices, fears of associated stigma, racial discrimination, and feelings of disrespect from professionals can also present as barriers. Such barriers have been shown to lead towards resistance to participation in any programme that may be helpful to children and families.

Past research has highlighted that programmes often fail to address these mentioned barriers in the recruitment process, which in turn, has the potential to limit the diversity of participants. It has also been noted that teachers and educators experience challenges to meet the contextually diverse social-emotional needs of children and their families (Lustick, 2016; Vincent et al., 2011). The increase in the community of contextually diverse families has heightened the risk of educators reacting negatively to challenging behaviours that do not relate to the dominant culture's expectations (Bermudez et al., 2011; Domenech-Rodríguez & Wieling, 2004; Fallon et al., 2012).

Consequently, there is a need for teachers and educators to consider the unique characteristics and circumstances of each family when developing engagement strategies and programmes with them. When such considerations are made for families, the barriers they may face in accessing and engaging in the programme can be reduced. Therefore, we can see that the role teachers and educators play in building a programme that is contextually responsive is vital. A teacher's or an educator's ability to reflect on and adapt their practices, according to the needs of the families and their individual contexts, is a skill that cannot be underestimated.

In an effort to be contextually responsive, many countries have their own policy frameworks that guide teachers and educators in such practices. For example, in countries such as Australia and New Zealand, the importance of teachers and educators embracing a contextually responsive programme is clearly identified in many of the early years' curriculum documents. Such documents include the Early Years Learning Framework for Australia (ELYF; Department of Education, Employment and Workplace Relations, 2009) the Victorian Early Years Learning and Development Framework (VEYLDF; Victorian Government, Department of Education and Training, 2016), and Te Whāriki He whāriki mātauranga mō ngā mokopuna o Aotearoa, the Early Childhood Curriculum of New Zealand (Ministry of Education, 2017). All three documents make references to how children's learning and development is impacted by their family's cultural histories. They also discuss how educators, teachers, and professionals need to value and recognise children's individual identities to enhance their wellbeing and identity. In addition, early childhood environments need to promote cultural awareness and understanding. The VEYDLF specifically states that "when children experience acknowledgement of and respect for diversity, their sense of identity becomes stronger" (Victorian Government, Department of Education and Training, 2016, p. 12) and they become more confident:

> A strong sense of identity enables a child to be confident and to recognise and accept that in any social setting there are consequences for their actions and behaviours … and learn how to interact with others with care, empathy and respect.
>
> *Victorian Government, Department of Education and Training, 2016, p. 18*

Combining the literature supporting the need for contextually responsive practices (Stern et al., 2015; Wyatt, 2014), and the explicit guidelines from early childhood curriculum documents, it is highly desirable that the programmes designed to teach young children social and emotional skills should embrace contextually responsive models.

Consequently, if a programme is designed to allow for flexibility in the delivery, taking into consideration the contextual aspects of the individual families and communities, then there is a possibility that it will have a greater and more sustained impact. Building a programme that is contextually responsive to the needs of the families, teachers/educators, and the early childhood setting may enhance the level of parental involvement. This is especially true when such programmes incorporate practices that are contextually relevant and provide meaning to the participants (Stern et al., 2015; Wyatt, 2014).

Collaboration with parents and educators

One way to build contextually responsive practice is to build and/or improve the collaboration with parents, teachers, and educators. When considering ways to be contextually responsive, it is important to recognise that collaboration between parents, teachers, and educators plays an important role when teaching children social and emotional competence skills – as does consistency between home and preschool. Collaboration between parents, teachers, and educators is vital. When such collaboration occurs, a common understanding of the practices and beliefs involved with the development of children's social and emotional skills can be achieved (Park et al., 2016; Sheridan & Kratochwill, 2007).

With young children constantly interacting with adults at home and at preschool, it is important that parents, teachers, and educators use consistent practices when teaching children. Cooperation and a strong partnership between a child's family and their educators can lead to several positive outcomes. They include an increase in a child's prosocial behaviours; an increase in positive attitudes towards school settings; and an increase in their academic achievement (Sheridan & Kratochwill, 2007).

Therefore, partnership is an essential element in successful early intervention programmes where a collaborative approach has been adopted. As noted previously, interventions that focus on the development of children's social and emotional skills are most effective when they occur early. They are even more effective when parents, teachers, and educators work together in partnership (Sheridan et al., 2012). In effective programmes, such as the previously mentioned CBC, parents are viewed as essential partners in the formation of effective interventions or education programmes (Sheridan et al., 2012; Sheridan & Kratochwill, 2007). In these programmes, parents, teachers, and educators work together and adopt a strength-based approach that enhances the social, emotional, and academic wellbeing of children. While such programmes contain strategies in developing children's social and emotional skills, they also form effective links between families, educators, and outside professionals.

Why the need for TOGETHER?

At the beginning of this chapter, you may recall we briefly mentioned three influential programmes in the development of TOGETHER: Incredible Years (Webster-Stratton et al., 2001), the Teaching Pyramid Model (Fox & Hemmeter, 2009), and

Conjoint Behavioural Consultation (CBC; Sheridan & Kratochwill, 2007). Each programme provides many evidence-based practices that lead to effective early interventions. Practices include the use of positive behaviour guidance strategies to build children's social and emotional competence. Each programme also offers training for parents, teachers, and educators. Programmes such as the Teaching Pyramid Model are now beginning to make inroads into ways they can be contextually responsive (with specific reference to culture, rather than context; Allen & Steed, 2016). The CBC programme specifically highlights the importance of collaboration and the development of strong partnerships between parents and educators as well as responding to the diversity of families and children (Sheridan & Kratochwill, 2007). So, you may ask, if such programmes offer ways to develop children's social and emotional competence, why the need for another programme?

Our answer is that while TOGETHER is informed by the other programmes, TOGETHER is designed to be short in delivery. TOGETHER is the first programme that requires minimal training time for parents, teachers, and educators. It has been designed to be easy to follow and to be adaptable across different contexts. It is also one of the first programmes to make the components of the training as user friendly as possible so that parents, teachers, and educators can work together without complex jargon. It has also been designed for the whole preschool community, not just for children who are identified as experiencing social and emotional challenges. TOGETHER offers a unique approach to developing children's social and emotional skills that is specific to various families and early childhood education contexts. As the driver, TOGETHER incorporates the contexts of the children, families, and educators in its delivery. Being responsive to a child's context is vital because it helps facilitate and understand the context of the family and their supports. Consequently, this information helps foster communication so that the family and educators collaborate to develop mutually beneficial activities to further develop the child's social and emotional competence.

In being contextually responsive, TOGETHER aims to reduce the effect of barriers such as social isolation, access to resources, and the demands of family life as well as the challenges associated with childcare, transportation, and time constraints. TOGETHER's objective is also to be accessible by providing strategies for developing children's social and emotional skills to parents, teachers, and educators at the same time. By bringing them all together, the programme provides a platform for a stronger parent–educator partnership. The course has also been designed to be short in nature so as to address the time barriers that affect families and educators. Additionally, it aims to reduce the fears of associated stigma and racial discrimination by being a preschool-wide programme that is available to all families and educators. Finally, TOGETHER takes a universal and preventive approach, which means that the skills taught to parents, teachers, and educators are applicable to all children, thereby reducing the need for higher-level interventions.

While TOGETHER provides strategies for both parents, teachers, and educators, it also recognises the trust teachers and educators already have with families. Early childhood settings are one of the first places where children experience relationships with adults other than those in their immediate families (Coleman et al., 2013). Therefore, TOGETHER aims to empower the teachers and educators with strategies to continue with the TOGETHER principles well after the training has been completed. Through empowering teachers and educators to feel confident to eventually facilitate the TOGETHER programme themselves, the hope is that more families will be reached. In turn, more children will have the opportunity to develop strong social and emotional skills.

In the following chapter, we introduce you to three important theories that have informed the development of TOGETHER. We then present to you a programme that is contextually responsive and promotes the parent–educator partnership. We show you how TOGETHER aims to reduce the barriers that families, teachers, and educators may face when trying to access early intervention programmes. As you begin to understand the rationale and theory of TOGETHER, we hope you will take away lessons that you can use to build your own contextually responsive and collaborative practices. We hope you can use such practices to assist you in growing children's social and emotional skills.

2

TOGETHER

What it is all about

In this chapter, our programme, TOGETHER, is introduced, which aims to help parents, teachers, and educators to understand strategies that will develop children's social and emotional competence skills. TOGETHER emerged from a need to not only assist with the struggles being faced by parents, teachers, and educators in developing children's social and emotional skills but to also share the knowledge of some simple, evidence-based strategies that really work when helping children develop social and emotional competence skills. TOGETHER aims to provide these strategies in a contextually responsive manner. While the strategies are simple, TOGETHER acknowledges that the hard part is being consistent with the strategies. Therefore, TOGETHER's objective is to create a platform that encourages collaboration between parents, teachers, and educators in order to develop consistency across the home and preschool settings.

Before we delve further into the strategies of TOGETHER, it is important to understand the foundation on which the programme is built. Therefore, this chapter begins with an overview of the three theories that have been combined to create TOGETHER's conceptual framework. Once the framework has been explained, the TOGETHER programme is then detailed. The chapter concludes with the research questions. These questions have been informed by both the conceptual framework and the TOGETHER programme as a response to the gaps that have been identified in children's social and emotional development.

The TOGETHER conceptual framework

The conceptual framework informs not only the development of the TOGETHER programme but also the research methodology and the analysis process that were used to develop the programme. The framework is a combination of several key theories that help to explain the development of children's social and emotional

DOI: 10.4324/9781003006466-2

skills. The explanations include how the theories work together to help us understand children's social and emotional development and the beliefs and practices of parents and educators. Also explored is how each theory considers the need for strong parent–educator partnerships and collaboration, and how these effect the development of children's social and emotional skills.

The framework incorporates the theoretical concepts from the social learning theory (Bandura, 1977), the ecological systems theory (Bronfenbrenner, 1986), and family-centred practice (Dunst, 1997, 2002; Dunst & Trivette, 1996). In short, the components of the conceptual framework were selected due to the complex systems that influence children's social and emotional development. For this research to understand how beliefs, practices, and relationships influence children's development, we must look at both parents and educators together, not separately. We must also understand the dynamic interactions that occur between home and preschool and the effect they have on children's social and emotional development.

Therefore, Figure 2.1 provides an outline of how each theory has contributed to the conceptual framework and helps to explain the dynamic interactions that occur between home and preschool. First, the social learning theory (Bandura, 1977) underpins the strategies taught to parents, teachers and educators in TOGETHER that relate to children's prosocial behaviours. The strategies include giving descriptive praise when such behaviours are observed, thus giving attention to practices that are strength based. Second, the inclusion of the ecological systems theory (Bronfenbrenner, 1986, 2005) allows us to explore the context – that is, the child, family, preschool, and community, all of which influence a child's social and emotional growth. Finally, the inclusion of family-centred practice (Dunst, 2002) forms the cornerstone of the TOGETHER programme, where families and educators collaborate and work in partnership to facilitate children's social and emotional development. The help-giving practices central to family-centred practice also align with TOGETHER's goal of empowering parents, teachers, and educators to teach the skills required to develop a child's social and emotional skills. Each theory is explained further.

Social learning theory

The introduction of the TOGETHER conceptual framework begins with the social learning theory (Bandura, 1977). In this theory, cognition, behaviour, and the environment are all linked to children's learning. Through this lens, children learn through observation, imitation, and modelling from the people that surround them and the environmental context in which they live. The TOGETHER training places emphasis on parents, teachers, and educators modelling prosocial behaviours. As children mimic these behaviours, parents, teachers, and educators are trained to recognise them through positive reinforcement. Positive reinforcement includes using descriptive praise, where a child's prosocial behaviours are clearly acknowledged and celebrated. It also plays an important role in the TOGETHER training programme because children develop hypotheses about what behaviour

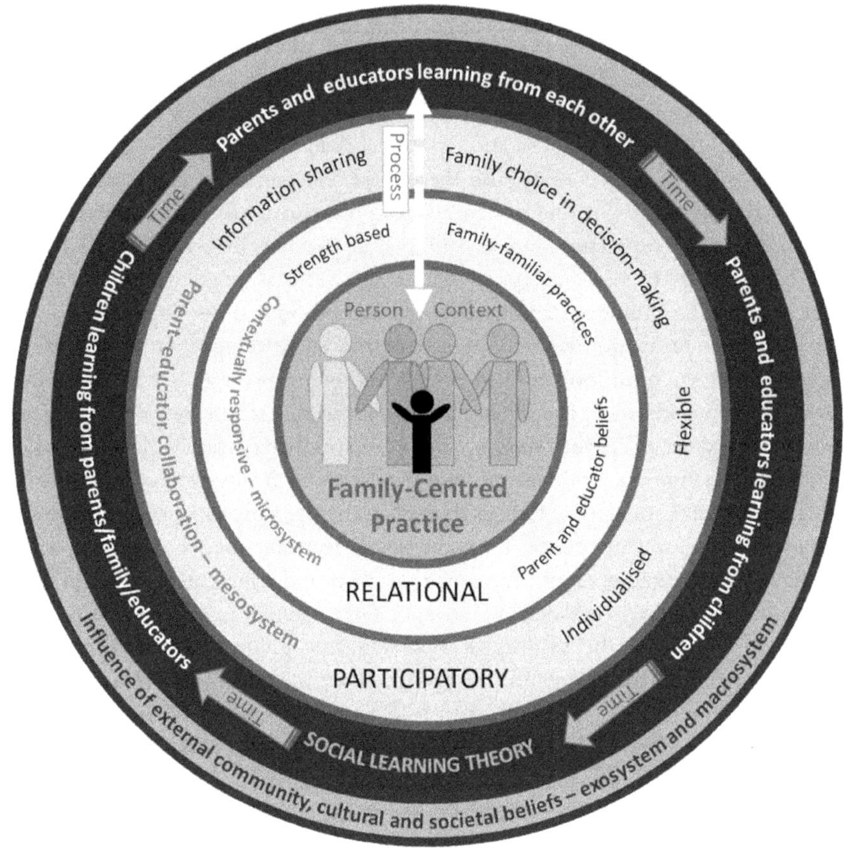

FIGURE 2.1 Conceptual framework of TOGETHER

Note. Adapted from "Ecology of the Family as a Context for Human Development: Research Perspectives," by U Bronfenbrenner, 1986, *Developmental Psychology* 22(6), "Family-Centered Practices: Birth Through High School," by C. J. Dunst, 2002, *The Journal of Special Education*, 36(3) and *Social Learning Theory*, by A. Bandura, 1977, Prentice Hall.

they perceive as appropriate and what behaviour is not appropriate. Using these hypotheses, parents, teachers, and educators can guide children in the development of their social and emotional skills. The adoption of this theory in the TOGETHER programme aids in understanding how children's social and emotional behaviours can change because of the role reinforcement plays.

Furthermore, the social learning theory also assists us to understand the change in parent and educator practices. Bandura (1977) discusses how cognitive processes, including symbolic rehearsal, have the potential to act as a reinforcer and thus change behaviour. In the TOGETHER training, parents, teachers, and educators are provided with reminder strategies to help them increase the number of positive interactions. These reminder strategies can be viewed as a tool for symbolic rehearsal. In the delivery of TOGETHER, we are interested in how we can motivate parents and educators to learn and undertake evidence-based practices to develop children's social and emotional competence. Bandura's theoretical positioning on social learning is valuable in this research. However, the contextually responsive and collaborative elements of TOGETEHR require further theoretical inclusions – hence, the inclusion of the ecological systems theory (Bronfenbrenner, 1986).

The ecological model

The ecological model complements the social learning theory by explaining that the contextual influences in children's development are shaped by a variety of environmental factors (Bronfenbrenner, 1986). Through this theory we understand how contexts and the perspectives, practices, and relationships of parents and educators influence children's social and emotional development. This theory acknowledges the interactions between the child, their family, the community, and wider society and how this influences their development. The theory is important to this research because it places the importance of studying children in multiple environments. For the case of the TOGETHER research, we are aiming to understand children's social and emotional development across the home and preschool settings. We also want to understand how the personal relationships between children and parents, children and educators, and parents and educators influence children's social and emotional development.

The ecological model proposes that children's development changes as they interact and engage with others and their environments. Building on this, Bronfenbrenner and Morris (2006) use the construct of process-person-context-time (PPCT) to illustrate the complex environmental interactions which influence a person's beliefs, behaviours, and overall development. The concept of PPCT is interwoven in the TOGETHER conceptual framework, as illustrated in Figure 2.1. Firstly, through acknowledging the influence of the process, we can develop knowledge about the interactions between the child, their family, the community, and wider society and how this influences their development. Secondly, through understanding the role of the person we can investigate how the beliefs and practices of parents, teachers, and educators influence children's development. In the same vein, understanding the influence of a child's characteristics on their social and emotional skills plays an important role in understanding their development. Finally, through acknowledging the influence of context and time we can understand the environmental features and changes which influence children's development.

Indeed, the influence of context and time is important to this research as it places importance on studying children in multiple environments. For the case of the TOGETHER research, we are aiming to understand children's social and emotional development across various contexts (the home and preschool settings) and periods in time (before and after training). The ecological model helps explain such influences. According to Bronfenbrenner (1986) children are placed at the centre of a set of five influential systems. These systems are the microsystem (environments of home and preschool), the mesosystem (the relationships between the home and preschool setting), the exosystem (the influence of external community aspects), and the macrosystem (cultural and societal beliefs), and the chronosystem (changes over time).

By understanding how children are nestled in these five systems helps with understanding how programmes like TOGETHER can assist with their social and emotional development. For this research, the personal relationships children have with their families, teachers, educators, and peers are especially important. It is these very relationships that TOGETHER focuses on at the commencement of the programme's implementation. In turn, the links made between home and preschool are vital in the programme's strategies. Of equal importance are the contextual elements – that is, the cultural and personal beliefs, the influence of parents' work, and the extended community – and the role they play in understanding the support required of those participating in the TOGETHER programme. Finally, through this research we also want to understand the influence change in parent, teacher, and educator beliefs and practices has on children's social and emotional development over time. By adopting the ecological model and including it in the TOGETHER conceptual framework we can acknowledge the influence of time.

However, the difference with the TOGETHER conceptual framework is that we see that centre of such a system slightly differently. For the framework, the child is placed in the centre together with their parents, and their teachers and educators, bringing us to the third theory of the TOGETHER conceptual framework –family-centred practice (Dunst, 2002).

Family-centred practice

Similar to the ecological systems theory (Bronfenbrenner, 1986), family-centred practice (Dunst, 2002) focuses on the social systems of families, which adds another important element to the TOGETHER conceptual framework. Specifically, it places importance on the relational and participatory practices between parents and professionals, such as educators. Relational practices are strength based, involve family-familiar practices, and encompass parent and educator perspectives.

Participatory practices, on the other hand, enable parent–educator collaboration and embrace flexibility. These practices can be individualised, and they encourage information sharing and family choice in any decision-making between the family, teachers, and educators. In other models, children may often remain the sole focus of early intervention strategies, whereas in family-centred practice, it is the whole family that is involved in capacity-building supports (Rouse & O'Brien, 2017).

The acknowledgment of these key relational and participatory practices plays an important role in the delivery of TOGETHER. Family-centred practice signifies the importance of being responsive to the contextual needs of children and families, celebrates their strengths, and encourages strong parent–educator partnerships (Dunst, 2002), all of which are essential elements in TOGETHER.

How do these theories work together?

The three theories introduced above have been brought together to create the TOGETHER conceptual framework, which has been used in both the development of the TOGETHER programme and to also help us understand the patterns that have emerged from the findings. As illustrated in the diagram in Figure 2.1 each theory is clearly visible and linked to the other two. First, the social learning theory (Bandura, 1977) surrounds the whole framework and is presented as a continual motion. This motion signifies the constant social interactions and the learning that occurs between the child, parents, teachers, and educators. Second, the influence of the ecological systems theory (Bronfenbrenner, 1986) acknowledges the contexts that surround the child, family, teachers, and educators. Finally, the contribution that family-centred practice (Dunst, 2002) gives to the TOGETHER programme is evident from the parents and the child being placed at the centre of the model with the support of the educators (holding hands). The child, parents, teachers, and educators are surrounded by relational and participatory practices that develop directly from family-centred practice that has been adopted for the TOGETHER programme.

The practices are presented in a circular motion due to the continual influence they have on the perspectives, practices, and relationships of parents, teachers, and educators, which are key factors in the TOGETHER research. The relational and participatory factors are also important due to the influence they may have on the social behaviours of a child. Incorporating these three theories into one conceptual framework has enabled the theory behind the TOGETHER programme to become clearer. Parts of the TOGETHER conceptual framework are featured in the discussions regarding the research methods, the five case studies, and in the description of the TOGETHER programme. So, let's find out a little more about TOGETHER.

The TOGETHER programme

TOGETHER: Growing Children's Social and Emotional Competence (TOGETHER) (Phillips et al., 2017) was born from recognising a need for a parent, teacher, and educator training programme that was contextually responsive and would encourage parent–educator collaboration. (Figure 2.2 is an image of the cover of the training manual.) It was also created to be more accessible, less time consuming, easy to follow, and ultimately empower participants to pass their new knowledge onto other families and educators in their community. The TOGETHER programme has been drawn from several established behaviour programmes such as the Teaching Pyramid Model for Supporting Social Emotional Competence in Infants and Young Children (Fox et al., 2010; Fox & Hemmeter, 2009) and the Building Cooperation in Three- to Five-Year-Old Children Teacher Training Manual and Workbook (Phillips, 2014; Phillips et al., 2013). TOGETHER has also been informed by the Incredible Years Teacher and Parent programme (Webster-Stratton, 1990; Webster-Stratton et al., 2001), the Parent Training Oregon

FIGURE 2.2 Cover of TOGETHER training manual

Model (Forgatch et al., 2004), and Conjoint Behavioural Consultation (CBC; Sheridan et al., 2005).

From the outset, TOGETHER aims to include the contextual needs of every participant. These needs are taken into consideration when deciding on the delivery and approach to training for each individual learning community. When needed, the approach includes finding ways to adapt the preschool programme to suit the needs of all children, parents, teachers, and educators. The programme is also focused on the development of contextual understandings between parents, teachers, and educators. The development of such understandings is that for contextual barriers to be reduced, an understanding of parents', teachers', and educators' views and beliefs are essential in the planning stages (Koerting et al., 2013).

From here, TOGETHER specifically aims to train parents, teacher, and educators side by side to increase children's social and emotional skills and encourage collaboration. The TOGETHER programme takes an individualised, flexible, collaborative, and strength-based approach towards training parents, teachers, and educators. The programme trains adult participants in positive behaviour guidance strategies and functional behaviour assessment and analysis. Positive behaviour guidance techniques include the use of descriptive praise and encouragement, increasing the number of positive parent–child or educator–child interactions, and recognising a child's strengths (Fox et al., 2010). Functional-behaviour assessment and analysis is a set of techniques and strategies that has been designed to ascertain the reason why a child engages in challenging behaviour and to identify strategies that teach prosocial behaviours – for example, identifying why a child may be having a tantrum (Hadaway & Brue, 2016). Is it because they are tired, overwhelmed by things in their environment, or because they are struggling with social skills such as turn-taking or sharing? The content of the TOGETHER programme has been designed to help parents and educators to:

1. Gain a common understanding about positive behaviour guidance strategies to build children's social and emotional skills.
2. Develop collaborative and trusting relationships between parents and educators.
3. Work together to develop and implement positive behaviour guidance strategies in the home and preschool, with the ultimate goal to improve children's social and emotional competence.

Getting started with TOGETHER

Before the delivery of the TOGETHER programme it is essential for facilitators to build an understanding of the contexts that are relevant to the children, their parents, the teachers and the educators, and the preschool in order to determine any barriers present that may reduce participation. To assist with these understandings, the TOGETHER facilitators ask each participating parent and educator to complete a communication styles and demographics (CSD) questionnaire prior to embarking on the programme.

The nine-question CSD questionnaire (see Appendix A, part 1) requests parent and educator demographics such as gender and nationality, the home language(s), and the teachers'/educators' education levels. The questionnaire also asks if there are any time constraints or barriers (such as access to childcare) that would create difficulties in accessing the TOGETHER training programme. It asks about any specific cultural needs, workshop time preferences, and preferred communication style. The questionnaire has been designed to provide demographic details and to ascertain the contextual needs of each parent and educator. Using this information, the facilitator can then adapt the TOGETHER programme to suit the needs of the individual participants.

The workshops

The TOGETHER workshops are intended to be welcoming and easy going. Via the self-developed CSD questionnaire and collaboration with the educating team, facilitators can determine communication preferences, accommodate the cultural practices used in each community, and determine if there are barriers that may limit participation. For each preschool community the circumstances may be different. One preschool community may require workshops to be run in the evening, some parents may require support with childcare, and the group's size may vary according to what parents, teachers, or educators are comfortable with. The CSD questionnaire provides initial information of the contextual needs of parents and educators. However, in the following description of TOGETHER, understanding contextual needs has also been built into the delivery of the programme, which provides a deeper understanding of everyone's contextual needs.

The TOGETHER programme includes the following content. It is delivered over two 120-minute workshops with a week's break between them. The first workshop includes:

(a) *An introduction to the Tree Model: Growing Children's Social and Emotional Competence (see Figure 2.3).* The Tree Model forms the building blocks for the TOGETHER programme. It provides parents, teachers, and educators with a visual representation of the essential elements presented in the TOGETHER training. Parents, teachers, and educators are encouraged to place the Tree Model in a visible place in the home or classroom as a reminder of the effective strategies that can be used to develop children's social and emotional competence.

    If you look closely, you will see that the Tree Model is linked closely to the TOGETHER conceptual framework. First, the child and their parents are placed centrally in the model, with the teachers and educators holding their hands in support. There are also links to building partnerships and relationships (family-centred practice; Dunst, 2002), understanding culture and context (the ecological systems theory; Bronfenbrenner, 1986), and strategies to guide children's behaviour to develop their social and emotional competence (social learning theory; Bandura, 1977). However, not every element is explained at the very beginning of training; rather, each element is carefully scaffolded as the parents and educators work through the programme.

(b) *Building relationships between educators, parents, and children.* As mentioned, central to the Tree Model is an image of a child with their parents who are holding the

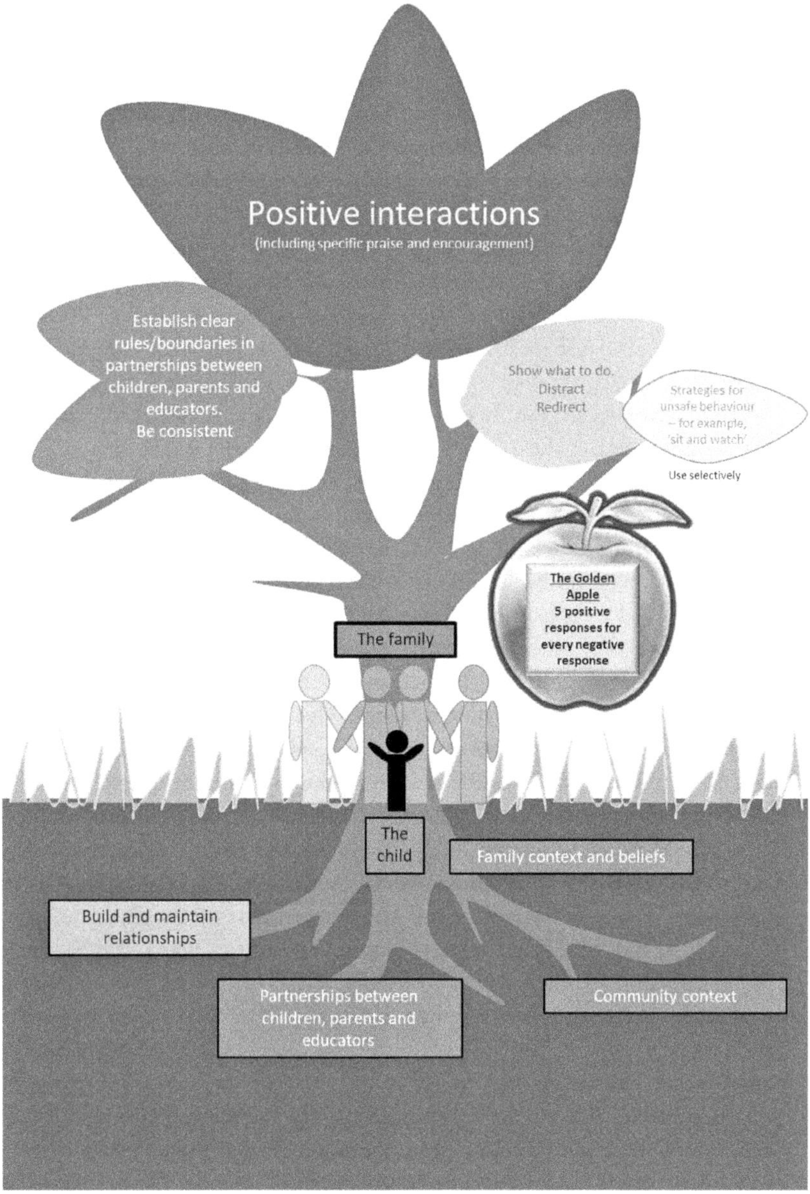

FIGURE 2.3 The Tree Model: Growing children's social and emotional competence

hands of the teachers and educators in partnership The image of partnership is important because it illustrates how TOGETHER has been designed for parents, teachers, and educators to work together. The image acknowledges that parents are the true experts of their child, and that the teachers and educators can be a source of support to both the child and the parents. The phrases "Build and maintain relationships" and "Partnerships between children, parents, and educators" have been placed at the roots of the Tree Model. Their placement illustrates that the development of strong relationships and partnerships with children, families, teachers, and educators from the very beginning will lead to the strong growth of children's social and emotional skills.

(c) *Exploring and understanding the context and culture of the children, their families, and the preschool/community.* You will remember that in Chapter 1 we mentioned that the contexts enveloping a child can have a profound impact on how successful they are in developing strong social and emotional competence skills (Murray & Farrington, 2010; Webster-Stratton & Taylor, 2001). But before this can begin, it is vital that parents and educators are provided with an opportunity to develop an understanding of each other's contexts. This is why we have placed "family culture and beliefs" and "community culture" at the strongest part of the Tree Model – the roots. At the very beginning of the TOGETHER workshops, parents, teachers, and educators are provided with a platform to come together and share cultural practices, family and preschool rituals, and important aspects of their beliefs and practices concerned with developing children's social and emotional skills.

(d) *The benefits and use of descriptive praise and encouragement.* Fox and Lentini (2006) demonstrated that when children receive feedback and specific encouragement when learning new skills, their perseverance increases. Webster-Stratton et al. (2008) have also shown that adults who provide higher levels of praise are more likely to encounter children with increased levels of social competence, emotional self-regulation, and lower levels of inappropriate behaviours. Descriptive praise has also been shown to improve intrinsic motivation in children (Henderlong & Lepper, 2002). The significant effects of descriptive praise and encouragement on children's social and emotional development is why "positive interactions" are placed on the largest leaves on the Tree Model.

In the TOGETHER training, parents and educators are taught to increase the number of positive interactions they have with children – essentially "catching children when they are being good". During this part of the training, participants are taught about the importance of describing the appropriate behaviour and to focus on the learning process (rather than the final product). They are encouraged to use proximity praise and encouragement and target specific behaviours according to a child's social or emotional needs. They are also taught that understanding social cues and developing emotional regulation takes time and for some children a higher number of positive interactions may be needed. To teach prosocial skills (and reduce challenging behaviour), parents and educators are also introduced to the "Golden Apple" – an essential part of the Tree Model where participants are encouraged to provide are least five positive interactions for every one negative interaction to effect change.

(e) *How to be a proactive parent or educator.* As mentioned earlier, the hardest part of the TOGETHER principles is getting parents and educators to practise the newly taught skills consistently. To do this, TOGETHER offers strategies to assist parents and educators to develop consistency, including the development of a basic positive behaviour guidance plan (see pages 29 and 54 of the training manual). Parent–educator collaboration is encouraged when coming up with reminder strategies and developing the plan to ensure it works for each parent, teacher, or educator, while developing consistency.

Between workshops, the teachers, educators and parents are encouraged to implement and practise the learnt positive behaviour guidance strategies in the preschool and home settings respectively. One week later, the parents, teachers, and educators regroup for the second workshop. The second workshop includes:

(a) *Reflection on how effective the previously taught strategies were.* On return from one week of practice, parents, teachers, and educators come together to reflect on their week of practising thc skills and to answer the following questions:
   i. How did the reminder strategies work for you in helping you deliver praise to children with challenging behaviours or the child who may be invisible or shy?
   ii. How did they help you focus on praise and encouragement?
   iii. How did it make you feel in your own practice? Did you notice a change in the child's behaviour?

By reflecting and sharing, parents, teachers, and educators are provided with another opportunity to collaborate, empower each other, understand each other's perspectives more, and begin to develop consistency in practices across the home and preschool settings.

(b) *Developing rules and boundaries, and managing misbehaviour.* Even though the focus of the TOGETHER training is to develop positive interactions, we recognise that there are times when children's behaviour can be very challenging and specific strategies are required. On the Tree Model the leaves become smaller for each strategy, illustrating to parents, teachers, and educators that while such strategies are important with assisting in challenging behaviour, it is the positive interactions that make the most difference to children's social and emotional development. During this part of the training, we begin by discussing the importance of establishing clear rules/boundaries in partnership with children, parents and educators, and the importance of being consistent with these rules and boundaries. We then move into the function of behaviours and the reason why children engage in challenging behaviour.

   It is carefully explained to parents, teachers, and educators that when we understand the purpose of the behaviour, then we can make better decisions on how we, as adults, will help the child to appreciate appropriate and inappropriate behaviour. We specifically ask parents, teachers, and educators to focus on what happened before the behaviour, what is the challenging behaviour, and what happened after? Following these questions, parents, teachers, and educators are able to identify the function of the challenging behaviour and then they are able to identify the appropriate response, such as redirecting, planned ignoring, natural and logical consequences, and the "sit and watch/cooling off" strategy. They are reminded about the Golden Apple throughout each strategy – five positive responses for every negative response.

(c) *Bringing all the skills learnt together.* In the final part of the TOGETHER programme, parents, teachers, and educators work together to develop a more detailed behaviour plan for each child, which includes understanding the reasons for the challenging behaviour (functional-behaviour assessment), identifying the challenging behaviours they want to reduce, identifying the opposite positive behaviours they want to increase, and then developing the prosocial and relationship strategies alongside some relevant descriptive praise phrases they could use.

The overall goal of the TOGETHER training is to build the capacity of the parents, teachers, and educators so that they become confident in building children's social and emotional competence independently from the TOGETEHR facilitators. However, it is important to recognise that the last workshop does not signal the end of the TOGETHER programme: parents, teachers, and educators are provided with additional coaching if needed. Additional coaching may include side-by-side assistance in the classroom, one-to-one meetings with parents, teachers, or educators, or additional workshops to scaffold on the knowledge acquired. The parents, teachers, and educators are also empowered to work together to coach and encourage each other. The style of the workshops often involves small focus groups where the parents, teachers, and educators practise producing strategies together.

The workshops are interactive and encourage collaboration between all participants, with the facilitator encouraged to take a step back while the parent–educator partnerships grow. By taking an interactive and collaborative approach in the workshops, it is anticipated that parents, teachers, and educators will become confident in the strategies taught. As their confidence develops, it is hoped that they can facilitate the programme with their family members or preschool communities themselves. The following research questions address the goals of TOGETHER, the effects the programme has on children's social and emotional development, and the effects on the parents', teachers', and educators' beliefs, practices, and relationships.

Does TOGETHER really work?

Now that you have been presented with what TOGETHER is all about, it is important to understand that such programmes require research to demonstrate their effectiveness. Therefore, the next chapter presents to you the approaches we used to investigate TOGETHER and its collaborative and contextually responsive programme design. Over a period of a year, we set out to find the answers to the following main question:

> What are the effects of the TOGETHER programme on the beliefs, practices, and relationships of parents, teachers, and educators in positive behaviour guidance and children's prosocial skills?

In order to answer this question, we also sought answers to the following three subsidiary questions:

1. What are the current beliefs, practices, relationships, and barriers to the training of parents, teachers, and educators in positive behaviour guidance?
2. How do parents', teachers', and educators' beliefs, practices, and relationships change after programme implementation?
3. How do children's social and emotional skills change after programme implementation?

These questions are addressed in the following five chapters: the approach for investigating TOGETHER, the three stories (presenting our findings), and the final discussion.

3

THE APPROACH TAKEN TO INVESTIGATE TOGETHER

You will recall from the previous two chapters that one of the purposes of TOGETHER is to build the knowledge and skills of parents, teachers, and educators so that they are confident in building children's social and emotional skills. The development of these skills in the early years is influenced by a number of different factors. Factors include the environment – such as a child's home and early childhood settings and adult–child, child–child relationships – and how parents, teachers, and educators interact or communicate with children (Shonkoff et al., 2017). Developing an understanding of these different factors, in terms of developing children's social and emotional skills, can appear overwhelming. To help such understanding, this book looks to the evidence-based methods because they examine and present the development of children's social and emotional skills on a deeper level. Such research has also helped to identify the influences that affect children's challenging behaviour.

In this chapter the approach taken to investigate the research questions outlined in Chapter 2 is introduced. The approach was designed to investigate the different elements of TOGETHER. The methods used in this research help us to understand the effects of TOGETHER on children's social and emotional skills. They help discover the current beliefs and practices of parents, teachers, and educators and how these change over time. Furthermore, the methods are used to investigate the parent–educator partnership before and after the TOGETHER training.

The approach

In order to investigate the effects of the TOGETHER programme, a case study approach was selected. This approach was used because the research included three participating early childhood communities, each with its own unique contextual needs, beliefs, and practices. When researching the changes in these varying contexts (such as child behaviour and adults' beliefs and practices) we needed to be prepared

DOI: 10.4324/9781003006466-3

for surprises; at times we also needed to rethink the approach. The case study approach enabled our research to be flexible and adaptable, not only in the delivery of TOGETHER but also in how the effects of TOGETHER were investigated and how the stories of TOGETHER were told.

What is a case study?

Investigating a case study is a common approach used in social sciences because it specifically enables researchers to examine phenomena in real-life contexts. A case study is an in-depth investigation of individuals (such as children, parents, teachers, or educators), a group (such as families or early childhood communities), or an intervention (Mac Naughton et al., 2001). When such an approach is used, the data is collected from a variety of sources, including observations and interviews. A case study serves to illustrate what happens to an individual or group in relation to a specific phenomenon. For example, looking at the changes in the behaviours of children, or the beliefs and practices of parents and educators, after implementation of the TOGETHER programme.

Why use a case study approach?

The rationale for using a case study approach in the TOGETHER investigation was two-fold. First, as indicated above, the three early childhood communities in which the TOGETHER training took place were each contextually unique from each other. The case study approach provided a range of different ways to collect information to determine whether the TOGETHER programme was working in each unique community. Second, such an approach enabled us to investigate the effects of TOGETHER in far more detail than might have been possible if we had been working with a larger population.

As is shown throughout this chapter, information was collected on the effectiveness of TOGETHER through a variety of ways. The reason for using different methods was because the use of only one method would not have produced a sufficient amount of reliable, rigorous data to understand the changes in the parents', teachers', and educators' beliefs, practices, and interactions. Neither would it have been enough to understand the changes in children's social and emotional skills. When researching early childhood behaviour, interventions and information/data collection methods need to include not only the voices of the parent, teacher, educator, and child but also other ways of recording and understanding their beliefs, practices, and behaviours in everyday life (Harris & Manatakis, 2013). When investigating the beliefs of participants, the use of "self-reports" are limiting and may not be a true representation of the actual beliefs and/or practices in which they actually engage (Gaete et al., 2017). Therefore, direct observation of what they actually do offers an alternative approach in providing a clearer picture of why parents and educators do things in certain ways. Direct observations are also helpful as the researcher is placed in the actual environment of where the change is occurring.

Researchers can see the behaviours, beliefs, and practice occurring in real time, and this may result in a deeper understanding of the changes occurring. By using different approaches to data collection, this research can expand on the findings, elaborate, and illustrate the results more clearly. Such an approach can also highlight any contradictions found in the beliefs, practices, and behaviours of the parents, teachers, and educators.

To collect parent, teacher, educator, and child information the following data collection methods were used:

1. A parent, teacher, and educator self-developed questionnaire especially designed for TOGETHER, called the **Communication Styles and Demographics (CSD) Questionnaire** (Appendix A, part 1). The CSD was completed with the parents, teachers, and educators before the training commenced. The questionnaire asked the participating children, their parents, and the educators to provide their details, and then the facilitators used that information to adapt the delivery of TOGETHER, specifically for those children, their parents, teachers, and educators.
2. An early childhood behaviour rating scale, the **Social Development Rating Scale** (SDRS) (Tyler-Merrick, 2015) (Appendix B). This Likert scale has 15 questions to rate the level of competence of the social and emotional skills that a child can perform and 15 questions to rate the level of competence of the social and emotional skills that the child finds difficult. If a child receives a score of less than 113, we then know the skills to specifically teach the child.
3. A self-developed questionnaire named the **Beliefs, Practices, and Relationships Questionnaire** (BPRQ) (Appendix A, part 2) (Phillips et al., in press-a). The questionnaire is used to help us understand the beliefs and practices of parents, teachers, and educators in relation to developing children's social and emotional competence, as well as understanding the relationships between parents and educators. The BPRQ consists of six Likert-type subscales – four subscales to measure authoritative, authoritarian, permissive, and cultural beliefs, a fifth subscale to measure practices, and a sixth subscale to measure relationships. Each subscale finishes with an open-ended question where participants can elaborate on their thoughts regarding their beliefs, practices, and the parent–educator relationship. A separate study to measure the BPRQ using Rasch analysis has been completed. The aim of that study was to use to Rasch analysis to assess the measurement properties, including reliability and validity, of the BPRQ for parents, teachers, and educators.
4. **Observations** of the children, teachers, and educators in the preschool and selected children and parents in the home. This was done by a dedicated researcher in the preschool and by the parents in the home via a small video camera, with responses marked on observation sheets (Appendix C). The observation codes and the recording form had been adapted from Phillips (2014). The duration of each observation was 30 minutes and occurred three times in each phase (before the workshops, during the teaching workshops,

and after the teaching workshops). For the second and third stories the home recordings were divided into 15-minute observations as the families found 30 minutes to be difficult to capture.

5. The direct observations focused on two dependent variables. The first was the teacher/educator or parent behaviour in response to the child's behaviour. The response codes included: (a) descriptive praise (praise that describes the positive behaviour – for example, "You have tried so hard to put on your shoes – great work"); (b) positive praise without description (for example, "Well done," or a smile or gesture in response to appropriate behaviour); (c) discouragements (negative responses to a child's behaviour or "stop" requests – for example, hitting); (d) planned ignoring (intentional ignoring of a behaviour such as a tantrum); and (e) non-contingent responses (this was recorded when none of the prescribed behaviours had been observed in response to a child's appropriate or inappropriate behaviour).
6. The second dependent variable was the children's appropriate and challenging behaviour: appropriate behaviour is defined as cooperating with an adult or peers and listening and engaging in socially appropriate activities with peers and other adults; challenging behaviour is defined as engaging in disruptive activities, not complying with adult requests, and displaying antisocial conduct such as hitting or having a tantrum.
7. Two postgraduate students were trained to assist with these observations. Their training included one, 1-hour meeting with the TOGETHER facilitator to clarify the codes, two half-hour training sessions that involved practising direct observation in another preschool class and from a sample video in a home setting. The practice included using the observation codes, and then scoring the children's responses. Once inter-observer reliability observations returned a result of 85 per cent or more, training was discontinued. This occurred on the second training session. Inter-observer agreement was calculated for 33 per cent of preschool observations across all phases and agreement occurred for 8 per cent of the observations.
8. **Recording workshop quotes,** where valuable conversations regarding the use of beliefs and practices to increase children's social and emotional competence were captured between the parents, teachers, and educators.
9. At the end of the TOGETHER programme, a short **follow-up questionnaire and interview** were completed by the parents, teachers, and educators to see if they had thought the programme was useful, what they liked and disliked about it, and if they would use it again in the future. The interview included three questions on: (1) how the educators' and parents' beliefs and practices regarding behaviour may have changed or not changed due to the TOGETHER programme; (2) if there had been changes in the parent–educator relationships; and/or (3) any suggested improvements for the TOGETHER programme.

Figure 3.1 shows that by using these different data collection tools, we could triangulate the questionnaires, scales, observations, and interview/workshop data

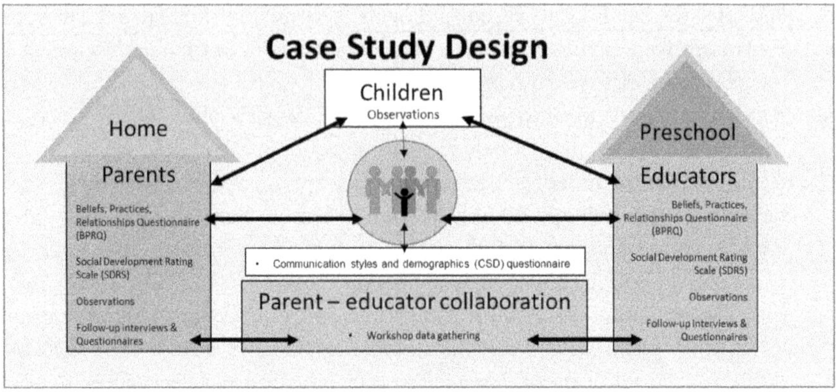

FIGURE 3.1 Overview of the research design of this case study

together to help tell the story of TOGETHER in each individual case study. Mathison (1988, p. 15) explains that triangulation provides researchers with a methodology to "construct meaningful propositions about the social world." Not only does triangulation assist in the convergence of a phenomenon but it also brings to light inconsistencies and contradictions in the findings, which then allows for a reduction in bias and an increase in validity and reliability. Through having multiple sources of information, we were able to further explore and explain the findings for any contradictions or new perspectives and investigate further ways to enhance the programme. Through this case study approach with multiple sources of data, we could also understand the elements that are highlighted in the TOGETHER conceptual framework as follows:

- First, using a case study approach – supported by parent, teacher, and educator questionnaires, child rating scales, and child, parent, teacher, and educator and child observations – assists us in understanding the contextual influences that relate to both the home and preschool settings. These influences link to the ecological systems theory (Bronfenbrenner, 1986).
- The case study approach also helps us to understand how relationships are formed, how practices can be adjusted according to family needs, and how parents, teachers, and educators can work together for the benefit of a child's development, which brings us to the elements of family-centred practice (Dunst, 2002).
- Finally, using the home and preschool observations helps to explain how the environment, social, and cognitive processes influence children's, parents', teachers', and educators' behaviours and practices, which is an important element of the social learning theory (Bandura, 1977).

Now that the reasoning behind the approach for investigating the effects of TOGETHER has been explained, we will turn to two more important elements that contributed to our approach – ethical and recruitment considerations.

Ethics and ethical considerations

Before embarking on any research project, ethical approval must be obtained from the institution to which the researcher belongs. In the case of the TOGETHER research project, ethical approval was received from Swinburne University of Technology's Human Research Ethics Committee. In addition, permission was also obtained from the management committees of the three preschools involved in this study.

There were several factors to address before we started the TOGETHER programme in each setting. First, we had to ensure that all the information we gained from the parents, teachers, educators, and children remained confidential. This meant that the names of the parents, teachers, educators, and children or the preschools would not be used by the researchers in any report, conference presentation, or publication on the project. Additionally, pseudonyms/code names were used to reduce the risk of identification.

Second, Australia is a multicultural nation. In 2012, the Australian Bureau of Statistics reported that over 18 per cent of Australians spoke another language other than English. Therefore, there was a high possibility that some parents, teachers, educators, or children involved in the three case studies may have English as a second language. To ensure we could include everyone, and with the assistance of the directors of the participating preschools, we identified the different cultural communities in each and then had the project invitations, explanatory statements, consent forms, and questionnaires translated into the languages that had been identified. Where other cultural barriers had been identified, we adapted the TOGETHER programme to suit the needs of those particular parents and educators.

Finally, participation in the TOGETHER research project was voluntary so parents, educators, and children could withdraw from TOGETHER at any time if they so wished. If they chose to withdraw, extreme care would be taken to ensure that the information that had been obtained from the questionnaires, rating scales, or observations relevant to them was destroyed.

Recruitment considerations: How we invited the children, parents, teachers, and educators

When undertaking research in early childhood settings and communities, it is important to identify and address the barriers in the recruitment process that would have the potential to limit the children's, parents', teachers', and educators' participation. These barriers would include such things as socioeconomic circumstances, language, social isolation, and mistrust (Bermudez et al., 2011; Domenech-Rodríguez & Wieling, 2004). Koerting et al. (2013) suggest that for the barriers to be reduced, an understanding of parents', teachers', and educators' views are essential in the initial planning stages.

Therefore, it is understandable that recruiting participants from early childhood settings is difficult. Enlisting parents for programmes (such as TOGETHER) where they learn to teach children social and emotional development skills is complex. Houle et al. (2018) suggest that all those involved with the family and child should be recruited. For example, the success of recruiting families would be dependent on the context of each community and the personal characteristics of the parents, teachers, and educators. Others who had direct involvement with participants would also need to be consulted, such as the management of the preschool. In addition, a strong parent–educator relationship could potentially lead to greater success with recruiting families. However, a lack of trust between parents, teachers, and educators, concerns about privacy, a stigma associated with involvement, or misunderstandings regarding the programme could lead to non-participation (Neuhauser et al., 2015). Therefore, the considerations that have been outlined informed our recruitment procedures in the following three stories.

The stories of TOGETHER

The three stories presented in this book are contextually different and offer in-depth illustrations of how TOGETHER taught the children positive social and emotional skills, influenced the parents', teachers', and educators' beliefs and practices, and successfully deepened the parent–educator partnership. The stories are named as follows:

- Story 1: Tamati and Henry
- Story 2: Recognising all children
- Story 3: The community hub

Before we delve into the journey of the participants in each story, it is important to understand how we came to form each narrative. We begin with how each early childhood community came to participate.

Recruitment for the stories

All the three preschools involved had expressed the need for additional training in developing children's social and emotional skills. They expressed their interest either directly with their early years management (EYM) or through an advertisement on a social media page for teachers and educators located in Victoria, Australia. Before we met with the teachers and educators, we met with the management of each centre. This included parent committees, the centre's EYM, or the head teachers. We specifically asked them how to best involve the parents, teachers, and educators. At these meetings, we identified the barriers that may have been present and then discussed the most appropriate means of addressing them. We discussed how best to communicate with families and how to work collaboratively with the parents, teachers, and educators on a plan for recruiting participants for the project.

We then invited teachers and educators to a one-hour presentation. The aims of the research project were explained, along with a brief overview of the TOGETHER programme. The teachers and educators were given a week to decide if they wished to participate before proceeding to parent and child recruitment. After they had decided to participate, the teachers and educators then needed to gauge if any families were interested in participating in the TOGETHER project. Once that interest had been confirmed, we collaborated with the teaching team to determine the best approach to encourage all the families of the children attending each preschool to participate in the project.

The reason for inviting all the families was that TOGETHER is a universal programme that has been designed for every child, parent, teacher, and educator. It has been designed to be accessible, easy to follow, and ultimately to empower parents, teachers, and educators to pass their knowledge onto others to develop positive learning environments in the home and early childhood centre. The TOGETHER programme is appropriate for all families, teachers, and educators involved in an early childhood community. The programme has been designed to include all parents, children, teachers, and educators so that any perceived stigma associated with involvement is reduced or eliminated.

However, in saying this, we were also aware of the additional barriers that at-risk families may face, such as poverty, language, social isolation, and mistrust (Bermudez et al., 2011; Domenech-Rodríguez & Wieling, 2004). Therefore, we provided additional guidance to the teachers and educators to identify children and families who may particularly benefit from the TOGETHER programme. Such guidance included developing alternative ways of communicating with families by engaging interpreters for any family where English was not their first language.

After consultation with the three preschools in relation to enrolling families for the project, the following recruitment process was adopted:

Story 1: Tamati and Henry

Story 1 is where the TOGETHER research began and serves as the pilot study. The teaching team approached us after hearing about the project through their management team. First, the teacher and educator gave informed consent to be part of the programme. They then chose to follow their usual methods of communicating with families, which included using an interpreter to rewrite the information in the languages of the early childhood centre where needed. Communication also included placing in parent pockets an information sheet that explained the aims of the project and a consent form. A one-page poster of the project's main points was also placed on the preschool's communication board. Finally, time was scheduled for families to meet the researchers for a short presentation of the TOGETHER project at the end of the preschool session, along with a copy of the information sheet and a consent form (in appropriate languages). The consent form could either be returned to the researcher or left in a labelled box at reception. In this centre, a total of 22 families were approached, with two agreeing to participate. The parents agreed for their child to be part of the child selection process and be observed in the preschool and at home, for them to participate in the parent–educator training, and to complete two interviews and two surveys with the researchers. The children were considered to have provided assent when they agreed to "be watched playing at preschool and at home" after being asked by their parents and educators.

The recruitment procedure in our first story taught us our first lesson, as outlined next, which needed to be reflected upon before we embarked on any further recruitments.

LESSON 1 – LOW PARTICIPANT RECRUITMENT AND BARRIERS TO PARTICIPATION

Despite the efforts made by the educators and the research team to reduce barriers to participation during Story 1, the uptake was low. The multicultural preschool community encompasses families from various socio-economic backgrounds and were of Australian, New Zealand, Indian, South East Asian, Middle Eastern, and European descent. However, the participating educators and families identified as predominantly Australian. While all the educators chose to participate, only two families gave consent, both of them being Australian.

Feedback from the educators suggests that barriers, such as time and language, had contributed to the low participation numbers, including not having enough quality time to connect with each family about TOGETHER. Educators made specific reference to parents often being at work and children being cared for by grandparents or being in family day care, which meant that connecting with a range of families was challenging. The challenges that emerged from the recruitment process in Story 1 demonstrate the need for more collaboration between teachers and educators before the recruitment process begins as well as coaching the teachers and educators in how to establish effective relationships with families.

Story 2: Recognising all children

In heeding the lessons from Story 1, the recruitment procedures for Story 2 followed the same protocols as for Story 1. However, minor adjustments were included to suit the needs of the preschool community and to reduce the effect of the barriers experienced in Story 1. We were approached by the preschool after a group email was sent by the local EYM on behalf of the research team. As there had been several staffing changes at the preschool, only the head educator decided to participate. After we had received the head teacher's formal consent, all families at the preschool were approached to gauge their level of interest and possible participation. They were invited, via email and the placement of notices in parent pockets, to attend a TOGETHER programme meeting. After a limited response from the families, a presentation was given at the end of a preschool session by the first author, where the aim of the research project and a brief overview of the TOGETHER programme was provided to the families. Given that both the centre director and the participating head teacher had developed a strong trusting relationship with the families, it was decided that after the first author had spoken, the presentation of the study and the programme would be continued by the centre director and the head teacher. At the end of the presentation, which was completed in approximately 15 minutes, we were available for questions and distributed explanatory sheets and consent forms to the families. It was this level of trust between the families and the centre staff that proved to be the most valuable element in the recruitment process for the research project. Of the 45 families that attended the centre, the parents from eight families gave consent for their child to be part of the child selection process and to be observed in preschool and home settings. The parents also agreed to participate in the parent–educator training sessions as well as complete two interviews and two surveys. The eight children were requested to provide assent

Story 3: The community hub

As with Story 2, the recruitment procedures for Story 3 followed the same protocols as for Story 1, with some minor adjustments to suit the needs of this particular preschool community. Again, we were approached by the preschool after a recruitment advertisement was seen on a social media site for early childhood teachers and educators. After giving a short presentation about the TOGETHER programme research project to the teachers and educators the parents of children in all the four-year-old kindergarten rooms were invited to attend the same presentation. Parents from two of the rooms decided to participate in the TOGETHER programme. Interestingly, we applied many of the recruitment lessons learnt from the first story; however, we continued to struggle to recruit families, with only three choosing to participate from both classes (66 families in total were approached). Each child from the three families provided assent. We worked closely with the teachers and educators to reach the parents who had been unable to attend the presentation due to their work commitments; however, contacting them still proved to be a barrier, even with the involvement of translators and grandparents. On a positive note, we had the highest number of teachers and educators participating in this story, with six taking part. In Chapter 6, there is an alternative approach to reaching parents, which may assist in breaking down the barriers to participation.

The settings

Let us learn about each of the preschool settings.

Story 1: Tamati and Henry

The setting for our first story is a small community-based preschool for children aged three to six years located in Melbourne, Australia. Our story is focused on one classroom from the preschool. In this classroom, at the time of the programme, 22 children were attending the preschool for two days a week for a period of 7.5 hours per day (a total 15 hours). The multicultural preschool community consisted of families from Australian, New Zealand, Indian, South-East Asian, Middle Eastern, and European backgrounds. From the self-developed communication styles and demographics (CSB) questionnaire and interviews (completed before the workshops commenced), we were able to identify the details of the participating children, their families, and the educators, and then use this information to adapt the delivery of the TOGETHER project specifically for them. The participating children, Tamati and Henry, along with their families, teachers, and educators are introduced in more detail in Chapter 4.

Story 2: Recognising all children

Our second story is set in a small community-based preschool that offered kindergarten programmes for three- and four-year-old children. The preschool was approached after it had responded to an invitation sent out through the EYM. Only families from the four-year-old kindergarten programme were invited to participate as the children attended for 15 hours, whereas the three-year-old group only attended for five hours. At the time of the TOGETHER project, this early childhood community consisted of one teacher and two educators, and 45 children and their families, who attended the preschool via a rotational system. The three educators attended the preschool Monday to Friday for five hours per day, while each child attended three assigned sessions (a total of 15 hours) per week. This multicultural preschool community consisted of families from Australian, American, Indian, Vietnamese, Chinese, Japanese, Middle Eastern, and European backgrounds; the participating families in the project were from Australian, American, and Chinese backgrounds. Again, the CSB questionnaire was used to identify demographics, communication styles, and the various needs of the children and their parents. As parents from three families needed assistance with childcare to attend the workshops, the workshops were conducted at the preschool with the children in attendance. However, the childcare was provided by a qualified educator who was not participating in the study. You can discover more about the children, their families, teachers, and educators from Story 2 in Chapter 5.

Story 3: The community hub

Story 3 is unique in that the participants are from a preschool that is part of a community hub, where a maternal and child health centre and a number of playgroups are also located on the same site. The preschool is divided into four rooms, with each providing a programme for four-year-olds. All four rooms share a large outdoor communal space. As previously mentioned, families from two of the rooms volunteered to participate in the TOGETHER project.

The two participating preschool programmes consisted of 33 children in each room. The six educators attended the preschool Monday to Friday for five hours per day, while each child attended three assigned sessions (a total of 15 hours). Three educators had been allocated to each room; however, both rooms shared a large outdoor space, which meant there were times when the children would interact with all six educators.

The multicultural preschool community consisted of families from Australian, Indian, Sudanese, Middle Eastern, Chinese, and European backgrounds. Two of the participating families identified as Australian and one family identified as Australian-Fijian-Indian. The educators identified as Australian, Mauritian, Malayan/Tamil/Indian, and Punjabi/Indian. The children, their families, and the educators are introduced in Chapter 6. As with Story 2, the parents needed assistance with childcare in order to attend the workshops, so they were conducted at the preschool with the children in attendance. Again, a qualified educator who was not participating in the study provided the childcare.

How we recorded the effects of the TOGETHER programme

To appreciate the narrative of each story, it is important to understand how we gathered information to enable us to tell each story. The procedures chosen for each story are similar, with some adjustments made along the way as we learnt important lessons in our TOGETHER journey.

The information for each story was accumulated from five different stages using an AB design. An AB design is a two-part study where information is collected before an intervention occurs (A), followed by phases after the intervention to investigate the programme's effectiveness. In other words, we collected information regarding child behaviour, parent and educator beliefs and practices, and information about the parent–educator relationships or partnerships before the TOGETHER training. This was followed by several phases, which allowed us to investigate the changes that had occurred in child, parent, teacher, and educator behaviour as a result of the TOGETHER programme. The particular design procedure was chosen so that the behaviour guidance practices of parents, teachers, and educators could be measured and recorded and then analysed to ascertain if the TOGETHER programme had led to changes in the behaviour of the parents, educators, and children. Each of the five phases is outlined as follows:

- *Phase 1: Two-step multiple-gating procedure.* A two-step multiple-gating procedure (Appendix A) uses an educator nomination form and the Social Development Rating Scale (SDRS; Church et al., 2006) to identify children with behaviour difficulties. The procedure involved teachers and educators nominating any child in their class who met a definition of "a child with behaviour difficulties." Children met the definition if they "(a) complied with teacher instructions much less frequently than other children of the same age, and any children who (b) engaged in antisocial behaviour much more frequently than other children of the same age" (Church et al., 2006, p. 2). In Story 1 this procedure was used as is. However, for Story 2 and Story 3 it was identified that the challenging behaviours of the child experienced by the parents were quite different from those experienced by the educators. Therefore, the SDRS was completed for all participating children by both the parents and the teachers and educators prior to Phase 2.

- *Phase 2: Baseline.* Baseline consists of the CSD questionnaire, the BPRQ, and preschool and home observations. The educators completed their questionnaires at the at the end of a working day two weeks prior to the baseline observations occurring. The parent questionnaires were completed via a phone call interview. The preschool observations occurred for three days over a period of two weeks. There were three 30-minute observation periods for each participating educator and child.
- In our first story, the observations occurred when a child was interacting with a teacher or educator. However, we learnt a valuable lesson during Story 1 in that we were capturing the change in only the child's behaviour (see our Lesson 2 reflection). Therefore, for Stories 2 and 3 the preschool observations included separate observations of the behaviours of each child, the practices of each teacher or educator, and their responses to each child's behaviour. Three 30-minute observation periods also occurred in the home setting over a period of two weeks for children who had been selected for home observations. The home observations occurred via a small easy-to-operate camera that the participating parent turned on during busy times of the day when they had difficulty with their child, such as food routines, bedtime routines, and playtime. At home, the observations included the behaviours of each child, the practices of the parent(s), and their responses to the child's behaviour.

LESSON 2 – PRESCHOOL OBSERVATION CHALLENGES

During our first story, the collection of observational data at the preschool did not capture teacher and educator practice and behaviour to its full extent. It was determined that the way observations were undertaken in the preschool setting needed to be investigated further for the change in educator behaviour to be more visible. The taking of video data in the preschool setting was compromised at the time due to privacy and consent restrictions. Additionally, due to time limitations and the placement of educators, there was inconsistency in how many times an educator interacted with each child. The inconsistencies meant that it was difficult to have a clear picture of the change in educator behaviour. The recommendation was that future preschool observations in other studies needed to include individual observations of each selected child and each participating educator (not just following the selected children). By adopting this approach, the researchers would have a clearer picture of the behaviour change for educators, parents, and children.

- *Phase 3: The TOGETHER programme intervention.* The TOGETHER programme was delivered over two, 120-minute workshops held one week apart, at a time which suited each preschool.
- In our first story children did not attend. The participating teachers, educators and parents were in attendance. The programme was also offered free to all families and educators in the preschool, and as a result, two additional educators and three additional parents from the preschool attended. In total, nine adults attended. In the workshops conducted in Story 1, we realised valuable discussions were being missed and learnt our third lesson, which is outlined in the Lesson 3 reflection.
- Therefore, for Stories 2 and 3 workshops were recorded. Due to the unavailability of childcare for participating families, their children also attended the workshops. A trained educator was employed to look after the children while the parents participated in the workshop.

LESSON 3 – THE CAPTURE OF DISCUSSIONS ON RELATIONSHIPS, CULTURE, BELIEFS, AND PRACTICE DURING WORKSHOPS

The two TOGETHER workshops conducted in the Pilot Study/Story 1 contained discussions between participants that gave valuable insights into their beliefs and practices (both related to culture and behaviour guidance practices), and how they had developed relationships with their children and with each other. Therefore, it became imperative that workshops be recorded at all future training sessions in order to capture the group conversations that would provide rich research data with genuine voices from the parents and educators.

- *Phase 4: Post-workshops.* The post-workshop and in-home observations replicated the same procedures used during the baseline for three days over a period of two weeks.
- *Phase 5: Follow-up.* The preschool and in-home observations replicated the same procedures used during the baseline and post-workshop phases. These occurred for three days over a period of two weeks. During the follow-up sessions, the parents and educators (only teachers and educators for Story 1) completed a second SDRS (Church et al., 2006) to determine if there had been a change in their perceptions of child behaviour. Parents, teachers, and educators also completed the BPRQ. The purpose was to see if a change had occurred in the beliefs, practices, and relationships of the parents and the teachers and educators. The participants were also invited to attend a feedback interview that would be conducted either face to face or by phone.

How the information was analysed

Having collected the information for each story, the next step in developing the stories was to analyse the data. Through analysis we could begin to see how the stories of each child, parent, teacher, and educator had evolved. We could then use this information to not only tell the story of each individual but also their community's story. In bringing these stories together, we could start to see patterns developing in the effects of TOGETHER.

The data analysis for each story was conducted through a mixed-methods approach. The quantitative approaches included a descriptive analysis of the SDRS (Church et al., 2006), preschool and home observations, and the self-developed BPRQ (Phillips et al., in press-b). The qualitative data was analysed through content analysis as outlined by Mac Naughton et al. (2001). The content analysis included the workshop audio data, notes from the observations, the open-ended questions on the BPRQ, and the follow-up interviews. The data analysis conducted for each instrument is described below.

Quantitative analysis

Analysis of the CSD

First, at the baseline the CSD questionnaire answers were categorised according to demographic information such as gender, age, nationality, education level, years of teaching, cultural considerations, group preferences, and communication preferences. The results were collated, tabled, and used to inform the delivery of the TOGETHER programme.

Analysis of the SDRS

A basic descriptive analysis was undertaken of the data from the SDRS (Church et al., 2006) to address the question regarding the change in child behaviour. The descriptive analysis for the SDRS included the median score and standard deviations for both educators for each participating child for the purposes of examining a change in child behaviour after educator and parent training. The descriptive data was collated and tabled.

Analysis of home and preschool observations

The frequency counts from the direct observations for each of the response codes (that is, praise, descriptive praise, and discouragements) were calculated and then placed in line graphs to determine whether there were differences between the baseline and the post-workshop response scores given by the parent and educator participants in each single-case study. The response types were *descriptive praise*, *general praise*, *non-contingent responses*, and *discouragements*.

Analysis of the BPRQ

Descriptive statistics were used to ascertain the differences and the changes in participants. The scores for each Likert-type question for each participant were entered manually into an Excel spreadsheet. For each individual case study, the results were tabulated and compared between participants and phases.

Analysis of the social validity questionnaire

A Likert-type scale, ranging from 1, representing a negative response to 5, representing a positive response, was used for the social validity survey for the first seven questions. The scores for each question were tabulated and compared between participants. The results were then combined and analysed using descriptive statistics that included the mean and standard deviation for each question.

Qualitative analysis of the BPRQ, qualitative notes from the observational data, social validity questionnaire, and the follow-up interviews

Content analysis, as explained earlier, was the process adopted to analyse the open-ended questions from the BPRQ, the qualitative notes from the observational data, the workshop audio data, and the follow-up interviews. The process involved the development of a category system from the data collected. Such a system was developed for the behaviours that emerged during the observations. Categories were also applied to conversation elements that had emerged from the thematic analysis (Nowell et al., 2017) of the BPRQ and the interview data. Such themes included specific practices and beliefs of the participants. The next step involved identifying the units of speech/responses/notes where each category was to be applied.

Once the units had been identified, they were then used to tell the story of each case study. As Mac Naughton et al. (2001, p. 133) state, qualitative data enables us to tell a story: "These stories are strengthened by using voices from the field, or detailed snapshots of the field, to bring to life the arguments being pursued in the research report." Thus, the units derived from the data were used to illustrate the effects of TOGETHER in the story and complement the quantitative data.

Triangulation of findings

One important element in the telling of each case study story and analysing the overall effect of TOGETHER is the triangulation of the data. Triangulation was used in the analysis to enable the range of trends that had emerged from the three stories to be understood. Figure 3.2 builds on Figure 3.1, where we indicated how the data collections tools worked together. Figure 3.2 illustrates our approach in

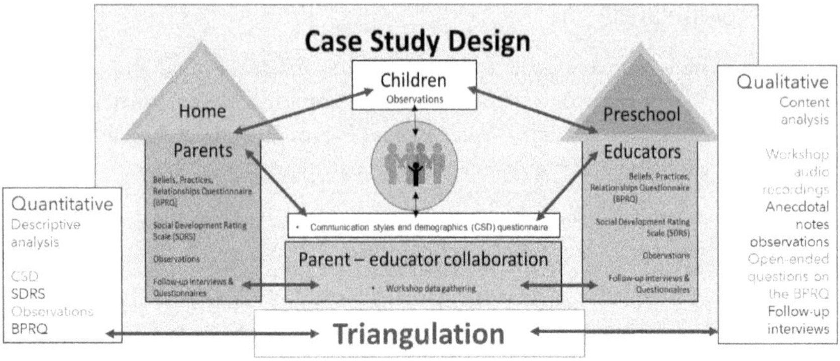

FIGURE 3.2 Triangulation of findings

using triangulation as a method to analyse each story. Rather than simply trying to confirm a hypothesis that had been derived from our investigation into the TOGETHER programme, we used triangulation in the analysis to deepen our understanding of the effect of TOGETHER in each case study.

Triangulation also helped to uncover the effect of context and relationships on the changes in the children's behaviour as well as the parents', teachers', and educators' beliefs and practices. Flick et al. (2012) states that data source triangulation enables researchers to understand the experiences and attitudes of participants through qualitative data. Such data can be used to further unpack the trends that have emerged. Additionally, Mathison (1988, p. 15) explains that triangulation provides researchers with a methodology to "construct meaningful propositions about the social world." Triangulation not only assists in the convergence of a phenomenon but also exposes inconsistencies and contradictions in the findings – thus reducing bias and increasing the validity and reliability of the findings.

The triangulation of the quantitative and qualitative data in the analysis phase occurred after each data collection method had been analysed. Triangulation was used as a tool to deepen the understanding of the trends that had emerged from each story. Triangulation also helped further analyse the trends in the children's behaviour, the parents' and educators' perspectives and practices, and the family–educator relationship before and after the workshops. Additionally, triangulation enabled the TOGETHER programme to be objective, which is an important consideration in reducing bias. As highlighted by Patton (1999), triangulation enables inconsistencies to be revealed between data sources as well as providing more profound insight into the analysis of the data and the phenomenon being explored.

Summary

This chapter has provided an overview of the data collection methods, the procedures, and the analysis required to tell the three stories. By taking a case study approach, using multiple data collection tools, illustrative evidence was produced that enabled the three unique narratives to be profiled in such a way as to demonstrate the changes that had occurred because of the TOGETHER programme. The nature of the parent, teacher, and educator relationships, and their collaborative practices, became more apparent through the application of the various data collection methods. Furthermore, the triangulation of the findings enabled the patterns of the participants' behaviours and practices to be viewed through multiple lenses, thereby providing a richer analysis of the changes that had occurred in each setting.

Chapters 4 to 6 present the results of each case study. They are presented in the form of stories to illustrate the effects of TOGETHER on the children, parents, teachers, and educators across the five distinct contexts. Each story celebrates the growth of the children's social and emotional skills, the changes in the parents', teachers', and educators' beliefs and practices, the deeper parent–educator partnerships that developed, and the empowerment of early childhood professionals to pass on their knowledge to parents and other participants in their communities.

4

STORY 1

Tamati and Henry

Tamati arrives at preschool with an eager smile and gives his educator, Ali, a huge high five. He bounds into the cloakroom and hangs up his bag, then rushes over to the blocks, giving his mum, Kiri, a huge hug and kiss to say goodbye on the way past. He then settles into creating his new block masterpiece. For 30 minutes, he is in his own world as he carefully places each block on top of the other and creates little "hidey holes" for his cars ... that is, until another child comes along and accidently knocks over a block. Tamati looks up in shock, then his face becomes angry ... he stands up ... then uses both his hands to push the other child over. The other child starts to cry and then Tamati follows suit. The peaceful play experience has now turned into a loud flurry of emotions. His other educator, Sue, walks over to assist both children, but the crying continues and she struggles to understand why. In fact, she has been struggling to understand why Tamati reacts the way he does most days. Is he just being naughty? Is he just being difficult? On the other hand, is there something more to his behaviour?

As teachers or educators, we have experienced similar challenges to Sue and Ali, both in the home and preschool. Ali, Sue, and parents reported that they had struggled with guiding children's behaviour and developing their social and emotional skills. Educators often cite that they don't feel they are well equipped with practical strategies to manage misbehaviour and parents often mention that they receive conflicting information on how they should guide behaviours (Carter & Van Norman, 2010; Reinke et al., 2012). With the increase in information, it is not surprising that teachers, educators and parents can become confused regarding what constitutes the most appropriate strategies – yet, as many programmes in positive behaviour guidance show, the strategies are surprisingly simple. So, how can these

DOI: 10.4324/9781003006466-4

strategies be learnt? How can teachers, educators and parents acquire these strategies together? And how can these strategies be adapted to suit the context of your home, preschool, or community? Let's explore one possible answer through our first story.

In Story 1, we present to you the pilot study of TOGETHER with two boys, Tamati and Henry. In this pilot study, we tested how feasible the programme was in a typical preschool setting in Melbourne, Australia. In this first story, we demonstrate how a positive behaviour guidance programme, such as TOGETHER, can improve children's social and emotional skills. We also provide insights into the effects the programme has on both parenting skills and educators' behaviour guidance practices.

Through this story, we illustrate the journey of one early childhood teacher and one educator as they worked with two children and their families in helping them to develop the children's social and emotional competence. We highlight the skills the parents, teachers, and educators learnt from the TOGETHER training, address the challenges they faced, and show how the practices they acquired guided the children in ways that were more positive.

The preschool setting for Story 1

As illustrated in Chapter 3, the setting for our first story is a small community-based preschool for children aged three to six years located in Melbourne, Australia. Our story is focused on one classroom from the preschool. In this classroom, at the time of the research project, 22 children were attending the preschool for two days for a period of 7.5 hours per day (a total 15 hours per week). The multicultural preschool community consisted of families from Australian, New Zealand, Indian, South East Asian, Middle Eastern, and European backgrounds. Through the self-developed communication styles and demographics (CSB) questionnaire and interviews (completed before the training commenced), we were able to appreciate the circumstances of our participating children, their families, and the educators, and used this information to adapt the delivery of TOGETHER specifically for these children, families, and educators.

The children and their families

Tamati

Our focus child, Tamati, is a five-year-old boy who lives with his mum, Kiri, his dad, Nikau, and his two younger brothers, Ihaka and Ari. The family arrived from New Zealand five years earlier and identify as New Zealand Māori. Tamati is a very curious child who has a love for everything mechanical. He enjoys playing with train sets, building intricate constructions, and exploring space-related concepts. He also loves riding bicycles, where he takes risks by performing balancing movements accompanied by extra little tricks, as well as reading with his mum and brothers. As an older brother, Tamati shows just how wonderfully caring he can be towards

Ihaka and Ari. However, there are times when Tamati struggles with his social and emotional skills.

At preschool, he was finding it difficult to share with others. If others tried to come and play in the same area at preschool, Tamati would often become irritated and, at times, aggressive, where he would push or hit other children. He was also finding it difficult to engage in reciprocal conversations with his peers and struggled to accept other children's perspectives. In contrast, however, he would relish delving deep into conversations with adults on topics that were of interest to him. He didn't participate well in group times unless, of course, they related to his own individual interests. Often at group times he would be restless and deliberately poke others, interrupt other children when they were sharing their ideas by yelling or screaming, or walk away within one or two minutes of the group time commencing and refuse to come back.

At home, Tamati struggled to follow simple instructions from his mum, Kiri, such as getting dressed. He needed constant reminding of the tasks he needed to do and at times he would become very frustrated with the morning routines by screaming, crying, or throwing himself on the floor. He would often become upset if one of his younger brothers interrupted his play and would hold his hand out towards them to indicate that he did not want them to approach him. He also found it difficult to express himself and communicate what he needed, often resorting to screaming.

Tamati's mum, Kiri

During the week Kiri would stay at home to look after her three sons while Nikau went to work. She has limited support from her extended family as they all live in New Zealand. However, the connection they have with their local church offers some support. She values the time her family spends together. She feels it is important to gather together each evening around the dinner table and spend time talking about their day. One practice they have as a family is choosing a book to read together at the dinner table – she feels that building a love for literacy at an early age is important. The family also has strong religious beliefs, which play a significant role in how they build relationships as a family. They spend time praying together and sharing what they value. Both Kiri and Nikau are very involved in the preschool community, with Nikau often offering his time at the weekend to participate in working bees at the preschool.

During our preliminary interviews, it became apparent that the morning routines were very stressful for Kiri when she was trying to get her three sons ready for the day as well as cope with Tamati's emotional and social needs. She valued the importance of having Tamati at preschool on time; however, there were some days when getting out the front door was a huge struggle. As previously mentioned in our description of Tamati, there were times when he would become very frustrated with the morning routines and would consequently scream, cry, or throw himself on the floor. Kiri had also become concerned about Tamati's speech and his difficulties in communicating his frustrations. His behaviours were impacting on her ability to get all three boys ready for the day.

Henry

As you may recall from Chapter 3, we chose children who had a variety of social and emotional needs to see if the educators would apply the same principles learnt in TOGETHER for all children, not just our focus child (Tamati). Therefore, we introduce Henry. He is also five years old and lives with his mum, Sonja, his dad, Tim, and his three-year-old sister, Lucy. Like Tamati, Henry has a deep interest in space-related subjects and putting together block structures. He also enjoys painting and activities that involve intricate crafts. He loves engaging in socio-dramatic play in the home corner and the cubby house.

Henry presented with more developed social and emotional skills than Tamati. At the preschool, he would watch other children play and carefully gauge their playing to ensure he would feel comfortable before joining them. As soon as he joined in with the group play he would become confident in contributing his own ideas and would be happy to listen to the ideas his playmates had. He would eagerly share with his peers and would always be excited to be part of the preschool's group times. At home, Henry's mum, Sonja, found him to be an easy child to manage throughout the day (yet she struggled with his younger sister, Lucy). Henry would follow Sonja's instructions at home and would always be keen to assist her in simple daily chores. She also mentioned that he was an extremely caring brother to his sister and was very tolerant of her when she tried to take away toys from him.

Henry's mum, Sonja

Sonja would also spend several days at home during the week with her children while Tim was away working. On two days of the week when she was working as a music teacher, Henry and Lucy would be looked after by their grandparents. Sonja reported that the time spent with extended family was very important to her as well as for Henry's and Lucy's development. She loved the idea that Henry and Lucy could get to know their grandparents more while she was working. Sonja's and Tim's love for music also played a big part in the family culture – they would use music to connect with each other and she had begun to teach Henry how to play the violin. Like Kiri and Nikau, Sonja and Tim would eagerly offer their assistance to the preschool community, especially with working bees and fundraisers.

While Sonja reported that at home Henry was a very placid and helpful child, she did struggle with Lucy. She hoped that the TOGETHER training would assist her with developing ways to help Henry and Lucy get along together.

Tamati's and Henry's educators, Ali and Sue

Tamati and Henry have two educators, Ali and Sue. Sue has a bachelor's degree in primary and early childhood education, and at the time of this research study had three years early childhood teaching experience. She had been employed at the participating preschool for one year. Ali has a diploma in early childhood education and had been teaching 16 years at the participating preschool. Both educators are Australian born and had grown up in the local community. Both reported that they struggled with guiding children's difficult behaviour. Sue also reported she struggled with forming effective relationships with the families at the preschool. In particular, she had a preference for speaking to the parents either over the phone or via email because face-to-face interactions would make her feel anxious:

> *Sometimes I lack confidence in approaching families around various issues with their child because I don't feel confident in my knowledge of child development, feel I lack experience and don't have good strategies to offer parents. I also feel worried about being culturally inclusive.*

Due to Sue's lack of confidence, additional coaching sessions on the content of the TOGETHER training were offered to her. This additional coaching was intended to reduce the concern she had about the potential face-to-face group work during the actual TOGETHER sessions. Interestingly, we found that in this study face-to-face meetings were the preferred means of the parents to learn about their children's activities at the preschool. Hence, it was important that both educators, especially Sue, were equipped with skills on relationship building that they could use during the TOGETHER training with parents.

What did we learn about the children, the parents, and the educators before the TOGETHER training?

In detailing Tamati's and Henry's stories, we have highlighted how their behaviour was manifesting, as well as the practices and beliefs around behaviour guidance before the TOGETHER training occurred for their parents and educators. In using the tools mentioned in Chapter 3, we discovered the patterns in the behaviour, beliefs, and practices of each of the participants.

What did we learn about Tamati's and Henry's social and emotional development before the training?

Tamati

As outlined in Chapter 3, Tamati was chosen as our focus child due to some concerns raised by Ali and Sue via the Social Development Rating Scale (SDRS; Church et al., 2006). Their concerns included Tamati's struggle to participate in group activities with his peers, his difficulty in taking turns and following Ali or Sue's instructions, his attempts to get his own way by throwing tantrums, his hurting of other children when they interrupted his play, his disruption of the play of his peers, his struggle to acknowledge peers during conversations, and his predilection for continuing to talk when others had indicated they wanted to say something.

The classroom observations also confirmed that Tamati was struggling with some social and emotional behaviours. For example, as highlighted in the introduction to this chapter, there were moments when Tamati was unable to express his frustrations after another child had disrupted his work. There were also occasions when he struggled to be part of the group: it was noted that at mat times he would often crawl between the other children who were trying to listen to Sue or would poke those beside him. When asked to be part of a group activity, he would often get up and walk away after a minute or so and would prefer to play on his own. Often Ali was observed redirecting his play to avoid conflicts with other children, or bringing him back to mat times when he had been struggling to join in.

At home the observations confirmed Kiri's concerns. Tamati struggled with following simple instructions from his mum, and when he was frustrated with not being understood, he would scream loudly or simply walk away. He would resist others by extending his arm out towards them with his hand raised and would then become upset.

Henry

Ali and Sue said they had no social or emotional concerns for Henry. In fact, they reported he would happily follow directions, participate and listen at group times, was able to take turns, offered toys to other children, and calmly played around others. Interestingly, though, the classroom observations revealed that while Henry was very compliant with Ali or Sue's instructions and was tolerant of other children, he did struggle to engage with his peers throughout the day. He would often follow Ali and Sue around the classroom to show them his creations; however, there was minimal response from his educators to his positive behaviours. He also had a tendency to watch what other children were doing from the sidelines and was uncertain how to approach them when they were engaged in group play. Henry was considered to be a "well-behaved" child. However, as evident from the classroom observations, this may have also meant that he was receiving little to no positive feedback for his appropriate behaviours. In addition, as Ali and Sue held no concerns for his social development, it could also be construed that some of the social delays Henry had been displaying were largely being ignored.

As we can see from the reported and observed behaviours of Tamati and Henry, both parents and educators had a role to play in each child's behaviour. Therefore, we continue this story by explaining the beliefs and practices of Kiri, Sonja, Ali, and Sue in relation to guiding children's behaviour and social and emotional development. We also begin to explore their perceptions regarding the parent–educator relationship.

As expected, the parents, Kiri and Sonja, and the educators, Ali and Sue, all had varying beliefs and practices in relation to building children's social and emotional competence and guiding their behaviour. From the BPRQ, interviews, classroom observations (of Tamati, Henry, Ali, and Sue), and home observations (of Tamati and

Kiri), we were able to discern patterns of behaviour and how this related to the beliefs of the parents and educators.

What did we learn about the beliefs and practices of Kiri, Sonja, Ali, and Sue?

We found that there were several key areas of behaviour where the parents and the educators had different viewpoints prior to the TOGETHER training. For example, not everyone agreed that children's behaviour needed to be praised or encouraged frequently. For example, Kiri was uncertain about this statement and felt that too much praise could be problematic for children's learning and development. When asked to reflect on her practice, she recognised that she would give more attention to Tamati's inappropriate behaviour than to his appropriate behaviour. She also reported that she would not return her attention to Tamati's appropriate behaviour after she had to redirect him. In addition, Kiri said that she would not share with others when Tamati had done something well and did not have a clear set of rules where she involved Tamati in producing them. Kiri's beliefs and reported practices were also reflected in the in-home observations where the only positive feedback she would give was with a few statements such as "good boy." She would offer very limited positive feedback in the way of descriptive praise or encouragement. Tamati would also receive more discouragements from his mother as a way of directing his behaviour and Kiri would often give directions without inviting any feedback from him.

On the contrary, Ali and Sue did report that they agreed that children's behaviour needed to be praised or encouraged frequently. They also reported that within their own practice, they would give more attention to appropriate behaviour rather than to inappropriate behaviour; they would return their attention to appropriate behaviour after redirection; they would share the child's appropriate behaviour with others; and they had a clear set of rules or guidelines for the children. However, the in-class observations contradicted their beliefs and reported practices. Both Ali and Sue gave very limited positive attention to either Tamati or Henry during the observations. In fact, they actually provided less positive interaction than Kiri (who recognised she gave limited positive interactions to Tamati). Ali gave a noticeably higher number of discouragements and there were a high number of instances where Ali or Sue would give directions to the children without inviting any feedback from them.

Henry's mum, Sonja, while not observed at home, did report practices that were more aligned with the educators. However, both Sonja's and Kiri's beliefs were more aligned with authoritarian parenting styles. They both believed that their sons should always do what they say. They felt that children should be told when they had not met their parents' expectations and that there would be times when they needed to use an angry voice. Sue disagreed with all these statements, and while Ali also disagreed, she did feel there were times when she needed to use an angry voice.

When asked about their perspectives on their child's role in the classroom, Kiri and Sonja had several views, which contradicted Ali's and Sue's. Both parents felt that children needed to work hard in school to achieve success, while the educators disagreed. Both parents felt that eye contact was important in communicating while the educators did not, and there was some disagreement on who had the primary responsibility for raising a child, with the parents believing it was more their role, while Ali and Sue saw raising children as a partnership between parents and educators.

What did we learn about the parent–educator relationships?

On a positive note, both Kiri and Sonja selected either the *agreed* or *strongly agreed* option in the BPRQ for the question of whether they believed they had good-quality parent–educator relationships. They also reported that they strongly agreed that the educators valued the strengths of their child and their family, that they were responsive to their needs, and that they were viewed as partners in their child's development. Interestingly, Sonja strongly agreed on all aspects of the parent–educator relationship, whereas Kiri felt that there was some room for improvement in the relationship. She also felt that the communication with Ali and Sue could be improved, as could their responsiveness to Tamati and his family's needs, and the valuing of his strengths. While Kiri felt that Ali and Sue considered her a partner in Tamati's development, she indicated that more could be done to strengthen this partnership. Both Ali and Sue reflected that while they agreed they had clear communication with the families, were responsive to the children and their parents, valued the strengths and cultures of the families, and viewed the families as partners, there was also a need to deepen the parent–educator relationship on all levels.

The responsive approach to being TOGETHER

As previously indicated, we had gathered information on the beliefs and practices of the parents and educators and developed an undertanding of the relationship between them. However, we still needed to collect information on how they liked to interact with each other. One of the main principles of the TOGETHER programme is to ensure that all parents and educators feel comfortable in the training environment. Therefore, in our preliminary interviews (and the CSD questionnaire), we gathered information regarding the way they would like to interact and communicate, and the venue and times that would best suit them for the training.

Tamati's and Henry's parents and educators had a preference to work in small groups and communicate face to face in more personal settings. Both the parents and educators desired the training to take place over dinner: "Would love a kid-free night where I don't have to cook … At the end of a long day at work it would be great to have some dinner ready and share with our families."

Now, imagine if we had decided to ignore these contextual variances and followed more traditional training scenarios such as booking the local school hall, lining the chairs up in rows, and presenting TOGETHER as a lecture? How would the parents and educators have felt? Maybe anxious? Maybe worried about sharing their experiences and ideas? It is a fundamental component of TOGETHER that we understand the communication styles and preferences of the participants to ensure that the parents and educators have been brought together in a way that is contextually responsive.

After consultation with Tamati's and Henry's parents and educators, the TOGETHER sessions were held at the preschool on two Monday evenings, one week apart. Working with Sue and Ali, a warm and welcoming environment was set up before the arrival of the parents. The arrangement included the placement of chairs in small circles, extra cushions, and a coffee table laden with food. Both Sue and Ali prepared one of their favourite dinner dishes, and though both Tamati's and Henry's parents weren't asked to bring any food, they still brought some. Ali said that the act of sharing food was often a way that they would come together and celebrate as a community; therefore, sharing a meal with each other added a welcoming element to the TOGETHER nights.

As the parents arrived, there was a warm flurry of conversation and laughter between the parents and educators. They appeared at ease, with open body language and a willingness to engage with each other. By developing an understanding of the contextual elements of the parents and educators in this small preschool community, we were able to adapt the delivery of TOGETHER to suit the communication and contextual needs of Tamati's and Henry's parents as well as Sue and Ali.

What happened during the training?

The principles of the TOGETHER programme (see Figure 2.3) in this preschool setting aimed to assist parents and educators to build their understanding of each other's context. Opportunities were initiated at the commencement of the training for both Tamati's and Henry's parents and their educators to develop an understanding of each other's practices and beliefs (including their beliefs related to guiding children's behaviour). They were also given strategies to develop collaborative relationships for the benefit of children's social and emotional development. The objective of the training in each of the sessions was for the parents and educators to exchange ideas in small group discussions in order to appreciate ways in which they could develop stronger relationships with the children and with each other.

As the training progressed, and the parents and educators shared their ideas, it was interesting to observe the point when the parents and educators realised that they had varying ideas on how they developed relationships. In sharing their ideas, the educators particularly were able to come up with new ways to build relationships with both Tamati and Henry in the settings of the preschool and learnt how to adjust their practices according to each child's needs. For example, both Sue and Ali were surprised to discover that Tamati's family bonded over books and that the family placed much importance on their faith. They also discovered the role music played in Henry's home life and how it provided an opportunity for connection between his mother and him. The discussions resulted in the educators commenting on how such information was vital to understanding the behaviours of each child. The information was also important in understanding the context of each family, which then assisted in the development of individual positive behaviour guidance plans. To enhance these plans, it was also helpful to note how positive praise and encouragement could be adapted to develop a child's understanding of social expectations that could help both Tamati and Henry develop useful emotional regulation.

Once the parents and educators had got to know each other better, the training focused on ways they could develop a child's social and emotional competence using positive praise and encouragement. The TOGETHER principles that were applied during this session included celebrating the positive interests/cultural practices that the children and their families connected with, and then using the parents' and educators' newfound understanding of each other to build positive relationships with the children. In brief, the focus was to increase the number of instances when a parent or educator would provide positive praise and encouragement to assist children in understanding the social expectations of them. From here, both the parents and educators were given the "homework task" of documenting how many times they gave positive attention and negative attention, with the aim to have at least five positives for every negative. Both Tamati's and Henry's parents as well as the educators, Sue and Ali, developed their own reminder tools, such as marking their hands with every positive interaction or transferring pebbles from one pocket to another each time they provided praise. They were asked to report on this in the next session.

On the second training night (after a week), the parents and educators reflected on how they had progressed in providing positive feedback to the children. In those reflections, they were asked to think about whether their feedback had had any impact on the children's behaviour. Ali reported that she had noticed the children had been starting to praise and encourage each other more so than before. Much to her delight, Ali added how the children had started to praise her as well. She also mentioned that the total classroom climate was more positive than usual and that she was pleased about that.

Not surprisingly, both Kiri and Sonja reported that it was often a struggle to remember to provide praise and encouragement to their sons, and at times it felt like they were forcing the positive feedback; however, they were beginning to see the "ripple effect" it was having on the siblings as well as on Tamati and Henry. They mentioned that the children enjoyed receiving recognition for when they did things well and it was exciting to see the pride on their faces when the encouragement was given.

However, the parents and educators also reported on the difficult behaviours and associated challenges they were experiencing at home and at preschool. This second-night reflection provided an ideal opportunity to present to the participants examples of lived experiences that would explain the concepts of functional behaviour analysis and the importance of recognising the reasons underpinning the behaviours. As the challenges were discussed, each parent agreed that they often experienced similar challenges, which led to the group developing a shared bond. These sharing moments potentially reduce any stigma a parent might feel in experiencing the challenges of coping with their children's behaviour.

One common recurring challenge for both Tamati's and Henry's parents and educators especially was the expectations relating to turn-taking. The children sometimes did not understand that if they did not take turns, they could potentially hurt each other. As the parents and educators worked together, they identified the behaviours they wanted Tamati and Henry to display. They progressed to discussing the possible reasons for each behaviour that they felt was inappropriate and devised together a number of proactive strategies as part of a positive behaviour plan that they could then use to encourage appropriate behaviours.

Sue identified the need to also have more private one-to-one parent–educator consultations after the training. Therefore, additional meetings were scheduled by both educators with each family to have a confidential but collaborative planning session. We provided additional coaching and words of encouragement via text or phone calls for the parents and educators. Interestingly, it was the educators that the parents approached for additional coaching rather than us. This turn of events demonstrated that both the parents and educators had developed a trust in each other to be partners in the children's social and emotional development.

After the TOGETHER training

It has been one month since the last observation of Tamati. He is back in the preschool with the building blocks again. He sees another child has built a tall tower and walks over to it, says how big it is, and then asks if he can knock it over. Ali quickly intervenes to help Tamati understand the importance of being respectful of others' work and suggests he build a tower of his own. Tamati listens and begins to build a tower next to the other child's. He is being careful of the other child's tower by moving very slowly every time he passes the tower. "You're being so caring about your friend's tower – great work," says Ali. Tamati smiles and continues to go back to his tower building. As the building progresses, Ali continues to give Tamati descriptive praise about how careful and respectful he is being. Suddenly, it is completed and Tamati stands back with his hands in the air. Ali looks over. "Wow! Nice job on building the tower. You have made it so big," she says. Other children come over and give Tamati the same feedback, impressed by his creation. Tamati smiles with pride and proceeds to tell his peers about his new creation.

After the TOGETHER training had been completed, it was observed that there had been a shift in Tamati's and Henry's behaviour, a shift in the beliefs and practices of the educators and parents, and a deepening of the parent–educator relationship. Again, by using the tools mentioned in Chapter 3, we were able to see and hear about these changes.

What did we learn about Tamati's and Henry's social and emotional development after the training?

Tamati

Both the reports from the educators, Ali and Sue, and the in-home and classroom observations indicated that Tamati's social and emotional skills had improved. They both identified that after the training had been completed, Tamati would follow their instructions more consistently and would participate more regularly in adult-directed activities. He joined in with more group-based activities, and he was interacting with other children more appropriately. When he became angry or frustrated, he was able to regulate his emotions and verbalise how he was feeling. He was also more willing to share with his peers and, in turn, was forming new friendships.

Tamati's behaviour change was also evident from the in-home observations (see Figure 4.1). In the weeks following the TOGETHER training, the number of appropriate behaviours steadily increased, and his inappropriate behaviours decreased. In

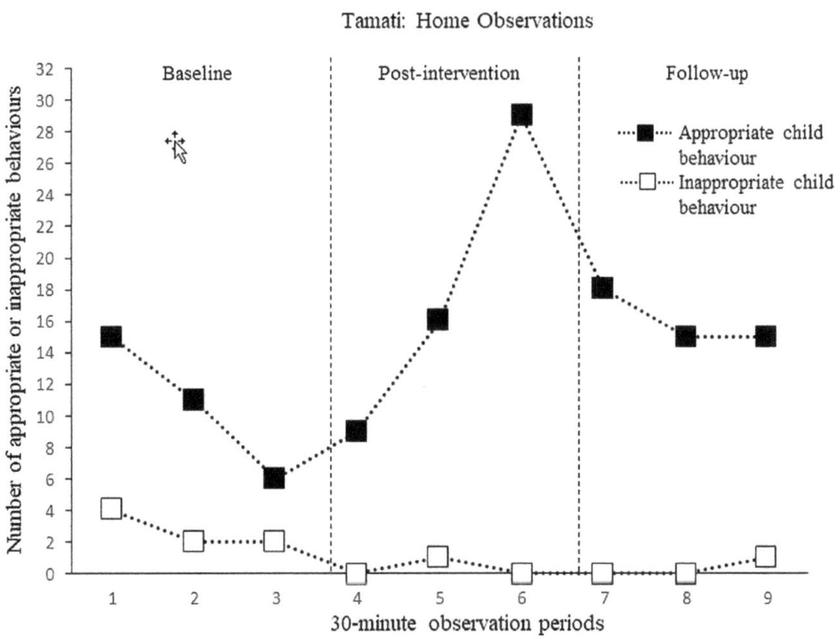

FIGURE 4.1 The number of times Tamati engaged in appropriate or inappropriate behaviour when interacting with his mother

the follow-up observations, which occurred six weeks after the training, Tamati's appropriate behaviours did decrease; however, the promising outcome was that his appropriate behaviours remained well above the number recorded before the training, and his inappropriate behaviour remained very low.

The classroom observations indicated that improvement in Tamati's classroom behaviours was not as visible when he interacted with Sue; however, when he interacted with Ali, his behaviours were much more positive.

Henry

As previously mentioned, Henry was chosen to be part of this case study because we also wanted to see how Ali and Sue would interact with other children who had not been identified as having behavioural needs. When Henry interacted with Ali, there was a noticeable increase in his appropriate behaviours. However, after the TOGETHER training had been completed, there were many instances when his appropriate behaviour was not acknowledged by Sue, and he would often experience long periods where no feedback would be given.

What did we learn about the beliefs and practices of Kiri, Sonja, Ali, and Sue after the training?

After the TOGETHER training had been completed, there had been a noticeable shift in the beliefs of the parents, Kiri and Sonja, and the educators, Ali and Sue. The responses provided in the BPRQ indicated a consistency that was emerging between all the participants. The responses from the mothers and educators also indicated that they understood the concepts of TOGETHER programme. Such concepts related directly to positive behaviour guidance strategies used to assist in the development of children's social and emotional skills. For example, after the training, they all reported they believed the children's behaviour needed to be praised or encouraged more frequently.

When it came to the positive behaviour guidance practices, a promising change had occurred with both the parents and educators – their responses had become more aligned. For example, everyone felt they could now give more attention to appropriate behaviour rather than inappropriate behaviour, they could let children know when they were doing great work, and that they could share how happy they felt when children were doing things well. There was also an acknowledgment of the importance of recognising children's appropriate behaviour after they had calmed down from being redirected due to inappropriate behaviour. The shift in the reported practices had also been noticed in the observed practices of Kiri and Ali, with both increasing the number of descriptive praise statements they made when they interacted with Tamati; however, the observed practices of Sue demonstrated that there had been little change.

Another change was that after the training had been completed, there had been a small shift by Kiri and Sonja to beliefs that were more reflective of a non-authoritarian style, such as using a calm voice when directing child behaviour. A greater understanding had also developed regarding the differences between bribes and rewards, with all agreeing that bribes were not helpful in directing behaviour. Another outcome was that Kiri, Sonja, Ali, and Sue had worked together on a set of guidelines for the children to follow and included the children in developing these guidelines. These practices had contributed to the improved consistency between home and preschool and, in turn, had deepened the parent–educator partnership.

Interestingly, Kiri's and Sonja's perspectives on their children's role in the classroom had not changed much after the training; however, their beliefs that related to the role of the parent, such as parents taking the main responsibility for raising a child, had changed slightly. While Kiri and Sonja still agreed with this statement, it had moved from *strongly agree* to *agree*, which indicated that there had been a shift in how the participants now viewed the parent–educator partnership.

What did we learn about the parent–educator relationship after the training?

While both parents and educators either agreed or strongly agreed that they had good quality parent–educator relationships prior to the training, there had been a shift from *agree* to *strongly agree* in several areas. Such results indicated that by undertaking the TOGETHER training programme, the parent–educator partnership had been strengthened. Both Kiri and Sonja reported that they strongly agreed with the statements that the educators valued the strengths of the child and their family, that they were responsive to their needs, and that the educators were viewed as partners in their child's development. Also, remember at the beginning of this chapter that Sue was concerned about her abilities in communicating with parents – well, after the training she reported that she felt more confident and clearer in her communication with the parents. Both she and Ali also reported that they placed more value on the strengths of the families.

Kiri's, Sonja's, Ali's, and Sue's views on the TOGETHER programme

While we collected data and reported on the changes that had occurred as a result of the TOGETHER training, it is also important to understand how the participants felt about the effectiveness of the programme to ensure it was relevant to their needs. Consequently, all four adult participants (Kiri, Sonja, Ali, and Sue) completed an anonymous social validity survey. The survey responses indicated that the training had met their expectations, that they were able to apply the knowledge they had learnt, and that the content was easy to follow. They also reported that they would continue to use the strategies they had learnt given that the strategies had proven to be an effective and efficient method for reducing behaviour problems.

When asked what could be improved, the participants' responses included:

- Scheduled follow-up for teachers.
- More real-life examples.

When asked what aspects of the training the participants had found useful, their responses included:

- Emphasis on specific praise.
- The opportunity to collaborate with parents.
- Planned ignoring and praising others.
- The strategies.

When asked if the training had influenced educator/parenting practice, the participants' responses included:

- It (TOGETHER) consolidated my education and beliefs. Tools were easy and effective to implement. Increased positive interactions with children. Increased positive interaction with families.
- Sometimes (influenced practice). Children are usually quite well behaved.

The short responses indicated that the participating adults had made several suggestions for modifying the TOGETHER programme. They recommended that the facilitator provide more "real life" examples because asking participants to provide examples could be too confronting for some of them. Another suggestion was the inclusion of a one-to-one follow-up session to discuss the behaviour plans or strategies that were being implemented. When asked what aspects of the training they found useful, the participants reported that positive praise, particularly specific (contingent) praise, was effective; the additional opportunities for parent–educator collaboration was valuable; and the provision of strategies to ignore inappropriate behaviours while paying attention to the positive behaviours was effective. The training was also considered to be successful in increasing positive interactions between the educators and the children and the children's parents.

An optional post-intervention interview was offered to enable educators and parents to provide additional feedback if they wished to do so. Both Ali and Sonja took up the offer. Both their responses to the interview questions indicated that they had become more aware of the need to provide positive responses to children's appropriate behaviours and they stated that more collaboration had occurred between the educators and parents due a feeling of "openness." However, their responses highlighted two key areas to consider for future implementation of the TOGETHER programme: one-to-one parent–educator meetings and the impact of time.

One-to-one parent–educator meetings

Sonja indicated a need for additional one-to-one meetings with the educators so that the two of them could discuss the child's needs with confidentiality and follow up on the child's progress.

Impact of time

Making additional time was an issue for both Ali and Sonja. Ali reported she found it difficult to collaborate effectively with families as she did not see them (referring to grandparents rather than parents bringing children to the preschool). She also mentioned that time and communication barriers, such as reduced connection with working parents, limited the opportunities of some families to become involved in the TOGETHER programme. Sonja expressed concern at the amount of time required to implement the strategies that she had learnt given that her busy family life meant that she sometimes struggled to interact positively with her children. She was often tired from work, needed to organise the daily dinner/cleaning/family routines as well as have a social life. She did report that the strategies were simple to use and she found that they helped her to encourage positive interactions when she was so busy.

What have we learnt so far about TOGETHER?

Story 1 regarding Tamati and Henry offers promising results in how to deliver a collaborative parent and educator positive behaviour guidance programme. The TOGETHER training taught both parents and educators effective positive behaviour guidance strategies in the same setting at the same time. As a result, there was an increase in Tamati's positive behaviours and a decrease in his inappropriate behaviours, and an overall improvement in his social and emotional skills. Henry's behaviours remained unchanged, though it was promising to see more positive interactions between him and Ali. There was also a positive change in Ali's and Kiri's observed practices relating to positive behaviour guidance strategies when they interacted with Tamati. Finally, consistency had developed between the parents, Kiri and Sonja, and the educators, Ali and Sue. Their beliefs and practices became more aligned regarding positive behaviour guidance and developing children's social and emotional skills.

However, the results also indicated that there were still some shortcomings that needed to be rectified, including how we collect the data and how we include a wider demographic of participants. Moving forward, the challenge was to investigate how the TOGETHER programme could be adapted to suit the diverse needs of both educators and parents while building common understandings and providing ongoing communication and support for all participants. The following two stories illustrate how TOGETHER was adapted to suit the needs of two more diverse groups of children, parents, and educators.

5

STORY 2

Recognising all children

Isabella watches on while three girls build an enormous house out of wooden blocks, big enough to fit her and the three girls. Isabella carefully places a block on the corner, looks up at the three girls, then quickly steps back and continues to watch. She appears unsure about how to join in. She looks over at her educator, Jia, who does not see her as she is busy helping other children at the craft table. Isabella turns back to the three girls and keeps watching them for another ten minutes. None of the three girls invites her to play, and when Jia walks past, she does not see that Isabella has been struggling to join in. Throughout the day Isabella quietly follows the directions of her educators; however, she is not confident in joining in with the other children. She either plays on her own or sits on the outside of other children's play groups. Isabella appears to be an invisible child. Because of her quietness and ability to comply with the educators' directions, it appears she is often forgotten. This is a concern as she appears to need an educator to help show her how to join in with the other children. At the moment, she is showing social delays, and these are being missed by her educators. If you were a parent or an educator of a quiet child, like Isabella, would you notice these behaviours?

All too often children are often identified as having social or emotional delays when their challenging behaviours become more noticeable. As evident from the vignette about Isabella, children's social and emotional needs may often go unnoticed, especially when they are compliant or follow all their educator's instructions. In their study, Woodruff and Lee (2011) demonstrated that children who have internalising behaviours, such as refraining from talking, avoiding social groups, and anxiety can develop more concerning social and emotional challenges when they are older,

DOI: 10.4324/9781003006466-5

including mental health disorders and substance abuse. While children may naturally be shy, when their behaviour reduces opportunities for social interactions, such as reciprocal conversations and joining in with group play, they are then at risk of not developing essential social and emotional skills later in life (Bongers et al., 2004; Whitted, 2011). Our second story demonstrates how the TOGETHER strategies can be used to develop a range of social and emotional needs in young children. This includes quiet children who are often unnoticed by confident children wanting their own voices to be heard.

In this second story we introduce our two focus children, Isabella (who you met in the opening paragraph) and Samuel, their early childhood teacher, Jia, and the children's parents. Two other parents who also joined the TOGETHER workshops and answered questions about their children, Julian and Ava, are also introduced. You will see that the contexts of each child have interesting similarities but also distinct differences. Through the TOGETHER conceptual framework, we are able understand the influence of their families' contexts while making links to the ecological systems theory (Bronfenbrenner, 1986), and how the principles of family-centred practice (Dunst, 2002) interlinked with TOGETHER.

The children, their families, and their early childhood teacher

Isabella

Isabella is a four-year-old girl who lives with her mum, Juan, her dad, Taio, and her six-year-old brother, Michael. At home Isabella enjoys drawing, reading picture books, and being in the outdoors with her family. Isabella was chosen as one of our focus children due to concerns raised by her parents, such as not following their instructions and having frequent tantrums. At home Isabella speaks Mandarin and Cantonese with her family and she is confident speaking English with her educators at preschool. The head teacher at the preschool and Isabella's educator, Jia, also speaks Mandarin, which was immensely helpful in assisting Isabella over six months to settle into the four-year-old preschool programme. While Isabella is confident with English, her mum, Juan, reports that by having her home language spoken at preschool she has appeared more at ease and is very comfortable around her early childhood teacher, Jia. During the previous two terms, Isabella had shown a high amount of anxiety about attending preschool due to finding it difficult to develop friendships with peers and being uncertain of the impending separation from her mother. However, the anxiety has now dissipated due to the additional attention Jia has given her when she arrives at preschool and the help she has received in transitioning to activities that she enjoys. At preschool Isabella is now content creating artwork and engaging in intricate tabletop activities by herself, such as puzzles and threading games. Despite being comfortable in engaging in activities by herself, Isabella struggles to interact/play with peers of her own age and this has been limiting her opportunities to develop strong social and emotional skills.

Isabella's mum and dad, Juan and Taio.

Juan is a busy mum caring for her two active children, Isabella and Michael, and dad, Taio, works full time. Juan identifies as Chinese and Taio as Taiwanese. Both Juan and Taio speak Mandarin and Cantonese as their first languages but are also fluent in English. Juan remarks that her and Taio's cultural practices are remarkably similar. As a family they have a love for the outdoors. They often go on camping trips and roast marshmallows on the open fire. Taio is also an avid fisherman who loves to share his skills with his children. Juan is very involved with the preschool community, often volunteering in the classroom, and often asking Jia how she can be of assistance with the daily classroom tasks, such as helping tidy at the end of the day. Juan was so pleased to have Jia as Isabella's teacher given her ability to speak Mandarin, which reduced any potential miscommunication between the preschool and the family. She was also delighted with Jia's responsive and caring nature in helping Isabella settle into the preschool.

Samuel

Samuel is a four-year-old boy who lives with his mum, Charlotte, his dad, Peter, younger brother Levi, and older sister, Bethany. Samuel was selected randomly from the children who were not identified as needing assistance with their social and emotional skills. Samuel was our second focus child. He is very curious and loves to be involved with anything new. In fact, when we began our observations at the preschool, he was curious about what we were doing and followed us around with his own clipboard, pretending he was taking observations too. At preschool, Samuel is eager to ask the educators questions and to offer his ideas. He gets very involved in group play, loves to use his imagination, and is frequently engaged with creative tabletop activities. At home, Samuel enjoys playing with craft-based activities with his older sister. His mum reports that he is really into creating things using tape and loves to describe his creations in detail.

Samuel's mum, Charlotte

Charlotte identifies as American and is very busy with her three children. She takes them to preschool, school, and sporting activities while Peter works full time. Charlotte has been part of the preschool community for the past few years and plays an active role, frequently volunteering to assist with classroom activities (including cleaning) and helping on preschool excursions to places like the zoo. She mentioned that Peter and she had recently been reading about the importance of positive feedback as a tool to develop children's social and emotional skills so she was eager to participate in the training to build on their new-found knowledge.

Julian

Julian is a four-year-old boy who lives with his mum, Lillian, his dad, Matthew, his older sister, Gloria, and his younger brother, Timothy. Julian was not selected as a focus child, so observations were not required of him at home or preschool; however, he is included in this story because Lillian participated in the workshops and reported on Julian's needs. She reported that at home he is generally well behaved, with the main challenge being sibling conflict when they are all together. She mentioned that Julian is quite independent and is helpful in looking after Timothy. She also said that he happily goes with the flow of the family. At preschool Jia reported that Julian easily makes friends, follows most classroom instructions, and is often involved in imaginative "superhero" games. He is a highly active child who likes to challenge himself on the climbing equipment outside and loves to explore the outside environment.

Julian's mum, Lillian

Lillian, who identifies as Australian, is busy with both raising her family and volunteering with local community charity organisations. She spends much of her time running between preschool, school, the children's sporting activities, and meeting her community commitments. Lillian feels confident in parenting her children; however, she mentioned that she was always eager to learn new strategies to help manage her family unit.

Ava

Ava, also four years old, lives with her mum, Zoey, dad, Jackson, and her two brothers, Hunter (six years old), and Lachlan (two years old). Ava was not selected as a focus child, so observations were not required of her at home or preschool; however, she is included in this story because Zoey joined in with the workshops and reported on Ava's needs. Zoey reported that at home Ava enjoys helping her around the house and shows her appreciation to others when they help her. She is generally good at taking turns and sharing with her siblings and takes a genuine interest in others when engaged in conversation. Zoey's main concerns are that Ava does not always follow instructions and struggles with her ability to express her emotions on occasions. At preschool Jia reported that Ava loves to play dress-ups with her peers, engage with books and puzzles, and explore her outside environment.

Ava's mum, Zoey

Zoey, who also identifies as Australian, had recently started a new job as an early childhood educator and her family had recently moved back to her parent's house. As a result, Zoey had been very busy trying to balance her work and family life. She mentioned that all her children had reacted to the change in the home situation, especially Ava's younger brother, who had been experiencing a high number of tantrums daily. Due to time constraints and trying to balance work and family life, Zoey required support in the way of additional coaching over the phone for her to join us in the TOGETHER workshops.

Early childhood teacher, Jia

Jia has a Master of Education and has been teaching in early childhood education for five years. Originally from China, she speaks both fluent Mandarin and English. She is the early childhood teacher for the four-year-old group and is assisted by two educators (who chose not to participate in the TOGETHER programme because they did not have the time). She has been teaching at the current preschool for the past two years.

What did we learn about the children, their families, and their early childhood teacher before the TOGETHER training?

What did we learn about Isabella's and Samuel's social and emotional development before the TOGETHER workshops?

You will recall from Chapter 3 that we asked the teachers and educators to complete the Social Development Rating Scale (SDRS; Church et al., 2006) to help identify the children who had social and emotional delays. Once Jia had completed the SDRS for each child in the class, her rating scores indicated that she had no concerns for the social and emotional development of Isabella, Samuel, Julian, or Ava. However, the results from the Communication Styles and Demographics (CSB) questionnaire, which we completed with the parents and in the conversations we had with Jia, revealed that all the parents – Juan, Charlotte, Lillian, and Zoey – had concerns relating to their children's social and emotional competence skills. Therefore, we asked each parent to also complete the SDRS. By having both Jia and the parents complete the SDRS, we were able to use the additional information to develop a deeper understanding of each child's social and emotional development as follows.

Isabella

At home Isabella's mum, Juan, reported that they had been struggling with Isabella engaging in several challenging behaviours, such as not following their instructions, having frequent tantrums, pleading when she could not get what she wanted, and often interrupting and annoying her older brother. Such behaviours were also observed in the home video recordings where, on one occasion, she had a tantrum for 30 minutes because she did not want to eat her dinner.

Interestingly, at preschool Isabella was different. She willingly followed Jia's instructions, sat with the group at story time and concentrated on class activities for extended periods of time. While the score from the SDRS completed by Jia did not indicate challenging behaviour for Isabella, it did show that there were concerns with her making friends and staying engaged with her peers. These concerns were also supported by the classroom observations taken before the TOGETHER workshops. For example, Isabella was not confident in asking her peers if she could join in, and she found it difficult to respond appropriately when other children tried to interact socially with her. She would not talk back but would nod, smile, or hand a toy to another child. She would not approach peer groups in a way that would encourage acceptance into the current group activity or conversation. Of greatest concern was that because she was so quiet and compliant with the classroom rules, she would often go unnoticed by her peers, by Jia, and by the other educators. Consequently, there were many missed opportunities for her to develop her skills in developing and maintaining friendships.

Samuel

Samuel's social and emotional concerns were more evident at home than at preschool. From the results of the SDRS, completed by his mum, Charlotte, and the home video recordings it became evident that Samuel was often disruptive during family gatherings as he struggled to listen to the ideas of others, had difficulty in compromising in group play, and would sometimes resist following instructions. Jia reported at preschool that while on some occasions he was disruptive at group times, she had no other concerns related to his social and emotional competence skills. This was noted in his classroom observations: he was often eager to engage with others in imaginative group play, would welcome peers into his play, and would confidently contribute to group conversations. At group times, in his keenness to get his ideas across, Samuel would sometimes struggle to let his friends talk.

Julian

Julian was not selected as one of our focus children, therefore, there were no home or preschool observations of him. However, the concerns of his mum, Lillian, which became apparent from both the SDRS and the parent interviews before the training in the TOGETHER workshops commenced, indicated that Julian's family were experiencing some challenges with his social and emotional development. Such concerns included not eating or drinking and misbehaving at mealtimes, often interrupting or annoying his siblings, and shouting at his siblings. Jia, on the other hand, reported no concerns for Julian at preschool. He eagerly joined in with his peers, was great at taking turns, engaged in reciprocal conversations, and followed Jia's instructions with confidence.

Ava

As with Julian, Ava was not selected as one of our focus children, therefore, there were no home or preschool observations of her. However, her mum, Zoey, indicated through the SDRS that the family was experiencing challenging behaviour at home from Ava. For example, there were times when she would ignore her parents' requests, interrupt or annoy her siblings, or plead or nag to get what she wanted. In contrast, however, Jia reported that she had no concerns with Ava. At preschool Ava would immediately follow classroom instructions, show an interest in others and what they were saying, and was confident in approaching others in group play.

What did we learn about the beliefs and practices of Jia and the four parents before the workshops?

To begin with there were several similarities in the beliefs of Juan, Charlotte, Lillian, Zoey, and teacher Jia that had been identified in the beliefs and practices section of the Beliefs, Practices, and Relationships Questionnaire (BPRQ). All believed that children's behaviour needed to be praised and encouraged frequently and providing affection to them was also important. They also felt that children needed to be spoken to calmly when they were misbehaving. However, discrepancies in other beliefs and practices did become apparent between the members of this small group. For example, while most of the parents felt that there were times when they needed to use an angry voice when a child was misbehaving, Jia did not agree with this statement. Isabella's mum, Juan, felt that an angry voice worked well in stopping Isabella's challenging behaviour from recurring. In the first BPRQ, she stated that "I do find punishment, like talking to them with an angry voice or have time out, for bad behaviour with my children works very well to stop it from recurring."

As mentioned, Jia did not agree with this statement. In fact, there were several instances where Jia's beliefs differed from those of the parents. While Juan, Zoey, and Lillian felt that bribes were valid tools to control children's challenging behaviour, Jia (and Charlotte) did not agree. This difference was also noticeable for eye contact when communicating: all the parents believed this was important, whereas Jia disagreed because she had observed that all children communicate differently. Her beliefs also extended to learning: while Jia highly valued free play as a form of learning, Juan, Charlotte, and Lillian believed that children should work hard to achieve success at preschool and Zoey felt children needed to sit quietly at preschool.

Such differences highlight how teachers and educators may often have different perspectives to parents on growing children's social and emotional competence and how to approach education. Jia was trained at an Australian University where play-based learning is regarded as best practice and recognising and responding to cultural differences is very important. Therefore, it is understandable that Jia recognises that not all children communicate in the same way; that she values children's contributions to group conversations; and that she sees play as an important part of education. Conversely, Juan, Charlotte, Lillian, and Zoey had views that had not been influenced by a teaching degree and had been more influenced by their contextual surroundings, including the way they had been brought up (think back to Chapter 2 and the ecological systems theory). Interestingly, Charlotte's view more closely aligned with Jia's in relation to directing behaviour, which may be explained by the fact that she and her husband had recently been reading about the importance of providing descriptive praise and encouragement to develop children's social and emotional skills.

The parents' beliefs also differed on what to do if a child has a tantrum. Isabella's mum, Juan, mentioned she did not feel confident in her parenting skills, and in preliminary discussions with Jia and the TOGETHER facilitator, she mentioned how she needed further guidance on how to guide Isabella when she had tantrums.

This was evident in the first home observation, where Juan and Taio (Isabella's dad) struggled with Isabella's tantrums for over 30 minutes at the dinner table. Juan had also recognised her struggles and her inconsistencies when she said that she had not given much attention to appropriate behaviours (as opposed to challenging behaviours), and that she had not calmly explained to her children why certain behaviours were challenging or inappropriate. In contrast, Charlotte, Lillian, and Zoey, as well as Jia in teaching these parents' children, felt that they let their children know when they were doing a good job; that they gave frequent compliments; they singled out appropriate behaviours; they immediately returned their attention to the appropriate behaviour after inappropriate behaviour; and they frequently let Isabella, Samuel, Julian, and Ava know they could succeed.

Interestingly, despite the responses from Charlotte, Lillian, Zoey, and Jia about giving positive attention to children, the home and preschool observations contradicted their reports. There was very little positive and descriptive feedback given to the children's positive behaviours by the three observed parents (Juan, Taio, and Charlotte). For example, both Isabella and Samuel consistently engaged in appropriate behaviour that was not recognised by their parents. On the other hand, sometimes the challenging behaviour was not addressed by Juan, Taio, or Charlotte, or their child would be redirected with no positive feedback once they had started to do the "right thing."

These inconsistencies were also noticed in the observations of Jia and her interactions with Isabella and Samuel in the classroom. Before the TOGETHER workshops, the observations of Jia revealed that she gave little descriptive praise or encouragement to Samuel and Isabella. She would often give directions, yet when the children followed her directions, no feedback was given. As mentioned earlier, Isabella shied away from interacting with peers during play, therefore, the small number of interactions with little to no feedback from Jia did not assist with developing Isabella's social and emotional development. Isabella was requiring assistance to interact with her peers; however, it appeared from the classroom observations that due to Isabella's quiet nature and the busy nature of the classroom, Jia was missing important opportunities to extend Isabella in these skills. As we continue with this chapter, you will be able to see that as a result of her participation in the TOGETHER workshops, Jia was able to develop skills to assist Isabella and the other three children. You will also see how the parents and educators worked together to develop consistency in their beliefs and practices, which Ava's mum, Zoey, believed was extremely important: "It is important that all carers are of a similar belief. This builds consistency. It also allows both parents and educators to learn what might work best for individual children."

What did we learn about the parent–educator relationships before the workshops?

Before the workshops commenced, all the parents reported through the data provided in the BPRQ that they felt the relationship they had with Jia was noticeably strong. For example, they felt there was clear communication due to the various avenues provided, such as Jia being available for conversations before and after the preschool sessions, frequent emails, a community noticeboard out the front, and individual parent pockets for paper communication. They felt that Jia was responsive to the needs of their children and family and recognised and valued their backgrounds through cultural celebrations (for example, Chinese New Year celebrations for Isabella and Halloween for Samuel). The parents also felt that she viewed them as partners in their children's development due to her responsive approach, while they valued her experience. As pointed out by Isabella's mum, Juan, Jia had established trust with the family: "My educator [referring to Jia] has my full trust as she has shown me how caring and responsible she is and that she is absolutely more experienced than me. I think this is very, very important to the children."

The responsive approach to being TOGETHER

The delivery of the TOGETHER programme for these four parents and their early childhood teacher, Jia, required a slightly different approach to our first story. From our initial meetings, and using information from the CSD, we were able to determine the interaction and communication styles of the parents and Jia, the most comfortable time and place for the families where we could implement the TOGETHER training, and any barriers they may have faced in accessing the training.

Both Jia and the parents felt that the training was best suited to be delivered at the preschool. As most of the families had school-aged children, we had a small window of time between 1 pm and 3 pm where the parents could meet after the preschool session but before they needed to go to the local school to pick up their older children. The four parents all mentioned they required assistance with childcare. To overcome this barrier, a qualified early childhood educator was employed to watch the children at the preschool while the parents participated in the training at the TOGETHER workshops. To make the meetings more friendly and welcoming, a light afternoon tea was provided for the children, parents, and Jia.

Ava's mum, Zoey, was unable to attend the first session due to job and family commitments, so the trainer provided the workshop content as well as additional coaching to her by phone to keep her up to date. By being adaptable to each family's situation, we were able to ensure the workshop information was the same for all the parents and Jia, which helped to build consistency between the preschool and the home environments.

What happened during the training?

In Chapter 3 we mentioned that we learnt a valuable lesson in how we missed opportunities to capture the discussions regarding the parents' and educators' relationships, beliefs, and practices during the workshops. Therefore, for our second story we recorded each workshop and were able to capture some important insights from the parents and Jia. The two workshops followed the same format as our first story.

Workshop 1

At the beginning of this workshop there was a feeling of excitement as the parents connected and their children realised that they would be staying at the preschool for a few extra hours. The fact that there would be afternoon tea at the preschool created a party-like atmosphere for the children. Several of the children were eager to join in for the first few minutes to see what their parents were up to. In fact, Samuel was eager to help with the presentation at the beginning, where he provided an opportunity for the facilitator to demonstrate the use of descriptive praise at the commencement. There was much laughter and conversation from all the children's parents and Jia, which indicated that everyone was very comfortable at the preschool and eager to participate.

After the parents and Jia were introduced to the TOGETHER principles at the beginning of the workshop, they opened their TOGETHER training manuals to page 11 (see Figure 5.1) and were then prompted to discuss how they could develop strong relationships with children and each other.

There were many contributions from the group. Jia initiated the conversation with how she had developed relationships with the children at the preschool, with a focus placed on following their interests:

> *I make an effort to have eye contact and also really listen to them. And then everything you do and you show that you are genuinely interested and listen to their thoughts. I remember when Isabella first started last year, she had Sarah as her teacher and she was a bit resistant to me, but I think over the time she can tell that I'm very interested in her and I want to make the relationships and I would just always be there for her if she needs help.*

Jia's comments prompted Charlotte to contribute how she had formed relationships with Samuel and his siblings at home through their interests, and how this focus had sparked conversations between her and her children:

> *Samuel is really into just sort of creating stuff and making stuff with paper and drawing and like taping more paper together… they spend a lot of time just making stuff. So, I find that if I give them the undivided attention of them explaining what they've done, like if in full detail of what they've created, all they've named it, all that sort of stuff.*

Juan was initially very quiet; however, we could see her confidence develop as Charlotte discussed her family and the way they had developed relationships between each other, which suggested that the small group setting was encouraging conversations between all the participants. Juan nodded in agreement with Charlotte's statement and then made specific references to how Isabella loved to

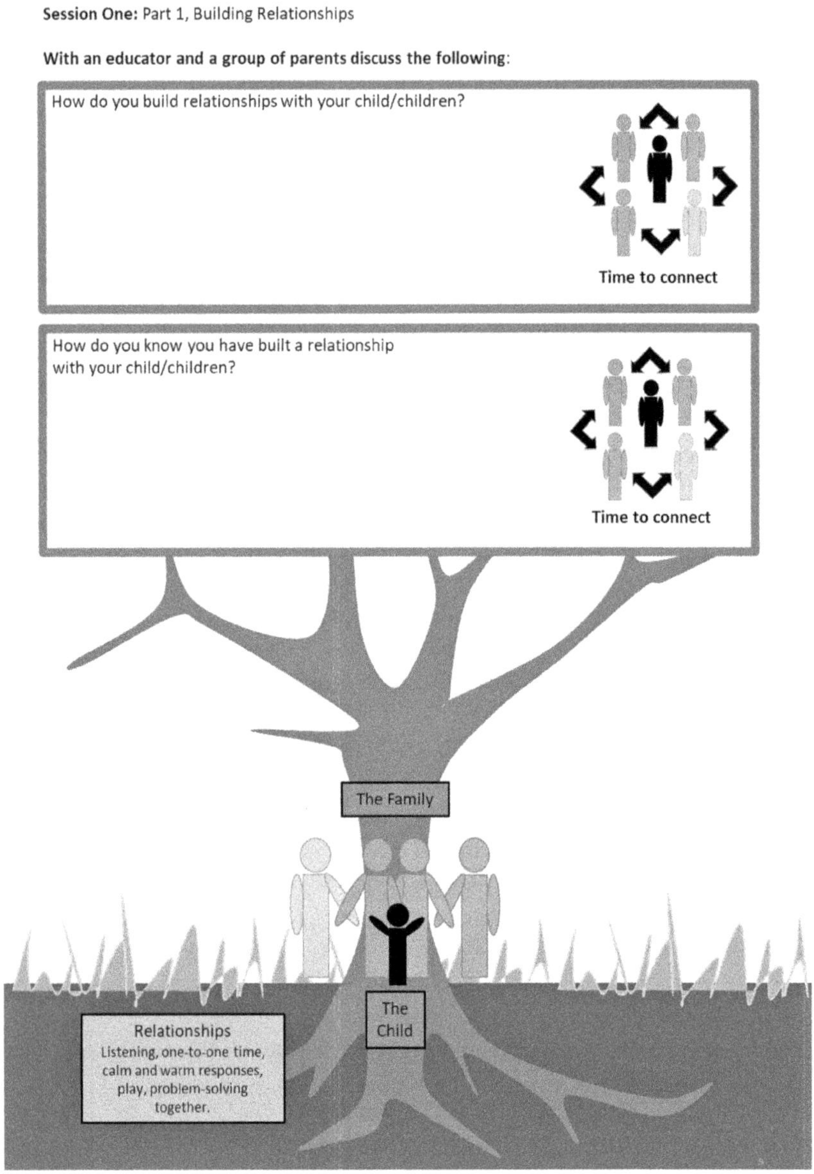

FIGURE 5.1 Session One, Part 1: Building relationships

copy the activities they had been doing at preschool when she was at home. For example, she mentioned the picture books that the children had created themselves, which was an initiative of Jia's, whereby she had introduced a platform for the children to express themselves and to build a connection between each of their homes and the preschool. Each child had drawn pictures and Jia had helped them turn their pictures into a story. All the parents agreed that the picture books had been helpful in creating a connection between the home and the preschool, and how proud the children had been in being able to share their "published" works with their families and their peers at preschool. For example, the following statement from Charlotte highlights just how effective these books had been in developing relationships:

> *I've actually been reading some of the ones like as a bedtime stories, I'll pick up they've (Samuel and his sister) drawn some pictures at kinder and then the kids will narrate what each page is. And I just write down verbatim what they say, which sometimes it's so silly and I'm like, we'll read them. They'll pick it out … he (Samuel) loves it. His story is getting read at bedtime.*

The conversations continued as the parents shared their cultural practices with each other, and how they used such practices to build relationships. For example, Isabella's dad, Taio, expanded on how they enjoyed camping, roasting marshmallows over the fire, and fishing as a family. Jia responded, discussing how Isabella would often talk about these experiences and how excited she was when her dad caught calamari. Charlotte listened and mentioned how as a family they would often celebrate the American holidays, which, of course, are not celebrated in Australia; however, at the preschool they did and this had made them feel very welcome. She also mentioned how as a family they loved to engage in dance parties and how this was extended at the preschool:

> *As a family we do a lot of dance parties. All three of them (children) get into it. During the day, at the weekends. They are inside and still moving around and it's hilarious … and we find that if I am grumpy that it can really turn all our moods around … we put just on upbeat music … it's the only tradition we really have … we do that a lot to reset …. Ever since Mr. George came in and did a little break-dancing class (at preschool), he likes to spin around on the floor. And he's Mr. George.*

As the conversations continued, it became quite evident that some strong connections had developed between Jia and the parents. Jia was very responsive to the families' interests and cultural practices. She mentioned how they made a point to celebrate different cultural celebrations of the families attending each year and was eager to discuss with the parents how she could incorporate more of the families' home practices at the preschool.

As the relationships between the parents and Jia deepened, we were able to move to the importance of providing positive praise and encouragement for the behaviour they wanted to see. Specifically, the focus was on how positive praise and encouragement have consistently been shown to develop children's social and emotional skills. It was discussed that adults who provide a higher level of praise are more likely to encounter children with increased levels of social competence, emotional self-regulation, and lower levels of inappropriate behaviours

(Webster-Stratton et al., 2008). The parents and Jia were shown types of positive praise and encouragement. They were provided with examples of positive strategies in action, such as focusing on the learning process rather than the final product and the use of proximity praise and encouragement. As the examples were being illustrated, the parents began bonding over the struggles they had been facing with their own child's challenging behaviour. Each parent felt relieved that the other parents had been experiencing similar struggles, and thus by sharing their experiences, they started to build a community of support. The comments the parents made truly highlighted the everyday struggles they were facing, such as Lillian saying:

> *It's more trying to take out the frustration ... why do I have to tell you 16 times to get out the door [referring to her children]! My daughter said to me, "You do that funny smile when I know you are not happy." That's because I'm trying really hard to, you know, not lose it ... to fake it until your make it ... forcing a smile can be really hard.*

Lillian bonded with Charlotte on this comment:

> *Sometimes it's about trying to stop the children from killing each other at the dinner table ... "He's making faces at me" ... "He's telling me I'm stupid" [comments her children make to each other] [I say] "You have come to the table and you are to sit really nicely." They don't know when to stop ... he doesn't understand when that limit is.*

And this was followed by Isabella's dad, Taio, who said, "I think she needs to control her temper. She throws a tantrum pretty easily when you say don't touch that ... We didn't have the same with her brother ... she is struggling with her emotions."

As a team, the parents and Jia (with the help of the facilitator) were able to come up with some proactive solutions for the struggles they had with the challenging behaviours of the children. Such solutions included the parents using descriptive praise when their children were doing the behaviours they wanted to see. By using the basic positive behaviour guidance plan (page 29 of the manual – see Figure 5.2) they were able to identify the behaviours they wanted to see less of, list the prosocial behaviours they wanted to see more of, come up with proactive and relationship-building strategies appropriate to their context, and list some useful descriptive phrases of praise and encouragement they could use to acknowledge when their child was being socially or emotionally appropriate. The parents and Jia also developed some reminder strategies to help keep their focus on the positive behaviours the children engaged in and worked towards the rule of "The Golden Apple" – five positive responses for every negative response (see Figure 5.3). For example, Charlotte mentioned how she would place five head bands on her wrist and transfer them to the other wrist each time she gave praise, and because she

Positive behaviour guidance plan

List the behaviours you want to see LESS of...	List the behaviours you want to see MORE of...	Proactive and relationship strategies (what we will do)	Praise and encouragement – useful phrases

FIGURE 5.2 Basic Positive Behaviour Guidance Plan

always had hand ties on her wrist, she felt this was a great tool. The parents and Jia were then given the homework task of practising the five positive responses for every negative one by using the basic positive behaviour guidance plan and the reminder strategies that they had developed.

FIGURE 5.3 The Golden Apple

Workshop 2

The second workshop saw the parents and Jia eagerly arrive ready to share their reflections on how they had progressed with giving more positive feedback than negative feedback to the children over the week. Charlotte began:

> *I did really try to praise good behavior every time I was seeing it. And not just, like you said, being very specific, sort of with the praise. I think we would just say, oh, good job. That's great. And I think we did that a lot. And we didn't really specify, so we've tried to do that. And even this morning, I noticed after having done that for not even a week, Samuel got dressed the first time I asked them, and then he came in to show me and he said, look, I put on my shoes without you even asking. So, I was like, oh, I love it when you get dressed the first time I ask you. I'm so proud of you, you knew you were leaving so you decided to put on your shoes all by yourself. I'm sure it was just a fluke, and that probably won't happen on Monday. But I tried to take advantage of that moment and just like really make them feel really proud of what he did, and that I was really impressed with it.*

Juan mentioned how before she had been like Charlotte and had not used descriptive praise until she began the TOGETHER training. While she was yet to see a change in Isabella's behaviour, she had noticed positive changes in herself:

> *Before I was like you [referring to Charlotte]. I just mentioned good girl. But this week I have been more specific but haven't seen a big change in her [Isabella], but I have seen a change from my side. I'm starting to enjoy her more instead of "Urgggghh!"*

Charlotte returned to her reflection and built on this:

> *I've noticed this even yesterday; I was walking home from kinder … Samuel would always say "I can't walk another step." … But we happened to be walking with his*

friend, and he walked the whole way by himself without complaining... So, I reinforced it yesterday how proud I was of him the day before for walking all by himself. And I was like, you must be getting big, so is Andrew. Your legs are getting stronger; you're getting so much bigger. Like, I'm so impressed at how you can do that all on your own. And he was just like, yes. And you can see him like, puffing his chest out.

After these reflections we then focused on developing rules/guidelines, redirecting behaviour, natural and logical consequences, and the sit and watch/calm down strategy. As the parents and Jia discussed the importance of rules, it became evident that many of the rules were framed in negative terms such as "Never talk over the teachers," "Don't touch," and "No talking at the dinner table." The parents also discussed how at home there was often inconsistency between them and their partners. These discussions led to points being made about having a set of three or four simple home rules, stated in positive terms, which all family members (or all educators) knew and were developed with the children to ensure consistency with parents and to also help with everyday routines at home and at the preschool. Such rules included "We use gentle hands," "We speak kindly to each other," and "We treat our toys nicely."

As we progressed to talking about the challenging behaviours that the parents were experiencing with their children, they were quite eager to share examples of what they meant with each other. As in Workshop 1, they continued to bond when they all recognised that they often felt the same way. Lillian started:

My kids fight all the time ... "He's got my things", "She's making a noise", "He's clapping, he's singing when I want to be singing". I think it's jealousy. There is this singing-in-the-car business – one wants to do it and the other wants to do it ... But I think that's just competition ... I want them to play nicely.

Charlotte had similar feelings, and made a point as to how time poor families can be:

And sometimes it is so time sensitive ... all of a sudden, just in that moment, just refused to walk away. He (Samuel) was trying to physically fight me to get in the car. It was like one of those moments where I was kind of letting it happen, but then I was like, you still have to go to school.

Zoey laughed and agreed with their frustrations:

I have that; you need to be in the car to go to school. Just they're just so slow. They just dawdle. Yeah, like half an hour, 40 minutes to eat a bowl of cereal. I'm like, are you kidding me.

As the parents discussed their frustrations and struggles, we were able to reflect on the previous discussion around positive forecasting (letting their children know that they believed they could get ready on time) and giving descriptive praise for the prosocial behaviour. Then discussions regarding children's tantrums became the next topic, with Juan mentioning her challenge with Isabella:

> *She is usually so reasonable. But when these things happen, that's why I feel so ill equipped to deal with it… I sometimes say to her, what do you actually want me to do in this moment? Look, sometimes she's just having a meltdown and I literally have no control over.*

Lillian agreed and offered her ideas: "In regard to my six-year-old, she absolutely loses it, and you can't reason with her. I'll often say, 'Go to the reset spot' … I do ask her to go somewhere else to calm down."

These examples of their struggles enabled us to discuss more about the reasons behind the tantrums and devise ways to recognise the behaviours that occurred before and after the tantrum. Specifically, their attention was drawn to page 42 of the TOGETHER training manual and the "A-B-C Identification" strategy (see Figure 5.4), where the parents and Jia were encouraged to reflect on the reasons why a child may be exhibiting challenging behaviours. They were asked to identify what happened before the behaviour (A = antecedent), what was the challenging behaviour (B = behaviour), and what happened after (C = consequence). For example, Zoey was able to use this strategy to illustrate an interaction she had with Ava:

> *I know often with her she is tired, and we had gone to gymnastics for two weeks in a row [A= antecedent] …. We had been going straight after school, and she had a meltdown, just burst into tears because we weren't having a hot dog for dinner [B = behaviour]…. Clearly, it was not about the hot dog. And I said, sweetie, we don't have to go to gymnastics. If you're tired and you need to go home and you need to relax. And you just want to sit at home and chill out, we can do that. I recognised that she needed to go home [C = consequence when Zoey took Ava home to rest].*

Jia also mentioned at the preschool they had quiet places such as the reading corner or tents where children could go if they needed some time to breathe and gather their emotions.

We then moved into discussing natural and logical consequences associated with the previously discussed behaviours that the parents had found challenging. For example, in Zoey's case, where her children were taking too long to eat a bowl of cereal (despite Zoey's best efforts to get them to eat) and the family needed to leave, the natural consequence would be that the child would miss out on breakfast and would need to wait until morning tea to eat. Or, in Lillian's case, where her children would constantly fight over who would get sing to their song, the logical consequence was that the music would be turned off. Once the siblings had worked out how to take turns and encourage each other, the music would be turned back on, and Lillian could give descriptive praise for the turn-taking and encouragement.

As the discussion progressed, the conversation steered towards more violent behaviour. Charlotte gave the example of Samuel's unawareness of his strength: "Samuel has no idea about his own strength; he's hitting us, pulling my hair out …"

Lillian was also having the same challenges with her youngest:

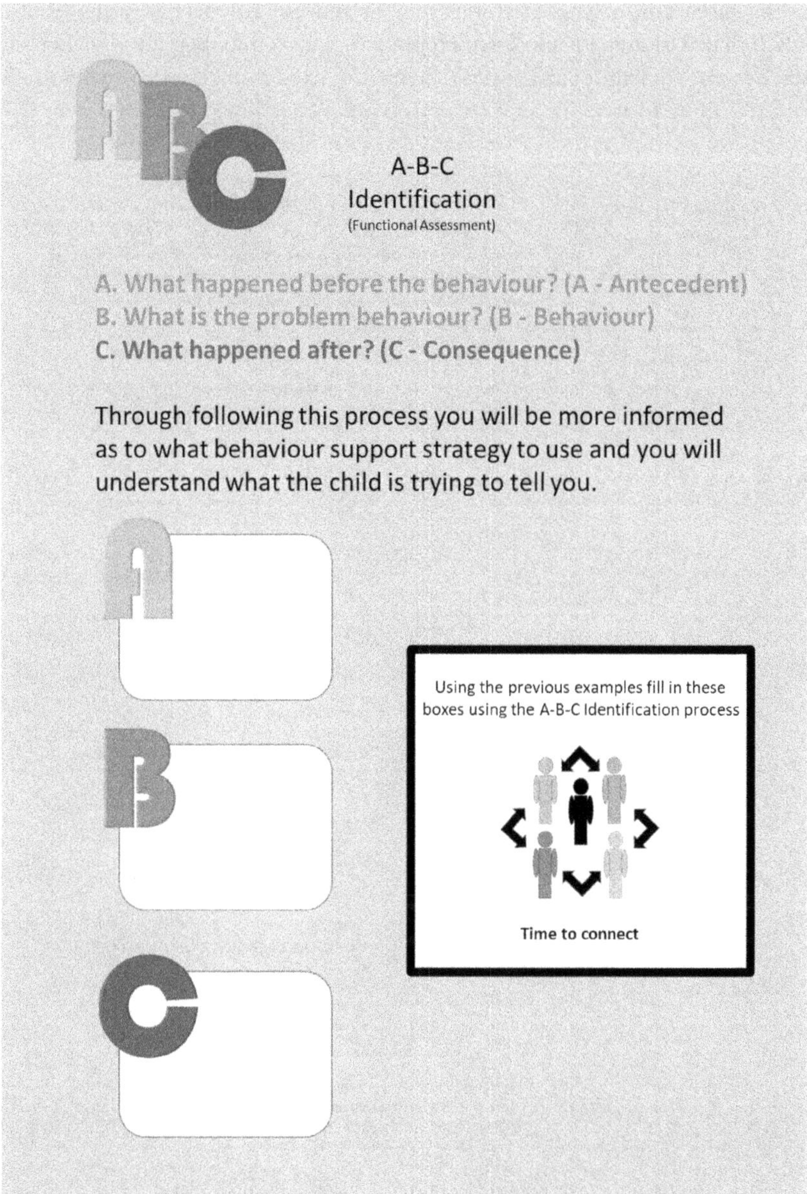

FIGURE 5.4 A-B-C Identification – Functional assessment

With the unsafe behaviour, it is fairly frequent, and he is my first terrible-two tantrumer. He will just continue for ten minutes, kicking and screaming, and I just have to put him in the car … He's literally ripping my hair out … he will scream the whole way to school and all the way back.

This discussion naturally led into the "sit and watch" strategy (page 49 of the TOGETHER training manual, see Figure 5.5). This is a strategy to use when children become violent. Lillian and the facilitator acted out a scenario where Lillian was pretending to have hit another person and needed help to calm down. Using

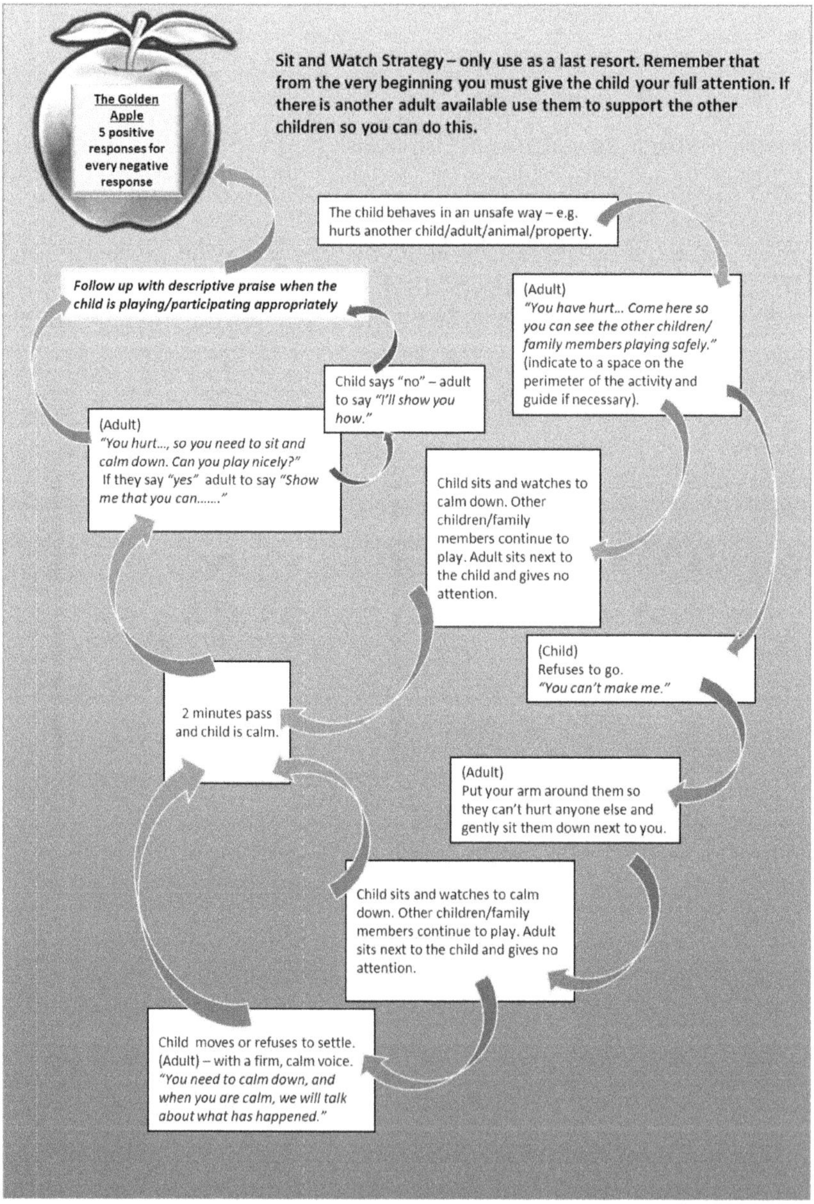

FIGURE 5.5 Sit and watch strategy

the map outlined in the sit and watch strategy, the facilitator acted out how to approach each stage of the strategy with assistance from Lillian. Emphasis was placed on reducing eye contact and attention, while staying beside the child until the child had calmed down. Then once the child had been calm for more than two minutes, strategies were given to the child to enable them to move to socially appropriate choices while remembering to follow up with descriptive praise once the child had been playing well again. When we were close to the conclusion of the session, the parents began reflecting on how the discussions had helped them realise that they were not on their own in their parenting journey.

Zoey mentioned the following:

> *I like that feeling like you are not the only one dealing with it [the behaviour] … like sometimes at a school pick-up you are … arghhh! You forget that on any given day someone else is going through their own struggles and it is not always talked about. I've been trying to be more realistic with them.*

Zoey was quickly supported by Lillian: "Yeah, maybe one of them [another parent] is in the car and struggling. I'm saying to myself, 'Thank goodness, it's not only me' and then feel better on the way to school."

What did we learn about the children, their families, and their early childhood teacher after the training in the TOGETHER workshops?

After the training in the TOGETHER workshops had finished, we continued with the preschool observations and Isabella's and Samuel's parents made video recordings at home. All the parents and Jia completed a second BPRQ about their beliefs, practices, and views on the parent–educator relationship, as well as the SDRS for their child (Jia did one for each child), and everyone participated in a final interview. The information collected from the questionnaires and the interviews indicated that many changes had occurred in the children, parents, and the early childhood teacher, Jia.

What did we learn about Isabella's, Samuel's, Julian's, and Ava's social and emotional development after the workshops?

Isabella

After the training, the video recordings indicated there had been an improvement in Isabella's behaviour at home. First, there were no signs of tantrums and she consistently showed progression in the development of her social and emotional skills. For example, she willingly followed her parents' instructions (including eating her food at mealtimes) and was using her voice to communicate when she felt frustrated or challenged by a certain task. Her perseverance with activities at home also increased when her mum, Juan, gave her descriptive praise for "doing the right thing." The completion of the SDRS by Juan supported the improvements in Isabella's social and emotional competence skills. She reported that Isabella was complying with her parents' instructions more often; she was eating and drinking appropriately at mealtimes; she was less likely to plead, nag, or demand things; and she was staging fewer tantrums.

The SDRS completed by Jia showed Isabella had improved in her confidence to interact with peers at the preschool; however, this had taken some time. Isabella continued to find it difficult to approach peers during play but would respond appropriately to them when they tried to interact with her by engaging in conversation. On several occasions Jia made the point of providing descriptive praise and encouragement when Isabella contributed to group play and scaffolded the interactions between Isabella and her peers. Jia also made an additional effort to include more of Isabella's interests in classroom activities, such as setting up a campsite (connected to Isabella's family's home practices and context). Through the campsite scenario, Isabella was more inclined to engage in play with peers as this was something that she was familiar with and, therefore, she was more comfortable.

By taking this inclusive approach, Jia had been able to provide Isabella with opportunities to practise reciprocal conversations with her peers, which enabled her to begin to form friendships – interestingly, Isabella and Samuel were observed frequently playing together after the workshops. Maybe this had something to do with the fact that they had spent time together outside the preschool session when their parents were attending the workshops. As time progressed, an improvement in Isabella's social skills when she was interacting with others had been noted. She had become more confident in offering her ideas during group times and there had been instances where she had initiated play with others. Isabella was no longer invisible to other children and she was receiving positive feedback from Jia (and other children), which was improving her confidence in the classroom environment.

Samuel

For Samuel there had also been a noticeable improvement in his social and emotional skills, which had become evident from the home video recordings, the preschool observations, the parent and educator reports on the SDRS and the final interview. He was more willing to share and was less disruptive. His mother, Charlotte, summed up his improvement well in her own words:

> *With Samuel we have seen several changes … He really, really responds well to the positive praise … like, it has just been amazing seeing him, like, puff up his chest and be proud when we give him that positive praise. Like, when he's being gentle with his younger brother, or when he's being really kind, you know, like sharing, and doing something special. So I definitely think it's improved [his behaviour] because he's more inclined to do those good behaviours because he knows he's getting "positives" back and that we are acknowledging them, and they [his good behaviours] are not necessarily going unseen.*

While concerns regarding Samuel's development were not an issue at the preschool, Jia said she had seen growth in his social and emotional skills. For example, she reported that he was now more willing to allow others to contribute their ideas during group conversations.

Julian

As mentioned earlier, Julian had not been selected as one of our focus children, therefore, there were no home or preschool observations made of him. The reports from his mum (Lillian) in the final interview indicated that, generally, Julian was engaging in more positive interactions with his siblings, which included agreeing to compromises during conflicts and being helpful with family tasks.

Ava

The SDRS completed by Ava's mum (Zoey) in the final interview also demonstrated improvements in Ava's social and emotional skills at home. Ava was following rules more easily and was responding to boundaries more positively. She was being more polite with her siblings, was more inclined to take turns when interacting with her siblings and would join in adult-directed activities when asked.

What did we learn about the beliefs and practices of Jia and the four parents after the training?

First, the BPRQ revealed that Jia and the four parents all strongly agreed on parenting and teaching beliefs that were more consistent with authoritative styles. By this we mean that children's appropriate behaviour needs to be praised or encouraged frequently and that when a child tries hard (even at the small things), they should be given praise and encouragement. Yet before the training in the TOGETHER workshops, Jia and the four parents did not believe this and were inconsistent in their beliefs. However, these inconsistencies did not translate to their practices. Jia, Juan, Charlotte, Lillian, and Zoey all reported that they would let children know when they were doing a good job; they would single out the appropriate behaviours they wanted children to do; they would share how happy they were when children did things well; and they would encourage children to talk about themselves in positive ways.

Interestingly, Isabella's mum, Juan, reported that she did not believe she gave more attention to positive behaviours than negative behaviours. However, the home observations clearly contradict this (see Figure 5.6). In fact, the observations reveal that Juan dramatically increased the number of her descriptive praise and encouragement statements. Before the workshops it was noted that there had been only six positive interactions provided by Juan to Isabella and over 18 discouragement statements made. After the workshops, Juan had increased the number of descriptive praise phrases given to Isabella, which averaged 25 per observation, and

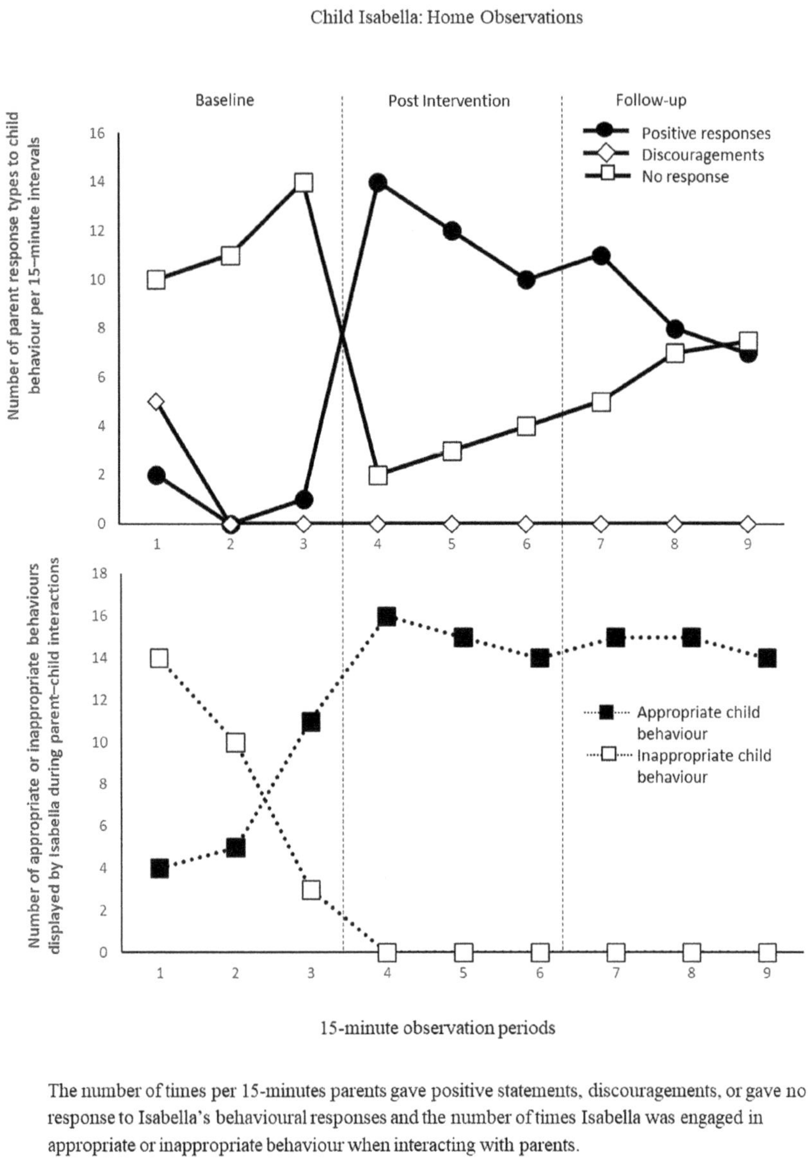

FIGURE 5.6 Child Isabella: Home observations

made only a few discouraging statements. It appeared that she had not realised just how much she had increased her positive interactions with Isabella. However, by the final interview she acknowledged the change:

> *I technically had heard about it [the strategies] before the training, but I didn't realise it was that effective … And, yeah, like I said during the first session, I would always*

praise her but use very general terms like "good girl" and "well done". Now I am being more specific, and I find it very effective. And the major thing is I actually really learn to enjoy her more. Before I was like, "Oh, you're so annoying." But now, actually you see the improvement little by little because you are looking for the good things she has actually done. So, yes, I enjoy her more.

For Samuel's mum, Charlotte, there had also been an increase in the number of descriptive praise and encouragement statements she had given to Samuel, although before the workshops began, she did have a good understanding of the importance of descriptive praise due to additional reading she had done before the TOGETHER workshops. As a result of providing more descriptive praise and encouragement to Samuel, she reported that she had begun to see a change in his behaviour and that the modifications she had made to her parenting strategies were working for the whole family. She was refreshingly honest:

You see such an improvement with all the kids [her three children] and how eager they are to please us. So, I think a lot of their behaviour comes from that. I've definitely seen a change since using that message [positive feedback] with them. Yeah, but it's not all puppies and rainbows. You know, there is still a lot of fighting and arguing. But I will say honestly that in the last four weeks we have noticed an improvement.

She continued by stating how the training in the TOGETHER workshops had helped develop more consistency in the strategies she and her husband were using in improving their children's social and emotional competence:

Since the training it has created conversation between me and my husband in that we had not talked about parenting before, so it has sorted of enabled us to bring to the table the things that I've learnt and sharing in the handouts you've provided. One of the techniques we really like, because it's really easy to remember, is the 5 to 1 in terms of every negative interaction. Trying to have five positive ones and sort of wipe the slate clean and negate that negative interaction. Especially because he [her husband] has such limited time with them [the children]. It makes us a united front in terms of consistency in our parenting, and I'm using similar techniques, so they're getting the same sort of parenting and response from both of us.

Lillian found that by practising the strategies she had learnt in the TOGETHER workshops, she was able to improve her interactions with Julian and found the sit and watch strategy particularly helpful. When asked about how her interactions had changed, she mentioned:

Yes, so mostly around that example that you gave around having the child sitting with you and explaining to them that they need to … When they are ready to behave in an appropriate manner that they can go and re-join what's happening. It is probably the biggest one. It doesn't quite work very well with a nine-year-old, but for the younger ones.

Zoey found that the TOGETHER training had challenged some of her previous practices. She referred to how she had been raised with different strategies and had been using them. However, after completing the TOGETHER training, she practised the new way of guiding her children's behaviour to develop their social and emotional competence:

> *I think it [TOGETHER] is quite positive, particularly if you have people who haven't been brought up that way. It has helped a bit as I had been brought up with you get the smack, but that doesn't particularly translate well and so that [the* TOGETHER *strategies] has been quite beneficial.*

For Jia, the preschool observations showed that, overall, she had tried to use more descriptive praise and encouragement when interacting with the children (see Figure 5.7). She mentioned that she had been trying to give more meaningful positive feedback. However, she did make the comment that she didn't really have any children in her class who had challenging behaviour. Her response indicates that she may have misinterpreted some of the TOGETHER strategies and, as a result, she was inclined to only give positive feedback to children who were struggling with their social and emotional competence.

What did we learn about the parent–educator relationship after the training?

As you would have realised from the parent and educator voices in our workshops, there had been some moments when the parent–parent and parent–educator relationships had been strengthened. The participants had found common ground on the challenges they were facing and then worked together to develop consistent strategies between their homes and the preschool. Before the TOGETHER workshops began, all the parents had reported that they had a strong relationship with Jia, which they reported continued after they had completed the training. Such reports were evidence of Jia's family-centred teaching practice (Dunst, 2002). Her approach had been noted by the encouraging comments from the parents, such as the one given by Charlotte:

> *Hearing how an educator deals with certain behaviours is helpful … like the educator's techniques … They [the children] have been very receptive with the educator but I like hearing the educator's approach as I think that's very helpful as a parent.*

When Juan was asked about her family's relationship with Jia, she reflected on just how helpful Jia had been in helping Isabella settle into preschool when her daughter was experiencing separation anxiety: "She has been great ever since the beginning because I have experienced some difficulty with Isabella settling at school. I was very upset and Jia was very helpful. So it was like the relationship was already perfect."

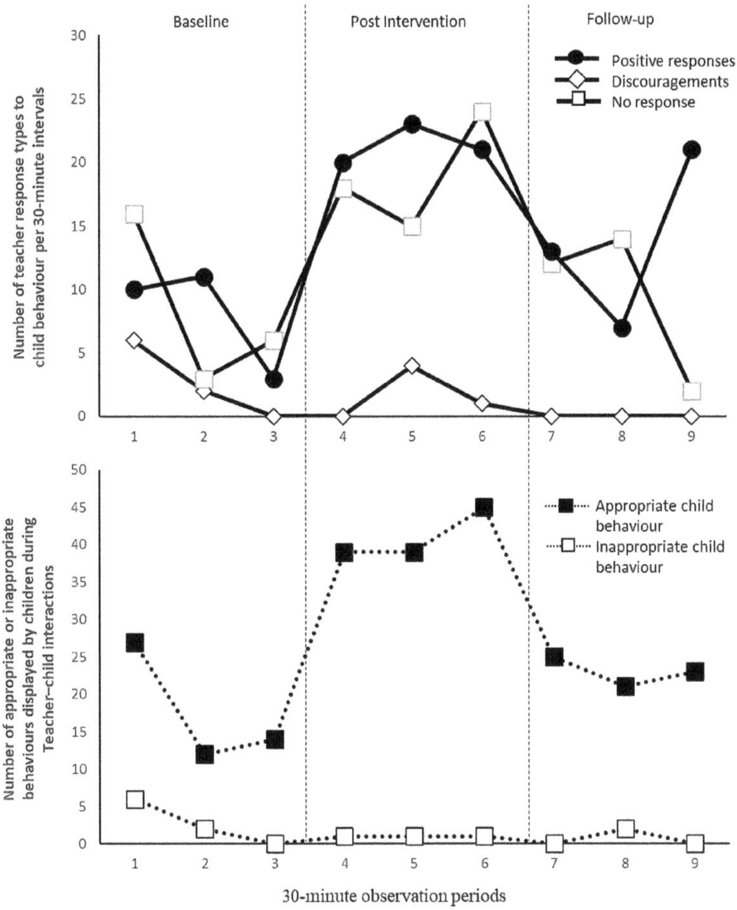

The number of times per 30 minutes Jia gave positive statements, discouragements, or gave no response to all children's behavioural responses and the number of times children was engaged in appropriate or inappropriate behaviour when interacting with Jia.

FIGURE 5.7 Teacher Jia: Preschool observations

Jia also indicated that she believed that the parent–educator relationship had improved between her and the parents who had attended the training:

> *We feel closer because we went through the training together and it's a great relationship-building exercise, and you also receive positive feedback from them. So definitely the relationship has strengthened. And it helped me to build the relationship with that child, which will help you deal with the challenging behaviour; and also the relationship with the family. It helps you build that partnership for dealing with the child's behaviour.*

When asked how the parent–educator relationship could be improved, the common response was that the parents would like to spend more time with the educator; that communication was the key; and that there needed to be consistency between what the parents do at home and what the educator does in the preschool. Juan felt that she needed more time with Jia to learn the strategies and would look to Jia for that support:

> *I think it's just like things we need to discuss and spend more time together so we can bring things up like again and again, you know what I mean? Even before the lecture, I had heard about it [positive praise and encouragement]. But after the lecture, I forgot things ... And after a couple of months I stopped ... not that I had forgotten the theory, but I had just forgotten to do it on a regular basis. So, if the educator somehow did a reminder ... not for like an hour lecture, just every now and then.*

In the next two chapters, you will see that we found that the trust parents have with an educator, like the trust Juan developed with Jia, is a vital element in helping families develop strategies to grow children's social and emotional competence. Read on to see how we have explored ways to empower early childhood teachers and educators to pass on the knowledge they have learnt from the TOGETHER programme to all the families they work with.

6

STORY 3

The community hub

Rishi is busy exploring outside. He loves to climb on the preschool's playground equipment and dig in the sandpit. Suddenly, it is time to come inside for group time. Naomi, one of his educators, had mentioned a few minutes earlier to the group that this would be happening. However, when she announced it was time, Rishi ignored her and continued to climb. Once all the other children were in, she walked over to Rishi, who smiled, then ran in the other direction of the door. After several reminders from Naomi, Rishi eventually came inside. All the other children were sitting on the mat listening to their other educator, Laura. Naomi needed to lead Rishi by the hand over to the mat and show him where to sit. He sat for a few minutes listening to Laura's instructions about how some children were able to share stories about their weekend. As each child began to take their turns, Rishi would interrupt, trying to tell his story, and speak over the other children. Naomi had to keep reminding him throughout the group time to let other children talk and to stop yelling over them. For most of the group time, Rishi struggles to join in and Naomi spends most of her time redirecting his disruptive behaviour. Is he just being naughty? Is he just being difficult? On the other hand, is there something more to his behaviour?

The two preceding stories have described the application of TOGETHER in varying contexts, including preschools and family circumstances. In Story 3 we introduce a new context – a community hub consisting of two preschool programmes. We explore how the context of the hub has contributed to the stronger relationships between the children, parents, teachers, and educators. Benjamin, Hailey, and Rishi are the three children that are central to this story, along with their mothers and educators. Through Story 3 we bring together components of the ecological systems

DOI: 10.4324/9781003006466-6

theory (Bronfenbrenner, 1986) by showing how the educators were able to respond to the contexts of Benjamin's and Rishi's disruptive behaviour. We also discuss how additional coaching empowered the educators to share their practices with other families who could not attend the TOGETHER training. This chapter also details the important role educators have in reaching out to families who may be hesitant about participating in the TOGETHER programme. The story uses family-centred practice (Dunst, 2002) to illustrate the important role educators have in empowering families with positive behaviour guidance skills, and the effect this has on children's social and emotional development. We also discuss why researchers and outside professionals need to value and utilise the trust educators have already cultivated with families when developing effective early interventions.

The preschool setting for Story 3

Story 3 is unique in that the participants are from a preschool programme located on the same site as a maternal and child health centre and a number of playgroups. The preschool is divided into four rooms, with each providing a programme for four-year-olds. All four rooms share a large outdoor communal space. This configuration is a recent concept that is changing how many early childhood centres operate in Victoria, Australia (Garvis et al., 2016). The concept is most often referred to as a community hub.

At the time of the research study, families from two of the rooms had volunteered to participate in the TOGETHER project. The preschool programmes delivered in these two rooms consisted of 33 children in each room. The six educators attended the preschool Monday to Friday for five hours per day. Each child attended three assigned five hour sessions (a total of 15 hours). Three educators had been allocated to each room; however, both rooms shared a large outdoor space, which meant there were times when the children would interact with all six educators. The multicultural preschool community consisted of families from Australian, Indian, Sudanese, Middle Eastern, Chinese, and European backgrounds. Two of the participating families identified as Australian and one family identified as Australian-Fijian-Indian. The educators identified as Australian, Mauritian, Malayan/Tamil/Indian, and Punjabi/Indian.

The children, their families, and their educators

Benjamin

Benjamin is a four-year-old boy who lives with his mum, Kelly, and his maternal grandmother. His mum grew up in the local area and the family identify as Australian. They have several family members who live nearby, including his cousins who are of a similar age. Benjamin shows much enjoyment in playing with others, especially when it is one to one. At preschool he will often be found building houses with large pieces of construction equipment, creating sandpit cities with the cars, engaging in craft-based activities, and climbing challenging playground equipment. At home he has a great interest in playing with Lego. With every creation he will have a special name for it and delights in telling his mum all about his Lego inventions. He also enjoys watching movies with his mum – it is their family treat. However, Benjamin finds it difficult to regulate his emotions and interact with large groups of children.

Benjamin's mum, Kelly

Kelly is a single mum who works long hours at a local supermarket. She ensures she can meet Benjamin's needs by adjusting her shifts to enable her to pick him up and drop him off at preschool. She feels it is extremely important to be available to talk to his educators when needed. Kelly reports that she finds it exhausting parenting Benjamin at times and she lacks confidence. She has been getting additional advice from an external psychologist to assist her with Benjamin's behaviour. She has started to employ some of the strategies she has learnt from his psychologist; however, she tells us that living with her mother (Benjamin's grandmother) makes things very difficult as her mother will often contradict the strategies that she tries to implement. Her mother will often tell her that she is not instigating the correct strategies. At times, Kelly feels quite isolated and the preschool has become, consequently, a place of trust for her. She has developed an especially strong relationship with Anika, one of Benjamin's educators. Anika herself is a single mother and Kelly feels she can relate to her and will often seek guidance and reassurance from Anika.

Hailey

Hailey is also four years old and lives with her mum, Diana, her dad, Paul, and her younger brother, Beau. The family has lived locally for all of Hailey's life and identify as Australian. Diana reports that Hailey enjoys spending time with her cooking – they often go to recipe website and pick out recipes. Hailey loves to paint her nails and play dress-ups. Her dad is a computer technician and, as a result, she has taken a deep interest in how computers work and will often ask him questions at the dinner table about his day with computers. Hailey also loves to be part of everything her mum does and will follow her around most of the day and help care for Beau. The family really enjoy going to the movies/cinema together, which forms much of their time connecting as a family. At preschool, Hailey often takes on a leadership role during play, she is good at negotiating and taking on the ideas of her peers. She enjoys being involved in socio-dramatic play and can often be found in the bamboo plantation outside or the family corner inside, pretending to cook, looking after the baby dolls, or going camping.

Hailey's mum, Diana

Diana spends most days caring for Hailey and Beau, while Paul works full time. Diana plays an active role in the preschool community and will often volunteer her time for fundraising and in-class help. She values the active role she plays in Hailey's life and cultivates their relationship through her love for cooking and baking. She feels confident in her parenting and actively seeks out opportunities to develop her knowledge as a parent, which includes reading parenting books and attending community playgroups. Diana has also developed a special friendship with Benjamin's mum, Kelly, and frequently organises play dates for Hailey and Benjamin.

Rishi

The third child in Story 3 is Rishi, introduced at the beginning of this chapter. From a Fijian-Indian background, he lives with his mum, Meleni, his dad, Jo, and his two-year-old brother, Adi. The family has had several personal challenges over the past year, with extended family members becoming ill. At home, Rishi loves to play chase and play-fight with Adi. He enjoys reading picture books with his mum and dad and practising his drawing. At preschool Rishi loves to move about his environment and is constantly exploring new ideas, especially when it involves testing out building toys, putting puzzles together, climbing on the outside obstacle course, and digging in the sandpit. However, Rishi has demonstrated several delays with his social and emotional skills.

Rishi's mum, Meleni

Meleni was willing to be part of the training and for Rishi to be observed at the preschool. However, due to time constraints and family illness, she was not able to participate in interviews.

Benjamin's and Hailey's educators – Emma, Anika, and Sukhleen

Of Australian descent, the head teacher for Room 1, Emma, has a Bachelor of Education (Primary and Early Childhood) with two years experience. The second educator, Anika, is from Mauritius, she speaks French and Creole as her first languages and has a Diploma in Early Childhood Education. She has been teaching in the early childhood sector for two years. She is also in the process of completing her Bachelor of Education (Primary and Early Childhood). The third educator, Sukhleen, also has a Diploma in Early Childhood Education. She identifies as Punjabi, speaks Punjabi and English, and has had four years of teaching experience. She has been in the current preschool for two years.

Rishi's educators – Laura, Sabeena, and Naomi

Laura is the head teacher in Room 2. She holds a Bachelor of Education (Early Childhood) and has been teaching for 15 years. She identifies as Australian. The second educator, Sabeena, has a Diploma in Early Childhood Education. She identifies as Malayan/Tamil, speaks Tamil, Hindi, and English and has been working at the preschool for the past two years. She has been teaching in early childhood for over ten years. She was also working towards her bachelor degree, which meant she was unable to be on site for all the observations during the data collection phase. The third educator, Naomi, also an early childhood teacher, has been teaching for two years and has a Bachelor of Education (Primary and Early Childhood). She also identifies as Australian.

What did we learn about the children, their families, and their educators before the TOGETHER training?

As a result of the baseline observations, surveys, and interviews, we were able to identify the patterns of behaviour and the beliefs of each participant.

What did we learn about Benjamin's, Hailey's, and Rishi's social and emotional development before the training?

Benjamin

Remember the Social Development Rating Scale (SDRS) from Chapter 3? The scores given by Benjamin's mum, Kelly, and his three educators indicated that Benjamin was struggling with his social and emotional development skills, so he was selected as one of our focus children for Story 3.

Kelly reported that Benjamin had aggressive outbursts of behaviour daily at home. He would often kick her, pull her hair, twist her arm, and scream extremely loudly when he became frustrated. Such behaviours were witnessed during the baseline video observations. There were times when Kelly was unsure what was triggering his tantrums. When he became upset, Benjamin found it difficult to explain to his mum why he had had the meltdown. She also reported that Benjamin found it difficult to follow instructions, such as when she asked him to get dressed. She reported that there would often be several instances during the day when he would not listen to her and would often walk away. At preschool, Benjamin would generally follow the educators' suggestions, which made his challenging behaviours less pronounced. However, his educators reported that there were times when he would struggle to understand the perspectives of his peers, take turns, focus on non-preferred tasks, and join in with group times. Over the term there had been several instances where he had hurt other children in order to have a turn with a toy, or had hurt someone when they had annoyed him at group times. His educators reported that he would often want to watch group times from a distance because larger groups of children appeared to overwhelm him. These behaviours had also been observed by our research team during the preschool observations.

Hailey

Hailey's preschool educators reported that the SDRS had revealed that she had reasonably strong social and emotional skills, but there were general concerns related to the struggles she had with joining in with peer groups and the preference she had for playing one on one. Her mum, Diana, reported that, at home, the main struggles they had with Hailey were related to her eating habits. At most dinner times, Hailey would find something wrong with the food, often describing things as being too grainy or too soft. Both the preschool and the home observations indicated that Hailey was quite eager to please others, looked out for her younger brother, and had established several close friendships with selected children.

Rishi

The SDRS was conducted by Rishi's educators, his mum, Meleni, declined to do the SDRS, citing time constraints. The scores given by Laura, Suhkleen, and Naomi indicated that there were a high number of concerns relating to Rishi's social and emotional development. The educators reported that he would often watch his peers playing from a distance and was very cautious about joining in with group play. Rishi struggled to take turns with other children, and if a peer stood too close to him when he was concentrating, he would often hit them out of frustration. He would also become aggressive if another child was playing with a toy that he wanted to play with. He would often interrupt other children during mat times and would resist coming inside when called. Rishi's family had given consent for Rishi to be involved in our research; however, due to family illness, his mum found it difficult to take part in the interviews. His educators reported that they had detected from the family that there was a general feeling that Rishi's behavioural concerns were more a result of the interactions he was having at preschool rather than any concerns at home.

What did we learn about the beliefs and practices of Kelly and Diana (the mums) and the educators before the training?

The following section uses the SDRS, the Beliefs, Practices, and Relationships Questionnaire (BPRQ) and the observations to gain some understanding of the children's, their parents' and their educators' situations before the workshops commenced.

First, the BPRQ indicated that Kelly and Diana held strong beliefs regarding the importance of praising and recognising children when they had done things well, as did the six educators who aligned with more authoritative behaviour guidance styles. However, the responses relating to authoritarian styles differed, with both Kelly and Diana believing that children should always do as they were told, the use of an angry voice and punishment was acceptable for inappropriate behaviour, and that parents should always be in control of their children. Conversely, the educators were divided regarding the use of angry voices, with some emphasising the importance of being calm at all times. In addition, while all the educators agreed that punishment was not an appropriate strategy for misbehaviour (they cited the importance of guidance), they did differ on the point of whether they should be in control of children and the use of an angry voice.

Kelly's and Diana's responses to the BPRQ also indicated that they believed that the primary responsibility for raising children lay with the parents, whereas the educators placed more emphasis on the idea that it took many people to raise a child. Kelly, Diana, and Anika also believed in the importance of children sitting quietly at school and that they would often require assistance with most things, whereas Emma, Sukhleen, Naomi, Laura, and Sabeena disagreed. They felt strongly that children should be able to look after themselves at preschool and that part of learning often involved much movement and play.

Regarding practices, Laura and Sukhleen acknowledged that they did not give more attention to appropriate behaviour rather than inappropriate behaviour, and this was confirmed in the classroom observations. Interestingly, Emma, Naomi, Sabeena, and Anika felt that they did give more attention to appropriate behaviour – as did Kelly and Diana – but it was only Naomi who was observed giving more positive attention to appropriate behaviours during the baseline observations. This suggests that while the educators felt they gave positive attention to children, the observations suggested that this was not always the case. Laura and Kelly also recognised that they were not consistent in their behaviour guidance strategies.

Regarding the parent–educator relationships, both parents and each of the educators felt that these relationships were strong. In fact, during the interviews this point was often cited by the educators as being one of the hallmarks of such partnerships:

Sabeena *By us respecting families at the beginning, you make good relationships, and then they trust you.*

Naomi *Across the board we put a lot of practice into our everyday interactions to ensure strong relationships are built from the beginning, such as getting to know their interests, open conversations, and purposeful listening so that they know we value what they talk about.*

The responsive approach to being TOGETHER

As with our previous stories, we adapted the delivery of the TOGETHER training to suit the needs of the families and the educators and to ensure all participants felt comfortable about participating. After our initial consultations (and the CSD questionnaire), we gathered information regarding the way the participants liked to interact and communicate, and the venue and times that would best suit them for the training.

Not surprisingly, all the educators mentioned that they were time poor and had a strong preference for the TOGETHER workshops to be held immediately after the preschool session at 2.30 pm, once families had left; any later would be difficult for them as they had their own families to tend to. Kelly, Diana, and Meleni also stated that afternoon workshops would suit them the best; however, they would need care for their children. Therefore, an external educator was employed to care for Benjamin, Hailey, Rishi, and their siblings during the training workshops.

Food also played a motivating factor for attendance, with the educators stating they would be tired after a five-hour shift and, understandably, the children and their mums would also be hungry. To help the mums, children, teachers, and educators, each workshop was set up like an "afternoon tea" session where food and drinks were provided. This set-up produced a relaxed atmosphere that was conducive to conversation from the moment the participants entered the room.

Sometimes it was hard for the parents to attend. Rishi's mum, Meleni, was unable to attend the first session due to a family emergency and Hailey's mum, Diana, was unable to attend the second session due to her car breaking down. Consequently, catch-up sessions were arranged for each of them via phone and face-to-face meetings. Due to the trainers' adaptability to each family's situation, we were able to ensure the same training was delivered to both the parents and the educators.

What happened during the training?

The two TOGETHER workshops provide us with a platform to assist the educators and the families and they enabled us to gain additional insights into the beliefs and practices of the parents and educators and the parent–educator relationship. The workshops followed the same format as explained in Chapter 4.

Workshop 1

As the first workshop progressed, both the parents and the educators bounced stories off each other as they shared their experiences about how they had developed relationships with the children and understood their needs. From the beginning of the training, the educators supported each mum in contributing and empowered them to share stories about their child. For example, Diana excitedly told the others about Hailey's passion for cooking: "Saturday is her involvement in cooking … we go through the Taste website … that's our little thing."

Hailey's educator, Emma, keenly took notes and mentioned that she had noticed this in the classroom and that she may need to include a cooking program at the preschool. Kelly then elaborated on Benjamin's love for Lego and how he enjoys playing with his cousin. She mentioned: "I feel like I am building a relationship with him when he says things are cool … as long as it makes him happy … that smile makes you happy and you are like, ahhhh, all good."

Rishi's educator, Naomi, supported Kelly in her statements and shared stories about her own experiences as both a parent and a teacher, and the need to sometimes adapt her interests to suit her own child's:

> *It's like pretending you are interested ... I had to pretend ... in my head I don't care about the game, but I care about you [referring to her own child and wanting to let the child know that she cared].*

The sharing of ideas continued as Kelly and Diana talked about their struggles at home and the educators offered their experiences in solidarity. As stories were recounted, both the mums and the educators showed more confidence in contributing to the group discussion. The trust the parents had in the educators became evident. For example, Kelly shared her struggles with trying to get Benjamin dressed and wanting him to listen. As the focus was on recognising and responding to positive behaviours, Emma shared how she would assist her nephew with his listening skills by giving him descriptive praise when he had listened well.

Towards the end of Workshop 1, Kelly shared her struggles with Benjamin hitting and kicking her. The educators were extremely supportive in helping Kelly produce strategies that would help her recognise when he was being gentle. Together they developed a positive behaviour guidance plan. However, it became clear that she also needed strategies to cope with Benjamin's aggressive behaviours when they were occurring. Consequently, some simple calm-down strategies were suggested, with the emphasis being placed on using the Golden Apple's principle of five positive responses for every one negative response. The trainers mentioned that the following week's workshop would include more strategies to assist with misbehaviour.

Workshop 2

The second workshop began with the parents and educators reflecting on their progress in giving more positive feedback than negative feedback, as well as the reminder strategies they had used over the past week since Workshop 1. The educators commented on how the reminder strategies had helped them become more aware of their practices. Each reminder strategy had been developed according to the needs of each participant. For example, Naomi and Laura began by noting on their hands with a pen when they had given positive praise and made the following comments:

> Naomi *It [the reminder strategies and the training] made you more aware of what you were saying ... looking through another lens was interesting.*
>
> Laura: *I was consciously thinking of the five positives if I had given a negative ... I was aware when I needed to factor that in and upping that a little more.*

For Emma, she placed small pebbles in her left pocket, which she transferred to her right pocket when she had given positive praise. She had an interesting reflection on her previous beliefs on positive praise and how after the first TOGETHER workshop, accompanied by her change in practice, these beliefs had been challenged. She made specific reference to her provision of descriptive praise during group times:

> *Over the past week it [the reminder strategies and the training] had made me think how much praise I had been giving in group times. In the past I would have focused more on the task. I thought that if I did that [gave praise], I would lose children … I have now changed my practice in that I am more flexible to talk to children about their positive behaviour. I thought it would hinder the concentration of the other children, but it didn't at all in the end. They would listen to the praise … then they all wanted the praise.*

Sukhleen, on the other hand, realised that without the reminders her practices would be harder to change. She was quite diligent in her role and admitted that she would often become caught up in the daily tasks. An educator's day can be extremely challenging in the education and care of children and the constant vigilance required to maintain cleanliness and complete everyday routines. Sukhleen gave an honest and valuable reflection about how it was hard to change her behaviour when she did not use the reminders: "I went back to my natural behaviour … and forgot it (to give praise)."

The remainder of the second workshop was focused on developing rules and guidelines, redirecting behaviour, natural and logical consequences for inappropriate behaviours, and the sit and watch strategy used to calm down children. We began with exploring the current rules or guidelines that operated in the home and the preschool settings, and it was interesting to note that while the parents had their rules set in their minds, the rules were only stated when the child had done something wrong and, therefore, were expressed using negative terms. For example, Meleni (who joined us for the second session), stated that she would tell Rishi and his brother that there is to be *"no screaming, no running, and no jumping on the couch."*

Kelly responded by saying that she would tell Benjamin that there is to be "no hurting, kicking, or hitting." The conversations with each parent provided a basis for suggesting new ways of introducing rules and guidelines for their children. Such strategies included stating the new ways of behaving in positive terms, with the focus changed to what the parents (and the educators) wanted their children to achieve and how important it was to involve their children in the establishment of the rules and guidelines so as to develop their social understandings. Kelly quickly adapted her thoughts regarding the rules she had told Benjamin: "I ask him to share and be nice to everyone … be kind to others … so, I could try to use gentle hands? … Yeah, I'll try that."

As we moved into why children may engage in inappropriate behaviours, the term *functional behaviour analysis* was introduced. The participants were assisted in exploring why a child may be displaying disruptive behaviours. It was encouraging to see how the parents and educators reflected on the times when a child may have a tantrum and discussed why this may have occurred in the first place. As the challenges were being shared and the mothers and educators in the workshop could relate to these experiences, a sense of camaraderie began to emerge. Through this sharing exercise, the parents and educators realised that they were not alone in their challenges in raising and guiding children. For example, in recounting her struggles with Benjamin, Kelly indicated that she would like guidance from the educators: "Let's say he is playing with Lego and he is concentrating, and it breaks … then he loses it. I can't do anything about that."

Together with the facilitator, Naomi, Emma, and Kelly discussed what may have triggered Benjamin's frustrations and the ways they could reduce the impact of these triggers when he was playing with Lego. They also talked about the importance of acknowledging him when he had been persistent with the Lego building task and congratulating him when he had been able work through his frustration. Offering him a space to calm down was also a strategy they discussed. Kelly did mention to the educators that many of the strategies appeared to be working because she had been astounded by the positive change in him over the past term already.

Moving on, we explored other strategies such as redirecting, natural and logical consequences for inappropriate behaviours, and the sit and watch strategy. Kelly and Meleni were also able to work together with their children's educators to develop a positive behaviour management plan for Benjamin and Rishi. Through collaboration, the parents, teachers, and educators were able to come up with a plan that would engender consistency between the practices of the parents at home and the practices of the educators at the preschool. With an increase in the consistency and collaboration between the parents and the educators, Benjamin's, Hailey's, and Rishi's social and emotional skills had begun to improve. Let us unpack these improvements and changes.

What did we learn about the children, their families, and their educators after the TOGETHER training?

Through the baseline observations, the surveys, and the interviews we were able to identify the patterns of behaviour and the beliefs of each participant.

What did we learn about Benjamin's, Hailey's, and Rishi's social and emotional development after the training?

Benjamin

Benjamin's mum, Kelly, and his teacher and educators, Emma, Anika, and Sukhleen all reported an improvement in his social and emotional skills. The changes that had been noticed were supported by the preschool observations and the SDRS that had been completed by Kelly and the educators. Both the preschool observations and the SDRS indicated that there had been an increase in appropriate behaviour from Benjamin in the weeks immediately following the TOGETHER training and that this continued during the follow-up observations. In particular, Benjamin was more eager to join in with group activities and would follow group instructions. He became more cooperative with games such as hide-and-seek and was able to accept the ideas of other children. He was also beginning to show an understanding of how his actions could assist others. For example, he was observed helping other children get their lunch boxes from their bags and was eager to assist his educators with tidying up. Benjamin was also demonstrating an understanding of when another child's behaviour was inappropriate by walking away before the situation escalated into a confrontation. Emma's reflection was a promising indication of the positive change that had occurred in Benjamin's behaviour, specifically relating to his emotional regulation: "From our perspective, he is a lot calmer than he was. He is such a different child. There was a lot of anger … he would get frustrated with other children."

Kelly reported that there had been a 50 per cent improvement in Benjamin's behaviour at home. She mentioned that she had noticed a shift in his ability to get along with others and was able to compromise with others when a disagreement arose. He was also following her instructions more regularly and the number of aggressive tantrums had reduced. Kelly found the strategies relating to redirecting were particularly useful in helping Benjamin regulate his emotional meltdowns:

> *It [the redirection] really does help. He was getting angry and sooking. I said how about we go and choose a movie [to help him calm down]. Sometimes it is so simple to refocus … it shortens the length of the tantrum.*

However, there were still many instances where she was struggling with his behaviours. She mentioned that consistency had been hard to achieve in the context of the family home and that there were ongoing challenges in the dynamics of the extended family they lived with. Halfway through the follow-up phase of the study, Benjamin and Kelly moved out of the family home, so the home context altered. This change increased Kelly's stress levels as she tried to manage a safe home environment for Benjamin, continue her role as a single mum and meet her work commitments.

Hailey

Hailey's social and emotional skills were relatively strong before the TOGETHER training except for a few challenges at home with her eating habits and her preference for one-to-one play. Her skills remained strong and the reports from Diana indicated that Hailey's behaviour at dinner had been improving. At the preschool it was encouraging to note that her positive behaviours, such as playing with other children and encouraging others, had been acknowledged by her educators through frequent positive feedback and descriptive praise.

Rishi

Rishi's educators, Laura, Sabeena, and Naomi, all reported an improvement in his social and emotional skills at preschool. As previously mentioned, due to family illness, his mum, Meleni, had found it difficult to take part in the interviews and therefore the change in his home environment was unknown; however, the improvement in his behaviour in the preschool setting was promising. The preschool observations and the SDRS completed by his educators indicated that there had been an increase in the number of appropriate behaviours exhibited by Rishi in the weeks immediately following the TOGETHER training. There had also been a slight rise in the number of inappropriate behaviours as well; however, they remained below the number observed before the TOGETHER training had commenced. Through the teachers and educators' actions in scaffolding on the behaviours they wanted to see, Rishi's aggressive temperament began to subside, such as in him hitting other children less frequently when he was frustrated with having to wait his turn. His educators made sure they gave him descriptive praise and encouragement when he was playing well alongside his friends.

In addition, Rishi was starting to regulate his emotions when he was becoming frustrated by remembering to walk away or asking teachers or educators for help. During the observations, both Laura and Naomi congratulated him on coming to them to ask for help when he needed it. He was also beginning to use polite remarks to engage with others, such as, "Can I please join you?" He was also happily joining in with group times and was becoming less inclined to talk over others during group activities. An encouraging remark was given by Naomi: "I feel like with Rishi and his behaviours he has grown so much and it has been a real positive for him."

What did we learn about the beliefs and practices of Kelly, Diana, and the six teachers/educators after the training?

The major shift in Story 3 relates to the change in the practices of the two parents and the six educators. This change, in turn, contributed to a deepening of the parent–educator relationship. After the training, the BPRQ showed that overall, the parents Kelly and Diana and the teachers/educators who completed the questionnaire (Emma, Anika, Naomi, and Sabeena) shared more beliefs and their practices were more consistent in developing children's social and emotional skills. There was an overwhelming consistency in response to the BPRQ questions that related to authoritative styles of behaviour guidance. The parents and educators all strongly agreed that a child's appropriate behaviour needs to be praised and encouraged frequently; that giving attention to their child was important; that when a child tries hard (even at the small things), they should be given praise and encouragement; and that it is important to be able to talk to their child about inappropriate behaviour in a calm manner.

Kelly's and Diana's beliefs regarding punishment also changed and became more aligned with the beliefs of the teachers and educators – specifically, the understanding that redirecting inappropriate behaviour should be framed by guidance rather than punishment. During the initial BPRQ, Diana noted her concerns that disciplining her daughter might lead to Hailey not liking her; whereas after the training, she was able to appreciate the value in redirecting Hailey when inappropriate behaviour occurred. As previous research has demonstrated, children of parents who have an authoritative style often exhibit higher emotional competence than children of parents who have an authoritarian style (Chan et al., 2009; Vartuli, 2005). In addition, educators who applied an authoritative style to their teaching often had children in their classes who were more engaged and responsive in their learning; whereas educators who practised an authoritarian style often had children in their classes who were more resistant to learning (Walker, 2008).

Consequently, these beliefs also aligned more with the practices reported on in the BPRQ: Kelly and Diana and the teachers/educator Emma, Anika, Naomi, and Sabeena reported that they gave more attention to appropriate behaviours rather than to inappropriate behaviours; they singled out the appropriate behaviours they wanted the child to practise; they were more consistent in how they addressed inappropriate behaviours; and they involved the child in creating the rules. However, Kelly reported that while she was making attempts to provide positive feedback to Benjamin, there were times when she was struggling and ongoing guidance was needed. After the TOGETHER training, Kelly would often connect with Anika on ways she could improve her positive behaviour guidance practice for Benjamin, highlighting how the educators were able to provide support and coaching with such skills:

> *I'm doing my best with him and doing a lot of praise. It was 50/50 really … yeah, I'm giving more positive praise when he lashes out … I don't know … I'm struggling a lot with his lashing out … In regard to behaviour guidance, I am not sure things are going well. I need a little bit more guidance on patience and dealing with that.*

The reports from the educators also showed that they were making attempts to reflect on their own practices of guiding children's behaviour and developing children's social and emotional skills. While the educators felt the strategies taught in the TOGETHER programme consisted of concepts they already knew, the two training workshops prompted them to reflect more on how they actually used the strategies they had learnt and, as a result, they began to change their practices. For example, Emma mentioned how she had moved from simply making requests of the children to ensuring that she had more positive interactions with them:

> *I think the training was already in line with what I believed, but my practices have changed … I think I'm more honest with myself … I was having shorter bursts. I was not connecting enough … I had to check to make sure I was giving feedback. I was giving requests rather than positive feedback.*

In addition, Naomi started to use the strategies with her extended family, as well as with her immediate preschool community, and recognised the importance of acknowledging all children when they were doing things well:

> *I knew a lot of the concepts and it [TOGETHER] has reinforced it. The conversations of how to support families and why children are doing these things was really helpful. It'll be in the forefront of my mind … I have even shared it with my sister and her*

> *son ... I'm trying to give more positives for children that are always the ones doing the right thing, too. When I'm just going past them I make an effort to give them positives ... for fourth term this is a good thing as it keeps them focused.*

The changes in practices had also been observed during the classroom observations (see Figures 6.1–6.5), where Emma, Anika, Sukhleen, Laura, and Naomi had noticeably increased the number of positive interactions they had with the children during the observations following the TOGETHER training. (Sabeena was only able to be observed four times during the data collection phase due to being on placement.) For example, during the second observation of Anika, she gave a substantial number of descriptive praise statements to the children:

> *I like your painting, it's beautiful ... You have all done great work, thank you ... Keep going, you are trying really hard ... Good boy, well done on packing up ... There is so much food here, great eating everyone ... Ah, I love your painting, I can see Santa ... Thank you for helping her.*

Sukhleen had paid attention to the processes involved in the children's learning, which demonstrated the shift that had occurred in her thinking. She now recognised the importance of acknowledging the steps the children had been taking towards their learning, not just the final product. For example, her comment to Benjamin when he was working on his building: "You're up in the universe? Wow, that's a cool world! Tell me about the universe ... wow! You know so much about the universe ... you're right, Benjamin."

She also celebrated Benjamin's achievements with her colleagues at the same time, which led to a sense of achievement for Benjamin: "I'm excited to see [as Benjamin led her by the hand] ... Emma, did you see Santa's house? It's so cool!"

Emma's practices had also changed after the TOGETHER training. During the training, one of the goals in Benjamin's positive behaviour guidance plan was to be able to join in, concentrate, and contribute to group times. The plan had been developed by his mum, Kelly, and his three educators (Emma, Anika, and Sabeena) and included several descriptive praise phrases, which could assist with his goals. Therefore, during group times, Emma would ensure that she gave Benjamin positive feedback and acknowledge the times when he was demonstrating appropriate behaviour. For example, during one observation, Emma gave the following descriptive praise phases, which resulted in Benjamin remaining engaged in the group time:

> *Benjamin, are you going to be able to sit there? ... Great choice, Benjamin, I can see you now ... Show me how you listen ... Would you like to stand up? [asking Benjamin to contribute to the group time] ... Thank you for sharing ... Benjamin, great listening ... Thank you, Benjamin. You can tell me your team name now ... You had your hand up; great work.*

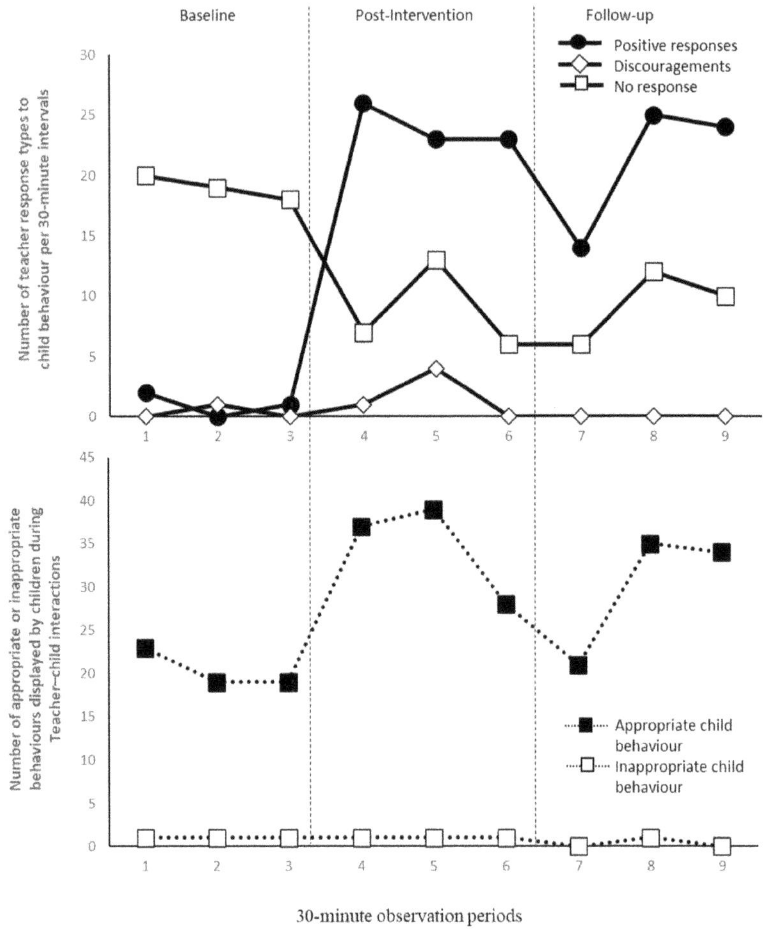

The figure indicates the number of times per 30-minute observation period that Emma responded with positive statements, discouraging statements, or no response to all the children's behaviour and the number of times the children had been engaged in appropriate or inappropriate behaviours when interacting with her.

FIGURE 6.1 Teacher Emma: Preschool observations

Emma also ensured that she gave positive feedback to other children during the same group time. Her responses not only assisted Benjamin in understanding the expected social behaviours but also ensured that the other children were receiving positive feedback for when they were doing things well. For example, she would frequently acknowledge Hailey when she was making positive contributions to the group: "Hailey, you have been sitting so nicely – would you like to pick the song today? … She (Hailey) is being a very good friend to you."

Like Emma, Laura understood the importance of providing positive feedback when children were trying hard at tasks that may be challenging for them. She was aware that Rishi would often wander around the room and find it difficult

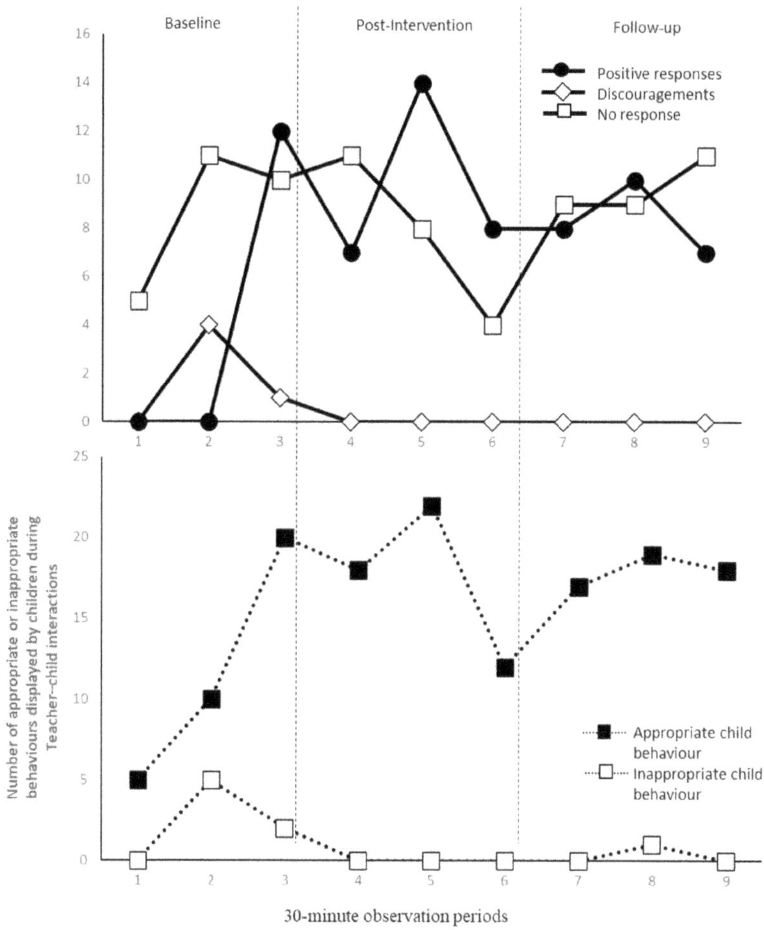

The figure indicates the number of times per 30-minute observation period that Anika responded with positive statements, discouraging statements, or no response to all the children's behaviour and the number of times the children had been engaged in appropriate or inappropriate behaviours when interacting with her.

FIGURE 6.2 Educator Anika: Preschool observations

to engage in a play-based activity for an extended period of time. When she was noticing that he was trying to engage in activities, she would give him encouragement throughout the process: "You worked really hard on this … Rishi, it looks amazing; I can't wait to see what it looks like when dry … Well done, Rishi, you got there in the end; it was a good choice."

The changes in practice were also seen in early childhood teacher Naomi. She provided regular positive feedback to the children before the TOGETHER training, but she increased the number of times she provided descriptive positive praise. In

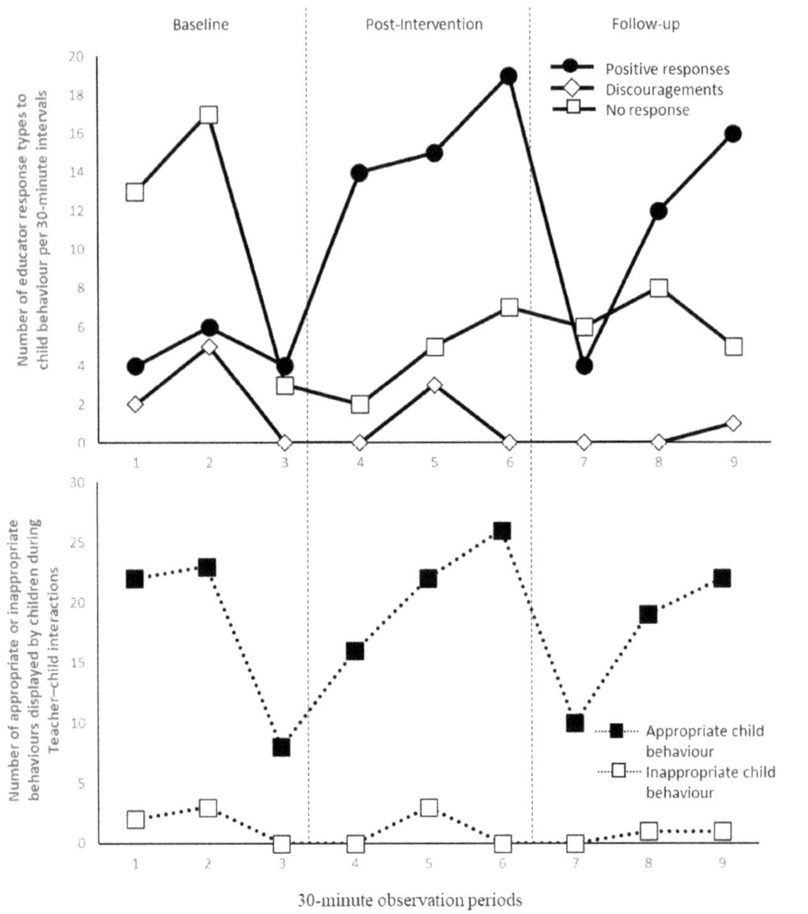

The figure indicates the number of times per 30-minute observation period that Sukhleen responded with positive statements, discouraging statements, or no response to all the children's behaviour and the number of times the children had been engaged in appropriate or inappropriate behaviours when interacting with her.

FIGURE 6.3 Educator Sukhleen: Preschool observations

particular, she made specific efforts to engage more with Rishi by ensuring that she provided more positive feedback when she had to give redirection to him:

> *I like the way you are sitting [after he had struggled to join in at group time and was sitting still] … You were already listening – great work … I loved how you put your hand up [after he had called out several times and needed to be reminded to put his hand up for his turn] … Thank you for sharing … Great question … You are right, great remembering.*

As with Naomi, Sukhleen and Anika they also increased their positive feedback during specific classroom routines, such as tidying up; however, their interactions with the children tended to more directive, with limited positive responses. Sukhleen mentioned that giving descriptive praise was a challenge for her during

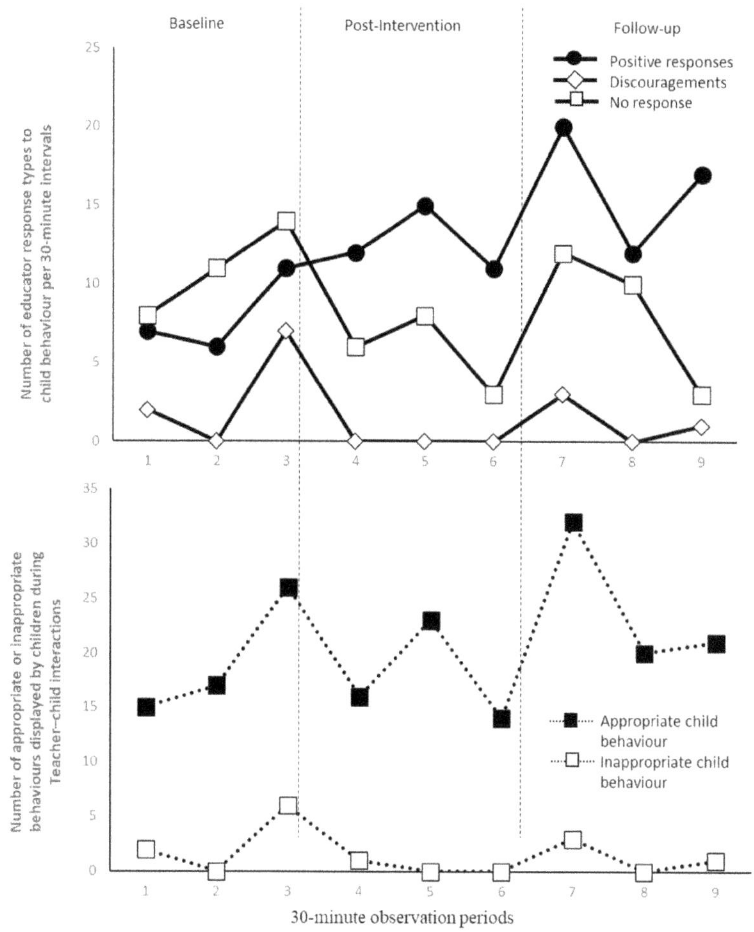

The figure indicates the number of times per 30-minute observation period that Laura responded with positive statements, discouraging statements, or no response to all the children's behaviour and the number of times the children had been engaged in appropriate or inappropriate behaviours when interacting with her.

FIGURE 6.4 Teacher Laura: Preschool observations

the day, especially considering the demands of the tasks that needed to be completed each day. She saw the value of providing positive feedback, yet she was refreshingly honest when she said that it would take time for her to change her practice. Such a reflection is important for any type of training programme because a shift in practice would often take some time for many participants.

What did we learn about the parent–educator relationship after the training?

The reports from the parents, teachers, and educators, as well as the classroom observations, indicated that consistent improvement had occurred in the practices

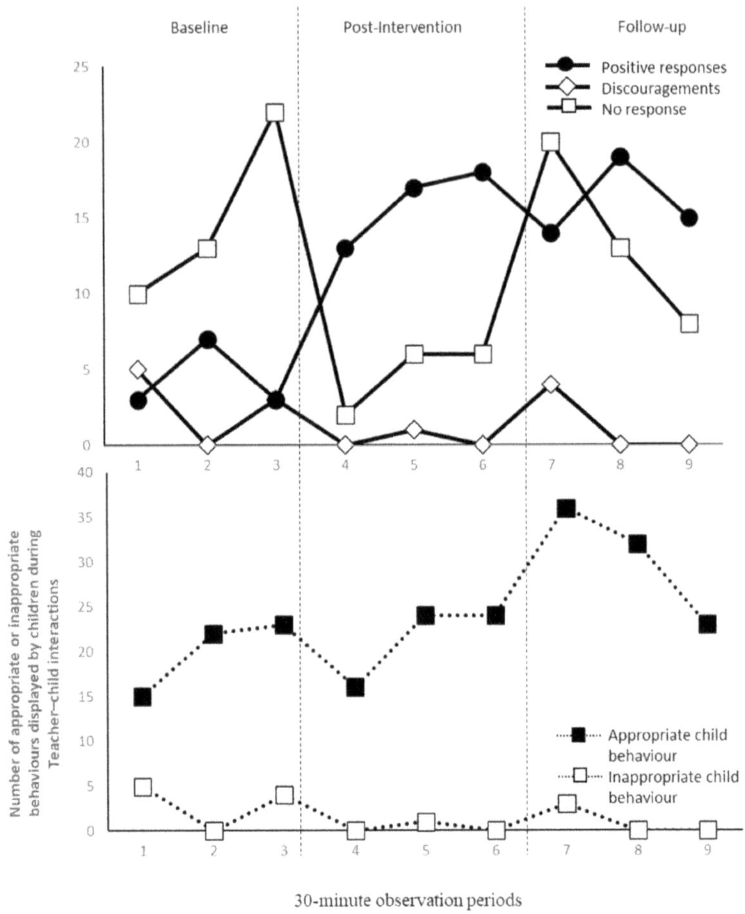

The figure indicates the number of times per 30-minute observation period that Naomi responded with positive statements, discouraging statement or no response to all the children's behaviour and the number of times the children had been engaged in appropriate or inappropriate behaviours when interacting with her.

FIGURE 6.5 Teacher Naomi: Preschool observations

of the parents and the educators after the training. Together with their improved practices there was also an improvement in the relationships between the parents and the educators.

For Benjamin and his mum, Kelly, the support from his three educators, especially Anika, became invaluable during this time, especially considering the challenges they had been facing at home. Each teacher and educator noted that there had been an increase in Kelly's interactions with them. She had begun to show a deeper trust in communicating the challenges that she was facing at home with Benjamin and regularly sought advice from his educators on the strategies she could use at home. Another encouraging outcome from the TOGETHER training was that the educators were sharing positive stories about Benjamin with Kelly, which she appreciated: "When I see them [the educators] and he's kind of upset, they'll take him aside and they let me know when he's been really good."

In Rishi's case, the educators were experiencing challenges in how best to communicate with his family. They recognised that developing a closer partnership with his family was going to take some time and that they needed to adapt how they interacted with his parents, especially his dad, Jo. They had started to see the positive changes in Rishi and that the partnership they had developed with his mum, Meleni, was assisting in his social and emotional development. However, as highlighted by Naomi, the relationship with Rishi's family was still developing:

> *Rishi's mum has spent more time with us and we have had more communication and reciprocal conversations with her. I feel like with Rishi and his behaviours he has grown so much, and it has been a real positive for him. With dad there is still a barrier … we need more time with him … I feel like we need to be positive rather than telling them things they don't want to hear. They want to hear that their child is happy and safe … We have more interactions with mum so we have more opportunity to connect … dad not so much. I don't know how [to connect] apart from organising more nights; he works full time … It's a real challenge … It's the same for lots of families.*

The teachers and educators also recognised that their own flexibility in how they communicated with all preschool families was pivotal in ensuring that they were being contextually and culturally responsive and family centred. There was an understanding that each child's parents communicated in different ways and that there were barriers as to how involved they could be with their child's preschool education. The educators in both classrooms recognised that many parents were time poor due to work and life commitments. For example, Laura reflected on the importance of building a strong rapport with families from the beginning and how technology was being used to communicate:

> *At the start it is about building rapport … breaking down the perceptions we had of families. We have had the intimate one on one and, wow, we were on a different page … it was rectified … They [the parents] were like, wow, you know what he/she is like … It is becoming more common to be sending emails … We need to be open to opportunities … Sometimes we get emails late at night … We need to be flexible in allowing the families to have the opportunity to touch base, even if it is later.*

Naomi also valued the importance of building strong relationships with families at the beginning and reflected on how the relationships were not only for the child's education but also for the wider preschool community. She touched on how every year they were presented with a new preschool community and therefore their practices needed to change in response to the needs of the different families in the community:

> *I'll build the relationship at the start ... We did our fathers' night ... Maybe we could have monthly family gatherings ... It's about being able to come into the environment and being not only about the child's education but about the community ... When you build that rapport with them [the families], and then when you do need to have those conversations about things that are developing, they may be more receptive to taking it on board without feeling it is harsh. Every year it is different with the community; it depends on the community.*

Emma agreed with Naomi while also recognising that families observed their practices as educators. She made specific reference to building relationships through community events at the beginning of the preschool year and how such events contribute to building trust between parents and educators, break down potential barriers, and increase the educator's approachability: "It's about the families and bonding [referring to community events] ... but the families are watching you, too. They see you are approachable ... It's those little chinks in the armour that have them see you as approachable."

Training/empowering teachers and educators through TOGETHER

As we continued with the observations and the final interviews, it became evident that the teachers and educators had developed strong and trusting relationships with Benjamin's, Hailey's, and Rishi's families. These relationships extended to many other families at the preschool as well. It was also apparent that despite our best efforts to recruit children and families to be involved in TOGETHER, it was not us, the researchers, who had the relationships with the families. While the teachers and educators participated in the recruitment process, there was still a need for the facilitators to develop trust with the families; however, as the teachers and educators' comments have highlighted, such trust takes time. Our own reflections informed us that empowering the teachers and educators to be facilitators of the TOGETHER programme in their own community increased the potential for more families to be reached. Therefore we proceeded with a third training session after our final observations, which was specifically designed to train the teachers and educators to become facilitators of the TOGETHER programme. As Naomi said: "Yes, I agree, they don't trust you (the researcher/facilitator) ... So it makes sense it comes from us ... The relationship is everything."

Naomi's statement clearly illustrates the need for additional coaching to train teachers and educators as TOGETHER facilitators. All six educators – Emma, Anika, Sukhleen, Laura, Sabeena, and Naomi – were eager to participate in additional coaching, which aimed to not only provide them with the training skills of the TOGETHER programme so that they would be empowered to continue to work in partnership with the children's families but also pass on their knowledge to the wider preschool community. A central element to the third session was the importance of building relationships with families in a contextually responsive, culturally appropriate, and family-centred way. The workshop and final interview discussions highlighted the interesting ideas that had emerged for developing relationships, establishing practices in positive behaviour guidance, and the value the educators placed on the TOGETHER programme.

It was encouraging to see that the teachers and educators had been able to recognise the strengths they had in establishing relationships with the preschool's families. They understood that the relationships and the trust that they had already established with the families would be of great assistance in building relationships and developing family partnerships in guiding children's social and emotional competence. For example, Anika, Sukhleen, and Sabeena all saw the value of speaking more than one language and appreciated how this ability could assist in building trust with families from different cultures. Many of the children were brought to the preschool by their grandparents who found it difficult to communicate with the educators as English was not their first language. However, with Anika speaking French and Creole, Sukhleen speaking Punjabi, and Sabeena speaking Tamil and Hindi, they were able to communicate with several of the grandparents who spoke languages other than English. This was not only beneficial for the children and their families but also provided another means of communication for all the educators. As Sabeena noted: "Most of the grandparents who come speak a different language, such as Hindi. So, it's easy for me to communicate with them and they feel comfortable."

As the teachers and educators discussed ways to move forward and involve more families in the TOGETHER programme, they saw how immensely valuable the additional languages that Anika, Sukhleen, and Sabeena spoke could be in responding to the context of each family. They also discussed how they felt small, intimate groups of families would be the best approach for any future collaboration with them. This reasoning was not only because of their own confidence in delivering the TOGETHER programme but also because they felt that the trust they had with the families could be better maintained in smaller groups. Through the coaching sessions, the teachers and educators were able to develop ways to facilitate the programme that were contextually and culturally responsive to their immediate community at the preschool. Some of the teachers and educators also discussed that maybe through team teaching, with the assistance of the TOGETHER manual, their confidence in facilitating the programme would improve. For example, in her final interview, Emma made the following statement:

> *The training manual is consistent … It reminds you that this is the path we are taking. It lies with my own confidence … and practising in front of my peers … I think it is just practice and the support of someone else, such as team teaching.*

While the outcomes of the additional coaching sessions were not measured, the workshop conversations and the final interviews gave some insight into how the educators had benefited from the additional training. The sessions also demonstrated how they could facilitate TOGETHER in the future, and that the trust they had already developed with families could be the key to reaching other families.

In understanding the backgrounds of the families they were working with, the teachers and educators were able to establish contextually responsive relationships, improve the consistency of their practices, and increase the children's social and emotional competence – all goals of the TOGETHER programme. With specific reference to her experience with Rishi, Laura acknowledged that understanding the family context and recognising how a child's behaviour manifested that context was an important component in facilitating future TOGETHER training.:

> *I think that once you know a bit more of the context of the family and the child, we know how to work with him … We need to give him a role, a purpose, and have control over the situation, and then we will get the best out of him that day … It's about understanding the function behind the behaviour.*

As our research moves forward, this third story has provided us with a new starting point – exploring how teachers and educators can be trained as facilitators of the TOGETHER programme.

7

LESSONS LEARNED

It is not all puppies and rainbows

Remember this quote from Samuel's mum, Charlotte in Chapter 5?

> *You see such an improvement with all the kids [her three children] and how eager they are to please us. So, I think a lot of their behaviour comes from that. I've definitely seen a change since using that message [positive feedback] with them. Yeah, but it's not all puppies and rainbows. You know, there is still a lot of fighting and arguing. But I will say honestly that in the last four weeks we have noticed an improvement.*

Charlotte was acknowledging the positive effects on her children after her participation in the TOGETHER workshops. As a result of the development of her parenting skills, with the assistance of the TOGETHER programme, Charlotte was beginning to notice the changes in all her children's social and emotional skills. However, she was also refreshingly honest in her reflections. She recognised that the role of being a parent is, at times, incredibly hard. But she also realised that by persisting with the TOGETHER parenting skills and practices, her children's positive behaviours had been increasing at home.

The stories of all those who participated in the TOGETHER programme, including Charlotte's, are important in helping us to evaluate the effectiveness of TOGETHER. You will remember that in Chapter 2 we explained the genesis of the programme TOGETHER: Growing Children's Social and Emotional Competence (Phillips et al., 2017). It developed from an awareness that there was a need for a parent, teacher, and educator training programme (in growing children's social and emotional competence) that was not only contextually responsive and encouraging of parent–educator collaboration but also (a) more accessible; (b) less time-consuming; (c) easy to follow; and (d) ultimately more empowering of participants to pass on their new knowledge to other families, teachers, and educators in their community.

DOI: 10.4324/9781003006466-7

So, what have the three stories told us about the effectiveness of TOGETHER? In this final chapter, we reflect on the three stories and use them to help us understand how TOGETHER worked across three varying contexts. Specifically, we offer our insights into the lessons the stories have taught us about developing children's social and emotional skills. So, how did we reflect? Do you remember towards the end of Chapter 3 that we mentioned the word "triangulation"? Using the method of triangulation, we were able to combine the different sources of information to help us understand the bigger picture. Sources of information include the Communication Styles and Demographics (CSD) questionnaire, the preschool and home observations, the Social Development Rating Scale (SDRS; Church et al., 2006), and the Beliefs, Practices, and Relationships Questionnaire (BPRQ). We were also able to gather important information from the parents, teachers, and educators through the workshops' recordings and interviews. There are lessons for us all: parents; early childhood teachers and educators; those who work directly with children in a professional capacity, such as education psychologists; and those who undertake research in early childhood education (ECE) and junior school education. Let us begin with the lessons we have learnt for some of the most important people in the lives of children: their parents, their early childhood teachers, and their educators.

Lessons for parents, early childhood teachers, and educators

In their early years, children will experience valuable interactions with their parents, their early childhood teachers, and their educators. Such interactions can enhance their social and emotional competence (Darling-Churchill & Lippman, 2016). The role such adults play in a child's life is vital for them to develop their social and emotional skills. Such skills include forming friendships, being able to participate positively in social settings, managing their emotions, and engaging in meaningful play and learning. Using the three stories, we will look at practical ways for parents, teachers, and educators to build children's social and emotional competence skills. Below are several important lessons for you to discover:

- Lesson 1: Responding to context through family-centred partnerships and teamwork
- Lesson 2: Praise and encouragement is key
- Lesson 3: Reflecting on your parenting or teaching practice to develop consistency
- Lesson 4: Bringing TOGETHER to your preschool community

Lesson 1: Responding to context through family-centred partnerships and teamwork

The building and maintaining of relationships and strong family-centred partnerships are critical elements in the social and emotional development of young children. Such elements are essential in helping teachers, educators, and programme facilitators to respond to the context of children and families (Barnett et al., 2010; Park et al., 2016; Sheridan & Kratochwill, 2007). Therefore, these elements form the basis of the TOGETHER programme, as seen in Figure 2.3 (see Chapter 2). Parent–educator relationships – which involve trust and cooperation, a strong, family-centred partnership, and a contextually responsive approach – lead to several positive outcomes. These outcomes include an increase in a child's prosocial behaviours, the development of positive attitudes towards school settings, and an increase in academic achievement (Sheridan et al., 2005). Therefore, it is essential that the parent–educator partnership is cultivated in programmes like TOGETHER. The three TOGETHER stories have illustrated that parents, teachers, and educators can build a stronger understanding of the family and community in which they live and work. The building of this strong relationship and common understanding provides a critical rationale for involving parents, teachers, and educators together in the contextually responsive delivery of the TOGETHER programme. As partnerships strengthen, so do the children's social and emotional skills.

Many teachers and educators understand the importance of establishing strong partnerships with families. Specifically, when we adopt a family-centred approach in building strong connections with families, this contributes positively to children's social and emotional competence (Sheridan et al., 2005). As you may recall, family-centred practice (Dunst, 2002) is a central component of both the TOGETHER programme and its conceptual framework (explained in Chapter 2). A family-centred approach places importance on the relational and participatory practices between parents and professionals, such as teachers and educators. Relational practices are strength based; they involve family-familiar practices; and they encompass parent, teacher, and educator perspectives. Participatory practices, on the other hand, enable parent–educator collaboration; they embrace flexibility; they can be individualised; and they encourage information sharing and family choice in any decision-making between the family and the educators.

Therefore, part of adopting a family-centred approach is ensuring we consider the context of the families (Stern et al., 2015). As identified in all three stories, there continued to be contextual barriers that stopped the parents from seeking assistance with their child's social and emotional skills. Such barriers included the demands of family life, challenges with childcare, and time constraints. The CSD questionnaire helped us to understand some of these barriers. In recognising the demands of the families' daily schedules, we were able to ensure the training was provided at times that suited them. By considering the challenges some parents had with childcare, where their families were often isolated with no additional support, the programme was able to cater for those situations by providing on-site childcare during the workshops.

In addition, through recognising how the parents, teachers, and educators connected naturally (such as informal lunches or afternoon teas), we were able to provide a setting for the workshops that ensured a relaxed and welcoming environment. Interestingly, across all three stories there was a high preference for small face-to-face groups and requests to have the training around food. For many of the teachers and educators they felt that creating events with food seemed to create relaxed atmospheres. Including food in events was already an integrated practice in developing partnerships with their families and therefore was integrated into the TOGETHER workshops.

Furthermore, being able to respond to each family using the language they spoke at home also assisted. In the case of the second story, Isabella's family were much more comfortable with the fact that Jia, her early childhood teacher, spoke Mandarin. Although the family did not require an interpreter, the fact that Isabella's parents could speak to Jia in their home language assisted with clearer communication. Interestingly, when Juan (Isabella's mum) was instructed in how to make the recording at home, she asked if we would prefer that the family speak in English. She was reassured that using their home language of Mandarin would be fine as it was important to see Isabella interacting in her natural environment. It was the same for the classroom observations. While Isabella spoke mostly English at the preschool, there were times when she interacted with Jia using Mandarin. To ensure the data collection phase also accurately captured Isabella's interactions, the research assistant for the observations also spoke Mandarin so that there would be correct translations. While Juan was confident in speaking in English, she did mention that having their home language spoken at preschool meant that Isabella appeared to be more at ease and comfortable in her interactions with Jia. In the school terms prior to the TOGETHER training, Isabella was exhibiting a high amount of anxiety regarding attending preschool. Juan mentioned that this was due to finding it difficult to develop friendships with peers and being uncertain about being away from her mother. However, the anxiety dissipated when Jia provided additional attention to Isabella upon her arrival at preschool, which included speaking Mandarin with her as she transitioned between activities.

Such sensitivity to a family's home language was also noticed in Story 3. Educator Emma recognised the language barriers relating to grandparents who did not speak English undertaking the drop-offs and the pick-ups at the preschool, which was limiting her effectiveness in communicating with them regarding the strategies from the TOGETHER programme. However, with Anika speaking French and Creole, Sukhleen speaking Punjabi, and Sabeena speaking Tamil and Hindi, they were able to communicate with grandparents who spoke a number of different languages. This was not only beneficial to the children and their families but also provided another means of communication for all the educators. As Sukhleen noted, her fluency in several languages assisted her fellow educators: "I always stand at the door and greet everyone ... then the parents and grandparents come and talk to us ... I can speak some of their languages and I can pass it on to Emma."

Consequently, as a result of the facilitators, teachers, and educators understanding the work, life, and language contexts of each family from the three stories, the TOGETHER programme could be adapted to the needs of each family. Koerting et al. (2013) concur with the need to be flexible. They state that early intervention programmes need to consider the unique characteristics and circumstances of each family when engagement strategies are being developed with families. When these considerations are taken into account, the barriers that families may be facing in accessing training can be reduced.

While some barriers had been reduced for the families from the three stories, there were still many other obstacles that existed within each preschool community. The main barrier that remained was that other families who had English as a second language were reluctant to attend the TOGETHER programme. This became evident in the recruitment process for all the three stories. The same reluctance was also apparent in families who were restricted by work or life interruptions. In the three stories some of the parents were unable to attend the workshops at the last minute due to unexpected developments. Yet, all the families associated with the preschool still required support. The solution was for the educators themselves to pass on the knowledge.[1]

While we had to think of new ways to reach families who could not attend, we also needed to continue to cultivate the parent–educator partnership for those who were attending. At the very beginning of the TOGETHER programme, the importance of relationships and the building of partnerships between children, families/parents, and educators is emphasised. Figure 7.1 illustrates a tool from the TOGETHER manual that can be used to begin conversations between parents and educators.

The focus of the tool is to ask parents and educators about how they build relationships with children and with each other. It can also be used to develop an understanding of each other's beliefs and practices as well as the contexts of the participants' lives. As the programme progresses, the focus remains on maintaining communication and promoting teamwork between parents, teachers, and educators. As the three stories illustrated, adopting a family-centred approach during training enabled the parents, teachers, and educators to strengthen their partnerships. Through these strong partnerships, consistency in the parents', teachers', and educators' practices between the home and preschool increased, which, in turn, led to an improvement in the children's social and emotional skills. Early childhood teacher, Jia, from our second story explained how the training had built the parent–educator relationship.

> *We feel closer because we went through the training together and it's a great relationship-building exercise, and you also receive positive feedback from them [the parents]. So definitely the relationship has strengthened. And it helped me to build the relationship with the child that will help you deal with the challenging behaviour; and also, the relationship with the family. It helps you build that partnership and dealing with the children's behaviour.*

Jia's reflection demonstrates that by providing opportunities to develop understandings at the outset, the first workshop built a strong foundation in which to help support the children in their social and emotional development. By taking the time to understand and develop these strong roots through building productive

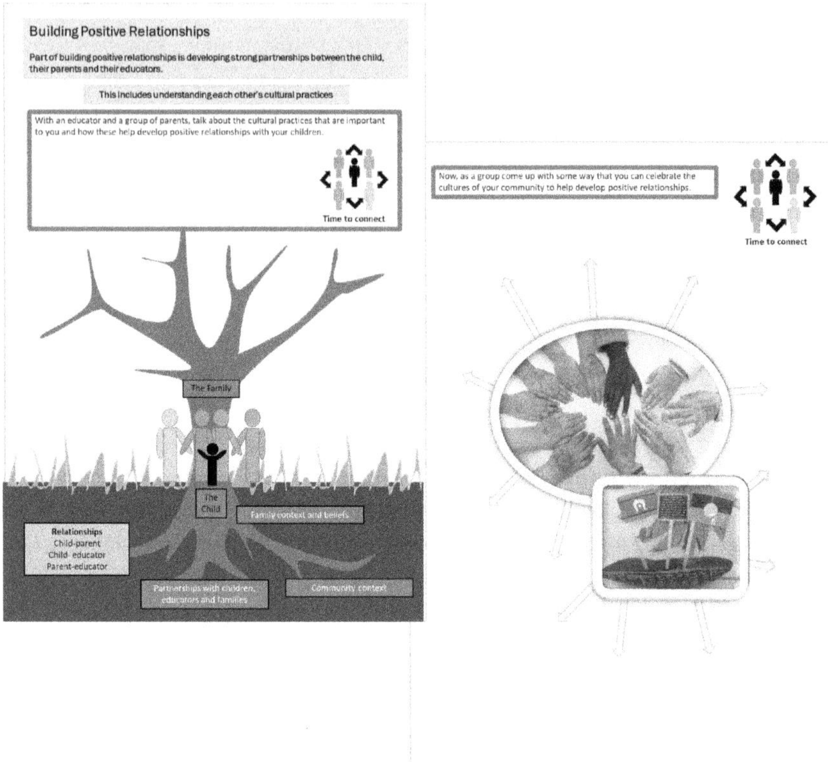

FIGURE 7.1 Building positive relationships

relationships and partnerships, positive outcomes will occur. One such outcome is that there is a higher likelihood that parents, teachers, and educators will be more effective in supporting the development of children's social and emotional skills (Sheridan et al., 2005). The establishment of strong partnerships between parents, teachers, and educators is vital because it provides a platform for developing a common understanding of each family's context and that of the preschool. It also builds a mutual understanding of the beliefs and the parenting and teaching practices that will influence the development of children's social and emotional competence (Barnett et al., 2010; Park et al., 2016; Sheridan et al., 2005).

In fact, the strengthening of such common understandings occurred in Story 1. Tamati's mother, Kiri, was provided with opportunities in the workshops to provide the background to her family's life. In particular, she mentioned how the family had bonded over books and that faith was an integral aspect of their lives. The educators commented on how this information was important because it provided them with an understanding of the context of Tamati's family and his needs. In understanding the family context, Ali and Sue were able to adjust the preschool programme to celebrate Tamati's interests. In turn, Ali and Sue were provided with more opportunities to provide him with more positive interactions.

While the sharing of such information may have seemed like a small gesture, it did lead to a much more positive learning environment for Tamati and his family.

Similar outcomes were also illustrated in the other two stories. In Story 2: Recognising all children, each parent mentioned the specific cultural practices that their family engaged in at home, such as the camping and fishing adventures of Isabella's family and the dance parties held by Samuel's family. As the parents discussed these practices, Jia, their children's early childhood teacher, was provided with new ideas for the preschool programme. Such discussions also provided additional opportunities for Jia to interact with these two children to discuss and affirm their family practices. For Isabella's social and emotional development, such information was vital in helping her feel more included at the preschool and being part of her community. The observations showed that Jia incorporated the "camping practices" of Isabella's family into the preschool programme. In turn, Isabella's social confidence grew when interacting with her peers. This was because she was able to engage in play-based learning that linked to her own family's cultural practices.

The improvement in Isabella's social and emotional development as a result of the development of the strong partnership between her parents and Jia is also supported by other evidence-based programmes. For example, Sheridan and Kratochwill (2007) state that such partnerships contribute to an increase in a child's prosocial behaviours; an increase in positive attitudes towards school settings; and an increase in their academic achievement. Hieneman and Fefer (2017) state that collaboration between families and professionals (such as early childhood teachers and educators) is a key component for supporting families. It is also a central element in decision-making and understanding why children may be struggling with their social and emotional development.

Furthermore, there were several instances presented in each story where the process of shared decision-making between parents, teachers, and educators had occurred. The TOGETHER programme provides consistent opportunities for explicit, practical parent–educator interaction. Specifically, the format of the workshops provides a platform for the teachers, educators, and parents to share their values on behaviour guidance. Such a platform is likely to enhance the parent–educator partnership. In the first workshop of Story 2, Kelly and Diana shared the struggles they had at home and the educators offered their experiences in solidarity. As the stories were shared, the parents, teachers, and educators showed more confidence in contributing to the group discussion. The trust the parents developed in the teachers and the educators became evident. For example, Kelly shared her struggles with trying to get her son, Benjamin, dressed and to listen to her. As the focus was on recognising and responding to positive behaviours, Emma, one of Benjamin's educators, shared how she assisted her nephew with his listening skills by giving him descriptive praise when he had listened well.

The collaboration and teamwork continued in the second workshop described in Story 2. As a result, the parent–educator partnership deepened. Through the sharing, the parents, teachers, and educators came to realise that they were not alone in their challenges in raising and guiding children's social and emotional skills. Benjamin's teachers, Naomi and Emma, discussed with Kelly the factors that may have triggered her son's frustrations and how these triggers may be mitigated. They also discussed the importance of providing descriptive praise when Benjamin was persistent with certain tasks and congratulating him when he was able to work through the frustration. Offering him a space to calm down was also a strategy that was shared. Kelly mentioned to the educators that many of the strategies seemed to work because she was astounded by the positive change in Benjamin over the past term already.

In addition, hearing how educators approached challenging behaviours appeared to reassure and empower the parents in each of the three stories. As with Kelly, Isabella's mum, Juan placed value on how the educators guided children's behaviour:

> *Hearing how an educator deals with certain behaviours is helpful … like the educator's techniques … They [the children] have been very receptive with the educator but I like hearing the educator's approach as I think that's very helpful as a parent.*

From the various scenarios described, the TOGETHER training provided increased opportunities for the parents, teachers, and educators to learn from each other. They were able to develop consistent practices in developing children's social and emotional competence through the workshop discussions. They were also able to work together to produce individual positive behaviour guidance plans for each child. The plans encouraged teamwork and consistency between the parents, teachers, and educators. Consequently, the children were provided with clear consistent messages about prosocial behaviours and how to regulate their emotions. Also with the development of such plans, the educators were able to implement consistent practices in the classroom and parents were able to share the strategies with other family members. In Story 1, Kiri passed on what she had learnt to Tamati's dad. In Story 2, Charlotte was able to teach her husband the skills she had acquired:

> *Since the training it has created conversation between me and my husband in that we had not talked about parenting before, so it has sort of enabled us to bring to the table the things that I've learnt and sharing in the handouts you've provided. One of the techniques we really like, because it's really easy to remember, is the 5 to 1 in terms of every negative interaction. Trying to have five positive ones and sort of wipe the slate clean and negate that negative interaction. Especially because he [her husband] has such limited time with them [the children]. It makes us a united front in terms of consistency in our parenting, and I'm using similar techniques, so they're getting the same sort of parenting and response from both of us.*

However, for those parents who were unable to attend both workshops, such consistency was much harder. Rishi's teacher Naomi, stated that she was able to make connections with his mum, Meleni, despite her not being able to attend all the training. Fortunately, she was able to find ways that she could pass on the

TOGETHER strategies to assist Rishi's family with the challenges they were facing. However, she felt the relationship with Rishi's parents was still developing.

> *Rishi's mum has spent more time with us and we have had more communication and reciprocal conversations with her. I feel like with Rishi and his behaviours he has grown so much, and it has been a real positive for him. With dad there is still a barrier ... we need more time with him ... I feel like we need to be positive rather than telling them things they don't want to hear. They want to hear that their child is happy and safe ... We have more interactions with mum so we have more opportunity to connect ... dad not so much. I don't know how [to connect] apart from organising more nights; he works full time ... It's a real challenge ... It's the same for lots of families.*

Naomi's statement would no doubt resonate with many parents, teachers, and educators; while she had developed a strong relationship with one parent, the connection with the other continued to be a challenge. Ali, the educator from Story 1, had also found that connecting with family members had been a challenge. In turn, this disconnection had been impacting on the effectiveness of the partnership. Ali reported that she found it difficult to collaborate effectively with families when she interacted with the grandparents rather than the parents. She also mentioned that time and communication barriers, such as reduced connection with working parents, limited the involvement of some families with the TOGETHER programme.

Interestingly, the feedback from Henry's mum, Sonja (Story 1), and Isabella's mum, Juan (Story 2), resonated with the teachers' and educators' feelings regarding the fact that time needed to be allocated for developing better connections between parents, teachers, and educators. Both Sonja and Juan felt that they needed more time with the teachers and educators to understand the ways in which they could support their children in their social and emotional development. Sonja mentioned that there was a need for additional one-on-one meetings with the educators so that they could discuss Henry's needs with confidentiality and follow up on his progress. Juan specifically stated:

> *I think it's just like things we need to discuss and spend more time together so we can bring things up like again and again, you know what I mean? Even before the lecture, I had heard about it [positive praise and encouragement]. But after the lecture, I forgot things ... And after a couple of months I stopped ... not that I had forgotten the theory, but I had just forgotten to do it on a regular basis. So, if the educator somehow did a reminder ... not for like an hour lecture, just every now and then.*

While this feedback indicated a need for more connection, Sonja's and Juan's comments also highlight just how much the parents in the stories valued the knowledge of their child's educators. Such comments, supported by the scores from the BPRQ and reports in the final interviews, indicated that the parent–educator partnership was strong across all three stories after the TOGETHER training. All the parents reported that they had experienced clear communication with the educators and that the educators had been responsive to their needs. The reports also revealed that the teachers and educators valued the participating families' strengths and cultural beliefs. The parent reports also indicated that they felt that they had been valued as partners in their child's education.

Overall, the trust the parents had in the teachers and educators has illustrated the vital role that teachers and educators have in developing the capacity of families to grow their children's social and emotional competence. Such trust cannot be underestimated given that early childhood settings are one of the first places where children experience relationships with adults other than those in their immediate families (Coleman et al., 2013). Early childhood settings are also a place where families can find support in raising their children. Therefore, early childhood teachers and educators are in an important position where they can build the capacity of the families they work with. As our three stories have illustrated, parents often look to their child's teachers and educators for guidance. In turn, teachers and educators can look to children's parents for guidance as to how they can best meet their children's needs.

The challenges presented in this section indicate that by adopting a family-centred approach, teachers and educators can appropriately respond to the particular contexts of the families they are working with and find new ways to accommodate their needs. Teacher Naomi recognised that the partnership between her and Rishi's dad was being impacted by the fact he was working full time. Ali also saw the impact of working parents on her ability to form valuable parent–educator partnerships. In consultation with teachers and educators, like Naomi and Ali, it is recognised that barriers that restrict families attending programmes such as TOGETHER continue to exist, as do the barriers for parents to connect with their children's teachers. The future challenge for many teachers, educators, and facilitators of the TOGETHER programme is to find ways that will enable them to continually adapt their practices to suit families' contexts. The three stories in this book are a good place to begin finding new ways of developing contextually responsive practices. Similarly, the three stories have also illustrated other ways parents, teachers, and educators can adapt their practices in the development of children's social and emotional skills. Such adaptations are outlined in our second lesson.

Lesson 2: Praise and encouragement is key

You may remember from Chapter 2 that "positive interactions" have been placed on the largest leaves of the Tree Model (Figure 2.3). They have been placed there because of the positive effect praise and encouragement has on children's social and emotional development. Their placement at the top of the model is because research has shown that adults who provide a higher level of descriptive praise are more likely to have a greater influence on increasing children's social competence behaviours (Fox & Hemmeter, 2009; Fox & Lentini, 2006; Webster-Stratton et al., 2001, Webster-Stratton et al., 2008). Children who have been exposed to more positive interactions also demonstrate improved emotional self-regulation and lower levels of inappropriate behaviour. One encouraging lesson from each of the three individual stories is that for each of the focus children there had been an improvement in their social and emotional skills because of one main reason: their parents, teachers, and educators all increased their attention to when the child(ren) was being "good" and encouraged them with descriptive praise rather than only giving them attention when they were being "bad."

Story 1 illustrates this phenomenon. We were able to see that Tamati's social and emotional competence had increased in several ways. First, the SDRS told us that after the workshops, Tamati was being more consistent in following instructions. He was also joining in with more group-based activities and having more positive interactions with other children, such as beginning to take turns. He was regulating his emotions when he was becoming angry or frustrated and verbalising how he was feeling. Second, the home observations confirmed the information from the SDRS. They revealed that as a result of Tamati's mum, Kiri, increasing the number of positive interactions she had with Tamati, his prosocial behaviours had correspondingly risen as well. Such improvements included his increased focus on completing tasks – for example, getting dressed. Another improvement was that he was getting along better with his two brothers. He shared more and took turns when they were all playing together. Kiri made a conscious effort to decrease her discouragements and focus on what Tamati did well by increasing the number of her positive interactions when he was "good." She made statements like "I really like your shapes" (referring to Tamati's playdough creations). During mealtimes she would make descriptive statements about how well he was eating. Interestingly, it was also observed that with the increase in Kiri's positive interactions, Tamati would pass on praise to his younger brothers, such as telling them they were eating well at the dinner table. There was also a focused effort from his dad to praise Tamati (and his brothers) when he was being "good." These results are consistent with the findings of Ogden and Hagen (2008), who also found that when parents reduced the number of negative interactions and moved their focus to recognising what their children did well, the children's prosocial behaviours improved.

Similarly in Story 2, the increase in positive interactions between the parents, teachers, educators and the children saw an increase in the children's social and emotional skills. Such a phenomenon was observed in the period following the TOGETHER workshops when Isabella's confidence was no longer "invisible"[2] to other children when she was interacting with them. Due to the support and positive feedback she had been receiving from Jia and the other children, her confidence grew in the classroom environment and she participated in group activities more. After the TOGETHER workshops, Jia would regularly congratulate Isabella when she had contributed to group play. As a result of Jia's positive feedback, Isabella had become more confident in offering her ideas during group times and was initiating play with others more often. At home, her mum, Juan, had also substantially increased her positive interactions and comments to Isabella. She was now playing close attention to when Isabella was following directions and trying hard at activities and would compliment her: "I believe you can do it," "You are really putting in an effort today because you have finished your colouring and you now know what it is," and "Yay, this is very tricky, but you found it" (followed by a celebratory two-handed high five from Juan to Isabella).

Isabella had also started to demonstrate behaviours that indicated she was believing in her own learning. For example, we started seeing instances where she was giving herself praise for her efforts – "It's so easy, I found the yellow, yay" – and persevering to finish tasks, saying "I want to finish; when I was a little I couldn't."

These interactions give a clear illustration of the importance of providing positive feedback when children are trying hard, even at the small things. By focusing on the process, rather than the final product, children can become more motivated to persevere with the tasks they need to complete. Whether it is persisting with the stages of an activity, completing each step in getting dressed, or achieving each step when learning how to use the toilet, there are always opportunities to recognise the small achievements as children work towards bigger goals. Fox and Lentini (2006) demonstrated that when children receive feedback and specific encouragement to each step when learning new skills, their perseverance increases, just like it did for Isabella.

Similarly in Story 3, there were promising outcomes for Benjamin's social and emotional development. Information from the SDRS completed by his mum, Kelly, and his educators, accompanied by the preschool observations, showed promising changes in Benjamin' s behaviour. His positive behaviour and his social and emotional skills increased when his mother and educators focused on catching him when he was "good" and commenting positively on what he was doing (rather than his "bad" behaviour). His teachers and educators gave him frequent compliments on joining in, putting up his hand, being gentle, and waiting his turn. They specifically developed a positive behaviour plan with Kelly, where they all agreed they would give descriptive praise and encouragement to Benjamin when he engaged in positive behaviour. As a result, he engaged in more prosocial behaviours. Such behaviours included joining in with group activities, following group instructions, and taking on the ideas of other children. He was also beginning to show an understanding of how his actions could assist others. For example, he was observed helping other children get their lunch boxes from their bags and was eager to assist his educators with tidying up. These behaviours had been promptly encouraged by his educator, Emma, with comments such as, "You are being such a good friend by helping" and "Thank you for helping tidy up." Benjamin was also displaying an understanding of when another child's behaviour was inappropriate by walking away before the situation escalated into a confrontation; previously, he would have hurt others as a way of resolving a disagreement.

Kelly also reported that he was improving in following instructions and that the frequency of his aggressive tantrums at home had lessened. The improvement in Benjamin's social and emotional skills helps us to understand that if we focus on the behaviours we want to see in children, they will be more likely to engage in such behaviours again. Creating a community culture where positive interactions between all those involved are strong may lead to an increase in positive praise and encouragement for all children. An outcome from all three stories was that most participants were able to increase their positive interactions with all children, not just the focus children. If we are wanting children to develop strong social skills – such as helping others, and regulating their emotions when they are frustrated – then it is important to recognise and give descriptive praise to all children when they exhibit these behaviours.

Such recognition is important because children who are struggling with their social and emotional competence skills have fewer positive social interactions. They are often viewed as being socially incompetent by either their parents, teachers, or educators, which can lead to the development of externalising and internalising psychological disorders (Bornstein et al., 2010; Wigelsworth et al., 2010). However, as the stories illustrate, a child's social and emotional skills at home may be different than at preschool. Therefore, it is important to recognise all children when they are doing things well. Remember that common saying – "Catch them when they are good" – and the Golden Apple in the Tree Model: "5 positive responses for every negative response" (see Figure 5.3).

In addition to descriptive praise and encouragement, consistency is also important. As previously mentioned, the TOGETHER programme focuses on teaching the use of descriptive praise and giving explicit feedback to children when they are doing things well. The programme also focuses on increasing the ratio of the number of positive interactions to the number of negative interactions. Such strategies appear simple in theory; however, the hardest part is developing consistency in parenting and teaching practices. There will be days when children's behaviours are extremely challenging, when parents and educators feel tired from life's demands, and time just doesn't seem to be on their side. Providing positive feedback may often be the last thing on their minds. Many of the parents, teachers, and educators in the three stories discussed similar challenges during the training. Charlotte's statement that it is "not all puppies and rainbows" may have added some humour to the conversation; however, it really shines a light on the fact that parenting is hard work. Recognising this fact is important in helping all of us to realise that it takes a considerable effort to guide children's social and emotional skills. There will be times when we will forget the importance of recognising when our children are doing things well. Therefore, part of the TOGETHER training involves developing reflective strategies to help parents and educators to remember to give positive feedback, which brings us to our third lesson.

Lesson 3: Reflecting on your parenting or teaching practice to develop consistency

As many early childhood teachers and educators will understand, reflecting on their teaching practice is an essential part of their role. In the same vein, parents regularly reflect on their practices but not to the extent that teachers and educators formally do. As a parent, you may often question your own practices. As you learn what works for your family, you may then modify your practices. In the same way, reflective practice is used as a tool to help teachers and educators improve their practice in building children's social and emotional competence. Reflective practice is also encouraged during the TOGETHER training because this encourages consistency in practice between parents, teachers, and educators. In turn, this benefits children's development. Early childhood teachers and educators who reflect on their practices have been shown to provide higher-quality environments for learning (Mac Naughton, 2003). Professional development programmes that include reflective practices have also been shown to effect more change (Riojas-Cortez et al., 2013). Similarly, parents who engage in self-evaluation (like self-reflection) become more self-sufficient and can make informed decisions on their parenting practices (Sanders et al., 2002).

By reflecting, the parents, teachers, and educators in each story were able to see how their change in practices had a positive impact on the development of children's social and emotional skills. For each story, reflections began during the second workshop. Even after one week, the parents, teachers, and educators from each story had begun to see positive change in their own practices. In Story 3, educator Emma reflected in the second workshop on how she had increased her attention to the positive behaviours she had observed in the children. Initially, she said she had been hesitant, which indicated that she was able to recognise her own bias on how effective positive attention may or may not be. However, over the week she discovered that by talking to the children about the things that they had been doing well, the children had increased their attention to their learning:

> *Over the past week it [the reminder strategies and the training] had made me think how much praise I had been giving in group times. In the past I would have focused more on the task. I thought that if I did that [give praise], I would lose children … I have now changed my practice in that I am more flexible to talk to children about their positive behaviour. I thought it would hinder the concentration of the other children, but it didn't at all in the end. They would listen to the praise … then they all wanted the praise.*

Emma had tried to increase her positive interactions not only between the two workshops but also in the months following the training. One way she had kept track of her positive interactions and reflected on her practice was by placing pebbles in her left pocket and transferring a pebble to her right pocket for each positive interaction she gave. While she had not done this every time she had given descriptive praise, she reported that having a simple reminder in her pocket in the form of the pebbles was helping her to remember to focus on the children's positive behaviour. Her change in practice had been visible in both the classroom observations, the BPRQ, and the interviews.

The same could also be said for most of the other parents, teachers, and educators in each of the three stories. The reminder strategies taught in the workshops are designed to be simple and fit in with everyday life. Parents, teachers, and educators are encouraged to come up with strategies that will work for them. In all of the three stories, the parents, the teachers, and the educators expressed how hard it could be to remember to give consistent praise and encouragement. They also mentioned the difficulty of remembering to catch children when they were "being good" and to follow up with five positive interactions for every negative one. It became evident that reminder strategies needed to be implemented. Such strategies included the wearing of elastic bands on a wrist and transferring one to the other wrist each time the parent or educator had given positive feedback. Another strategy involved simply carrying a pen in a pocket and using it to mark a cross on the hand for a negative response and a tick for a positive response. These reminder strategies enabled parents and educators to reflect on their practices. Reflection was demonstrated in the third story, where the parents and educators commented on how the reminder strategies had helped them to become more aware of their practices and to be more consistent. Educators Naomi and Laura were making marks on their hands with a pen when they were giving positive praise, and made the following comments:

Naomi: *It [the reminder strategies and the training] made you more aware of what you were saying … looking through another lens was interesting.*

Laura: *I was consciously thinking of the five positives if I gave a negative … I was aware when I needed to factor that in and upping that a little more.*

Sukhleen, on the other hand, understood that without reminders her practices were harder to change. She was diligent in her role and admitted that she would often get caught up in the daily tasks. However, in Story 3, the educators realised that consistencies between their practices would result from them working together. Sukhleen and her colleagues, Emma and Anika, worked together to devise consistent ways that would improve Benjamin's social and emotional competence. For example, they reflected on the behaviours Benjamin was struggling with. They then discussed the prosocial behaviours that they wanted Benjamin to achieve. They recognised that he had been finding it hard to join in with group play (such as turn-taking), staying focused on non-preferred tasks, and not lashing out when someone upset him. The three educators then reflected on their own practice. They realised they had been more focused on giving instructions and intervening when Benjamin engaged in inappropriate behaviours. They reflected they had given little attention to him when he had joined in well with a group or had been playing happily alongside another child. After reflecting on their practices, Sukhleen, Anika, and Emma decided to give descriptive praise and encouragement to Benjamin when:

- he was playing happily alongside his peers
- he was trying to listen to the ideas of others
- he was trying hard, even at the small things (praising perseverance and the steps of the process).

The three educators also wrote some descriptive positive praise phrases they could use when Benjamin was doing things well. Such phrases included "You are playing so nicely with ____ and have listened to their ideas" or "Great work on waiting for your turn."

As a result of the descriptive praise and encouragement given by the three educators, Benjamin's classroom behaviours improved. He was able to follow instructions during group times and was listening and following the ideas of other children. He was also showing an awareness of other children's feelings and could recognise when his peers needed help. He was more consistent in regulating his emotions and would walk away before a situation escalated into a confrontation. The following reflection from Emma indicates that Benjamin's educators were encouraged by the positive changes in his behaviour that specifically related to his emotional regulation: "From our perspective he is a lot calmer than he was. He is such a different child. There was a lot of anger … he would get frustrated with other children."

Moving on from Benjamin, let us bring you back to Story 1 and four-year-old Tamati. Before the TOGETHER training, Tamati had been struggling with his social and emotional competence. He was finding it difficult to share with others. At the preschool, if other children were attempting to play in the same area as he was, he would often become irritated and at times aggressive, which would often lead to him pushing or hitting the other children. He was also finding it challenging to engage in reciprocal conversations with his peers and to accept other children's perspectives. He was not participating well in group times unless it was related to his own individual interest. Often at group times he would become restless, deliberately poke others, or walk away within one or two minutes of the group time starting and refuse to come back.

During the TOGETHER training, Tamati's educator, Ali, and teacher, Sue, were proactive in developing a behaviour plan for him. They used the plan to help them reflect on the proactive and relationship strategies that they could use in guiding and increasing Tamati's social and emotional competence skills. Figure 7.2 outlines the plan that they had developed for Tamati (the training manual includes a blank plan for the reader). You will notice that Ali and Sue had reflected on the social and emotional behaviours that were of concern. They then identified possible reasons why Tamati engaged in these inappropriate behaviours, and this was followed by a discussion on the behaviours they were wanting to see. From there, they were able to think about how they could change their own practices and interactions with Tamati to help grow his social and emotional competence skills. Consequently, the behaviour plan assisted in developing Tamati's social and emotional skills. With an increase in positive attention to Tamati's prosocial skills from his teacher and educator, especially from Ali, an improvement in his overall social and emotional skills was observed.

The above examples demonstrate the importance of parent, teacher, and educator reflection. When we understand how our own practices and behaviours affect the growth of children's social and emotional development, positive changes can

Behaviour Plan for: *Tamati*

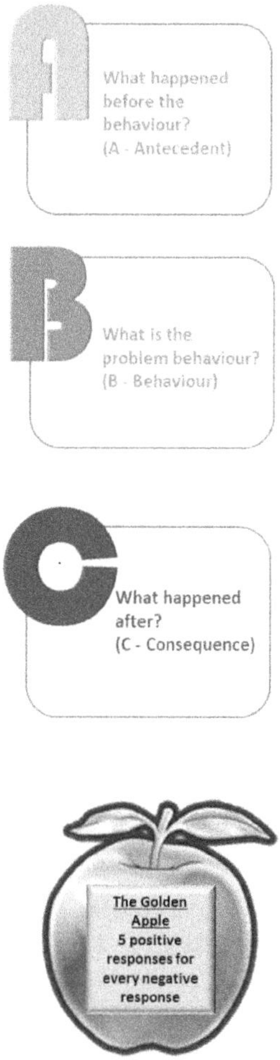

List the behaviours you want to see LESS of...	List the behaviours you want to see MORE of...	Proactive and relationship strategies (what we will do)	Praise and encouragement – useful phrases
Hitting and pushing others when upset Possible reasons for negative behaviour *Finding it hard to express how he feels when someone plays close to him*	*Regulating his emotions when he is angry or frustrated and verbalising how he is feeling*	*1. If he is becoming frustrated with peers be beside him to provide him with phrases to communicate his feelings if needed.* *2. Redirect him to a preferred activity if needed to help him calm down.* *3. As a last resort (e.g. he has hit someone), use the sit and watch strategy.*	*"Tamati, great work on letting me/peer know how you are feeling. Thank you."* *"You are playing so gently with your friend, well done."*
Walking away from group times Possible reasons for negative behaviour *Finding it difficult to remain focused. Distracted*	*Joining in with more group-based activities*	*Use positive forecasting. Give descriptive praise throughout the group time – begin with the moment he arrives.*	*"Tamati, I'm looking forward to you joining us at group time soon."* *"I love that you have joined us, Tamati."* *"Tamati, you are doing such a great job at sitting and listening."*
Taking toys from others Possible reasons for negative behaviour *He wants the toy, but is unsure how to ask for a turn*	*Being able to take turns and listen to the ideas of others*	*Set up activities where Tamati can practise turn-taking with peers. Include activities he enjoys such as block building. Model turn taking with others and provide him with phrases he can use to ask for turns. Give descriptive praise when he takes turns etc.*	*"Tamati, thank you for passing the block to__. You have made them feel so welcome."* *"Thank you for letting ____speak. They had a great idea. what is your idea Tamati?"*

FIGURE 7.2 Positive Behaviour Guidance Plan

then be made. In each of the TOGETHER stories, there were several examples of parents, teachers, and educators reflecting and then changing their practice to include more positive interactions with children. As the positive interactions increased, the children's social and emotional competence grew. The phenomenon of positive interaction had also been observed in the programmes that informed the development of the TOGETHER programme. For example, the Incredible Years programme (Webster-Stratton, 2000) found that with an increase in educator descriptive praise, improvements would occur in children's social competence. The

Teaching Pyramid Model (Fox & Hemmeter, 2009) also found that when educators adopted these strategies, positive outcomes for children in their care were observed, especially for those identified as "at risk."

In these similar programmes, children developed higher levels of positive social interaction skills once their teachers had participated in the training sessions. Therefore, it is vital that any programme that aims to improve children's social and emotional competence allocates time for parents, teachers, and educators to reflect on their practices. The participants also need time to reflect on children's specific individual needs and increase their positive interactions with the children they teach and care for. Equally important is that parents, teachers, and educators develop ways to build consistency in strategies between the home and the preschool. This brings us to the next important lesson about how the TOGETHER programme can reach other families and colleagues in the early childhood community.

Lesson Four: Bringing TOGETHER to your preschool community

Early childhood teachers and educators are placed in a unique and important position when working with families. First, they may be a child's first connection with another adult outside their family. They are part of an important step in a child's and their family's life as they begin to immerse themselves in the wider world. Early childhood teachers and educators often develop stronger relationships and have usually cultivated a deeper trust with families than researchers and other professionals (Santiago et al., 2016). Therefore, the trust that parents place in the hands of their child's teachers and educators cannot be underestimated. While parents are often viewed as a child's first educator (Victorian Government, Department of Education and Training, 2016), it is through the partnerships that parents create with teachers and educators that a child's learning early in life is often enhanced.

The parent–educator partnership is a central element of TOGETHER's conceptual framework, which was introduced in Chapter 2. Part of the framework has been built from the ecological systems theory (Bronfenbrenner, 1986). This theory acknowledges the reciprocal interactions and influences that operate between the child, their family, their teachers, and their educators (as well as the wider interactions and influences of community and society). As a teacher or educator, your involvement in the early years of a child's and their family's life is incredibly important. As the ecological system demonstrates, the attachments children form with their parents, teachers, and educators have a powerful effect on their development, as do the interactions between children's families, their teachers, and their educators.

A critical component of such interactions in the parent–educator relationship is the trust that parents develop in their children's teachers and educators (Adams & Christenson, 1998; Santiago et al., 2016). The importance of trust is also championed in the work of Dunst and Trivette (2009) and involves family-centred practice, which is another major element in the TOGETHER conceptual framework. Specifically, trust, combined with mutual respect and shared decision-making, is an essential ingredient in the parent–educator relationship (Dunst & Dempsey, 2007).

Developing trust takes time and is embedded in reciprocal relationships between a child's parents, their teacher, or their educator (Santiago et al., 2016). Therefore, it is understandable that engaging parents in programmes such as TOGETHER requires a level of trust between all parties. What became evident in all three of the stories was that a sense of mistrust acted as a potential barrier to additional participation from other families in the TOGETHER programme. Specifically, during the recruitment phase for each story, the first author assisted with the invitation process for families. Despite having received the endorsement of the teachers and the educators, the family buy-in was not strong. Quite possibly, the families were wary of a university researcher with whom they had no connection. Or maybe it was the general sense of mistrust associated with the TOGETHER programme being in a research setting. While such observations may be speculation, what the three stories did tell us was that the teachers and educators not only had strong and reciprocal relationships with the families involved in the training workshops but also with other families who were not involved with the programme. It became evident from each of the three stories that in order for other families to benefit from the strategies developed in the TOGETHER training, it would be the responsibility of the teachers and the educators who had completed the workshops to reach out to them; not the researchers; not other early childhood professionals. The trust lay with the teachers and the educators.

So, how can this trust be cultivated to grow children's social and emotional competence? First, the fundamental premise of the TOGETHER programme is to establish strong positive relationships between children, parents, teachers, and educators. It is also about building effective parent–educator partnerships. This foundation is needed for consistency and collaboration to occur between parents, teachers, and educators. When there is consistency in beliefs and practices, as well as a strong collaborative parent–educator partnership, the climate is then optimal for the social and emotional competence of children to develop (Barnett et al., 2010; Park et al., 2016; Sheridan et al., 2005). Therefore, it was encouraging to see that all the parents in each of the three stories believed that the teachers and the educators considered the parents to be partners in their child's development.

They also reported that the teachers and educators were responsive to their needs, valued their strengths, honoured their cultural beliefs, and treated the families with dignity and respect. Before the TOGETHER training had even commenced, it was clear from all three stories that strong relationships already existed between the parents, the teachers, and the educators. While some teachers and educators did report that they felt less confident in their relationships with the families (such as Sonja in the first story), it was unequivocal that the parents felt that the relationships they had with their children's teachers or educators were strong. The teachers and the educators in Story 3 also saw the value in building strong relationships and partnerships. As Sabeena and Naomi both clearly stated:

Sabeena: *By us respecting families at the beginning you make good relationships, and then they trust you.*

Naomi: *Across the board we put a lot of practices into our everyday interactions to ensure strong relationships are built from the beginning … such as … getting to know their interests, open conversations, purposeful listening so they know we value what they talk about.*

While the parents, teachers, and educators reported initial strong relationships between each other, the TOGETHER programme offered strategies to enhance these relationships and improve the parent–educator partnership. As the three stories demonstrate, after the TOGETHER workshops, the parent–educator relationships were even stronger. Through the strengthening of these relationships, the trust the parents had in the teachers and educators deepened. As these relationships and partnerships grew, so did the children's social and emotional skills. For example, in the first story, educator Ali stated that as a result of the TOGETHER programme, there were "increased positive interactions with children and increased positive interaction with families."

And for educator Naomi (Story 3) she found that after the TOGETHER workshops there was an important shift in the partnership she had with Rishi's mum, Meleni. While they had already developed a strong relationship before the workshops, Naomi stated that the partnership had been strengthened. Naomi reported that they had more opportunities for communication and connection, and as a result Rishi's social and emotional skills had increased:

> *Rishi's mum has spent more time with us and we have had more communication and reciprocal conversations with her. I feel like with Rishi and his behaviours he has grown so much, and it has been a real positive for him. We have more interactions with mum, so we have more opportunity to connect.*

Such observations are important to acknowledge as it indicates that in programmes like TOGETHER, it is the teachers and the educators who will ultimately make one of the biggest differences. Again, it is not the researchers. It is not the other early childhood professionals. While such professionals have an important input into children's social and emotional competence, it is the early childhood teacher or educator who has already developed the strong relationships with the parents and the extended families. As confidently stated by Emma in Story 3, where we discussed the parent–educator relationship with her, she stated that "Yes, I agree. They don't trust you [the researcher/facilitator] … so it makes sense that it [the TOGETHER training] comes from us … the relationship is everything."

So, why do early childhood teachers and educators already have strong relationships with parents and families? An early childhood teacher or educator will most likely have a strong theoretical and practical understanding of the importance of establishing relationships with parents and families. Specifically, in the context of the three stories, the teachers and educators followed the curriculum mandated in Victoria, Australia, encompassing the Early Years Learning and Development

Framework for Australia: Belonging, Being, and Becoming (EYLF; Department of Education, Employment and Workplace Relations, 2009) and the Victorian Early Years Learning and Development Framework (VEYLDF; Victorian Government, Department of Education and Training, 2016). Both these policy documents emphasise the building of strong partnerships with parents and families. In the ELYF it states that "educators' practices and the relationships they form with children and families have a significant effect on children's involvement and success in learning. Children thrive when families and educators work together in partnership to support young children's learning" (Department of Education, Employment and Workplace Relations, 2009, p. 10). It also says that:

> Learning outcomes are most likely to be achieved when early childhood educators work in partnership with families. Educators recognise that families are children's first and most influential teachers. They create a welcoming environment where all children and families are respected and actively encouraged to collaborate with educators about curriculum decisions in order to ensure that learning experiences are meaningful.
>
> *Department of Education, Employment and Workplace Relations, 2009, p. 13*

In the VEYLDF, the same sentiments are celebrated, including making strong links between home and preschool:

> Every partnership will be unique, just as each family is unique with different values and priorities. Early childhood professionals work in partnership with all families within communities to build links between home and other settings a child attends. This provides greater consistency and complementarity for the child.
>
> *Victorian Government, Department of Education and Training, 2016, p. 9*

The document continues, saying teachers and educators are required to "establish partnerships where information sharing supports families' confidence, identifies what families do well, and recognises the family's critical importance in their child's life" (Victorian Government, Department of Education and Training, 2016, p. 9).

When such documents stipulate the importance of strong relationships and partnerships between parents, teachers, and educators, it is understandable that teachers and educators place value on such practices. It also once again reinforces the fact that as a teacher or educator, you are placed in a position where such relationships can be cultivated. In addition to the trust being developed through strong parent–educator relationships and partnerships, it is important to acknowledge that many parents and families have placed their trust in you due to your experience. Take for example the comment from Isabella's mum, Juan: "My educator [referring to Jia] has my full trust as she has shown me how caring and responsible she is and that she is absolutely more experienced than me. I think this is very, very important to the children."

As a result of their years of training, many teachers and educators will have a gained a strong understanding of child development. Parents will, therefore, often value the knowledge that teachers and educators bring to the partnership. Recognising the strengths that everyone brings to a partnership is an important element in family-centred practice (Dempsey & Dunst, 2004). It is also important to focus on the strength of the whole parent–educator partnership itself (Sheridan & Kratochwill, 2007). By focusing on both the strengths of the individual and the group, social supports are strengthened and the outcomes for children's social and emotional skills improve. Therefore, it is important to understand that the knowledge you bring to the parent–educator partnership is truly valuable. As illustrated by Juan's comments in Story 2, parents do consider teachers and educators to be a source of knowledge and assistance:

> *After the lecture [the workshops] I forget things … And after a couple of months I stopped … not that I had forgotten the theory, but I had just forgotten to do it on a regular basis. So, if the educator somehow did a reminder … not for like an hour lecture. Just every now and then.*

Such a comment indicates that Juan felt that Jia, her daughter Isabella's teacher, could help her with additional training and reinforcement. It became clear from each story that it was the teachers and the educators who would be better placed to eventually train parents and other family members in the TOGETHER programme. Therefore, it is important that programmes like TOGETHER investigate ways to empower teachers and educators to deliver the workshops or pass on the strategies through other means. Remember, teachers and educators are in a position where they are likely to have the most connection with the families compared to any other professional.

Realising that teachers and educators could be further empowered, we took their training to another level in the final story. In Story 3 we recognised that it may be the teachers and educators who are better positioned to assist parents and families in developing children's social and emotional competence. By utilising the experience of teachers and educators, and the strong partnerships that they had no doubt already developed with their students' families, we believe that barriers to families accessing programmes like TOGETHER can be mitigated. Therefore, we invited all six educators – Emma, Anika, Sukhleen, Laura, Sabeena, and Naomi – to participate in additional training.

While the outcomes of the additional training sessions have not been measured, the workshop conversations and the final interviews detailed in Chapter 5 provide some insight into how the educators had benefited from the additional training. First, the additional coaching demonstrated how teachers and educators could facilitate TOGETHER in the future. It also indicated how the trust that they had already developed with the participating families could be the key to reaching other families. Second, through developing the teachers' and educators' understanding further, several outcomes began to emerge. The teachers and educators were able to establish more contextually responsive relationships with their families and improve consistency in their practices, which are essential goals of the TOGETHER programme. Laura recognised that understanding the family context and recognising the function of the child's behaviour was an important component in facilitating future training, with specific reference to her experience with Rishi:

> *I think that once you know a bit more of the context of the family and the child, we know how to work with him ... We need to give him a role, a purpose, and have control over the situation, and then we will get the best out of him that day ... It's about understanding the function behind the behaviour.*

Our overall message for parents, teachers, and educators

The overall message we want parents, early childhood teachers, and educators to take away from the three stories and this conversation is that their role is invaluable in a child's life and the child's family's life. First, the knowledge that parents have about their child is important in understanding the context in which the child is developing. Essentially, the parents are the experts on their own child. Second, teachers and educators are placed in a valuable position of trust with children and their families. Through such trust, parents may be more inclined to share about their child with the teacher or the educator. As illustrated in all of the three stories, when parents and educators work together in partnership and share their knowledge, mutual understanding increases. With this increase in understanding, teachers and educators are better equipped to respond to children's social and emotional needs. In turn, parents and teachers working together can develop consistent practices that will lead to the children having a better understanding of social and emotional expectations in each setting. As children's understanding of such expectations grows, the prospect of their social and emotional skills improving is greatly enhanced.

As our three stories have shown, the parents, teachers, and educators were able to improve their teaching practices in growing children's social and emotional skills. These improvements were achieved not only through the TOGETHER workshops, but through family-centred and collaborative parent–educator partnerships. In all three stories the parents, teachers, and the educators found the TOGETHER programme:

(a) was easy to follow
(b) reinforced their previous knowledge in growing children's social and emotional competence
(c) enabled them to pass on to others the knowledge they had learnt from TOGETHER
(d) relatively short in terms of the time commitment required to learn the strategies from TOGETHER, especially considering the positive results observed

in children's social and emotional skills as a result of the parents, teachers, and educators improving their practices.

As the three stories have shown us, it is the parents, the early childhood teachers, and the educators who will have the greatest impact on the development of children's social and emotional skills. Therefore, we would encourage you to use the online TOGETHER training manual. We believe that the manual, together with your previous knowledge and experience, will enable you to learn the strategies. The manual is presented in such a way that it promotes collaboration between parents, families, teachers, and educators. You will be able to use the manual as a tool to not only develop your own parenting and teaching practice but to also develop consistency in responding to children's behaviour between the home and preschool settings. You will be able to embed the TOGETHER training into your everyday practice, thereby potentially growing the social and emotional skills of every child you teach and care for.

Implications for early childhood education (ECE) policy and early childhood professionals

The three stories provided us with valuable insight into families, teachers, and educators from varying backgrounds as they worked towards developing strong social and emotional competence in their children. Each story demonstrated that the parents, teachers, and educators observed an increase in the children's social and emotional skills as they increased their positive interactions. Such results are common in other programmes as well, such as the Incredible Years (IY; Webster-Stratton et al., 2001), the Teaching Pyramid Model (Fox & Hemmeter, 2009), and Conjoint Behavioural Consultation (CBC; Sheridan et al., 2012).

TOGETHER is based on many of the principles of these programmes. We expected some similarities with the parents, teachers, and educators in our findings, including the use of positive behaviour guidance strategies to build children's social and emotional competence skills. The IY, the Teaching Pyramid Model, and the CBC programmes also suggest ways to be contextually responsive and promote positive parent–educator partnerships. The difference between the TOGETHER programme and these three programmes is that the parents and teachers attend the workshops together and there are only two workshops.

Another difference with TOGETHER is its shorter delivery time. Potentially, its brevity was more appealing to the parents in the three stories because they felt they could accommodate TOGETHER's shorter time commitment into their busy family life. TOGETHER aims to reduce the barriers, such as being time poor, and any associated stigma that some families and educators may face when trying to access early intervention programmes. TOGETHER also relies on the trust that early childhood teachers and educators have formed with children, their parents/caregivers, and extended family. While our research into the effectiveness of the TOGETHER programme has produced the promising results illustrated in the three stories and our conversations, there are still many unanswered questions that require further investigation. Through the three stories, we identified several lessons for researchers and other professionals as we moved forward in the TOGETHER journey.

Reducing barriers to involvement in early intervention

Our first lesson focuses on the barriers that continue to lower participation levels in the TOGETHER programme. One barrier often cited by parents, teachers, and educators is the time commitment. Teachers and educators would often mention time limitations when they were contemplating enrolling in professional development programmes. The same could be said for parents (Koerting et al., 2013). Most of the parents, teachers, and educators in our three stories mentioned during the preliminary interviews that time was a barrier to them being able to attend workshops. Yet, so many early intervention programmes that train teachers and educators in developing children's social and emotional competence require substantial time commitments. Consequently, the TOGETHER programme has been designed to reduce the required time commitment from participants.

So how does TOGETHER reduce the time factor? As the three stories have illustrated, the structure of the programme is two 120-minute training workshops where the participants work through an easy-to-follow manual. Additional coaching is provided in some cases. However, the visual images in the manual have been created to remind teachers, educators, and parents of the TOGETHER strategies. It is a tool they can revisit without having to enrol for further training. In addition, the format ofTOGETHER involves collaboration between the teachers, educators, and parents. By training together, more support is provided by the teachers and educators to the parents, as illustrated throughout the three stories. There is even support given from parent to parent. Such support reduces the need for continual connection with other early childhood professionals. The support may also reduce the stigma parents often feel when asking for assistance for their child's challenging behaviour.

Of course, as we look to the future, more research is needed into how early childhood teachers and educators can continue to provide support to parents and extended family members after the TOGETHER training. It is also important to explore how early childhood teachers and educators can pick up a simple programme like TOGETHER and eventually facilitate it themselves. When teachers and educators are empowered to facilitate a programme such as TOGETHER, there is a possibility of reducing other barriers such as contacting hard-to-reach parents and families.

One solution to this dilemma is to have the teachers and educators attempting to reach parents and families who are less inclined to participate due to their work commitments or the general demands of life. A hindrance that is consistently raised is the difficulty of contacting parents or family members who are working. In Story 1, educator Ali reported that it was challenging to collaborate effectively with families when she would only meet the child's grandparents, not the parents who were working. She also mentioned that time and communication barriers, such as the minimal level of connection with working parents, limited the extent to which some families could commit to the TOGETHER programme. Such sentiments regarding time also featured in the other two stories. For example, in Story 3, teacher Naomi mentioned that it was challenging to connect with Rishi's father due to him always working. In fact, except for Isabella's parents, it was only the mothers of the children who attended the TOGETHER training.

The gap in the level of connection with other family members, particularly fathers and grandparents, has become a point of concern. Research indicates that inconsistency between the practices of carers can lead to negative outcomes for children's social and emotional development (Claessens & Chen, 2013). Therefore, in early childhood settings, where children are often receiving care and education from multiple sources (for example, parents, extended family members, teachers, and educators), it is important that future research explores how partnerships can also be developed with other influential family members or carers, not just the immediate carers.

This point brings us back to the notion that most teachers and educators are already connected with parents and families. They have often developed a sense of trust with parents and families, which researchers and other professionals may struggle to achieve. If programmes such as TOGETHER are to reach families from a wide variety of contexts, we need to value the role of the teacher and educator. As illustrated in the three stories, it is the teachers and educators who understand the contexts of the families attending their preschool better than any other professional. Therefore, in early intervention programmes, it is important to explore ways in which teachers and educators can be empowered to facilitate programmes such as TOGETHER.

In many of the early intervention programmes, the teachers and educators are trained in positive behaviour support strategies (Fox & Hemmeter, 2009; Sheridan et al., 2012; Webster-Stratton et al., 2001), as we do in TOGETHER, yet they are often overlooked as potential facilitators of these early intervention programmes. Just imagine what could be achieved in growing children's social and emotional competence if teachers and educators were empowered to run programmes such as TOGETHER themselves. Imagine the possible barriers that could be removed or minimised for parents and families. Imagine the decrease in the stigma often associated with parents and families if they could connect with someone they trusted. Imagine how much more contextually responsive TOGETHER could be. Imagine the implications for future research.

Consequently, further study is required to explore how we can assist other family members to access the TOGETHER programme. One possible line of enquiry may be how to reach other family members through their children's teachers and educators, who are often enthusiastic to participate in programmes such as TOGETHER, as discussed in the next section.

Teachers, educators, and professionals empowering each other

Let us step into a lecture theatre filled with pre-service teachers. Now, let us ask these education students what would be one of the most pressing subjects where they felt they needed more training. In the same vein, let us step into the staffroom of a preschool or early primary school. What do you think the topic of conversation would be regarding the challenges that the teachers and educators were facing? In many cases, you would no doubt hear repeatedly that the teachers and educators were struggling with children's challenging behaviour. In other words, they would be struggling with helping children develop their social and emotional skills. It is concerning that early childhood teachers have continually reported that they need assistance in addressing delays in children's social and emotional competence (Carter & Van Norman, 2010; Reinke et al., 2012).

Such concerns were also highlighted during the recruitment phase for the three stories. Interestingly, enrolling teachers and educators for the TOGETHER programme was not a challenge. In fact, during the initial recruitment stages, over 100 early childhood teachers and educators responded to an online invitation in the space of one afternoon. Considering the capacity of the current TOGETHER research project, including all the interested teachers and educators was not possible, so we had to close the invitation portal one day after advertising the project. However, such a response gives an indication that there are many early childhood teachers and educators who are struggling with developing children's social and emotional skills. Such a response also signifies that there is a considerable demand for in-service training. This demand is concerning, however, considering the importance of the early childhood teachers' and educators' roles in children's social and emotional development. The demand is also troubling when it is the teachers and educators who will often have the strongest partnerships with children's families (Coleman et al., 2013).

Therefore, from both our observations during the recruitment phase for the project and the research of others, there would appear to be insufficient training available to assist teachers and educators in developing the skills necessary to improve children's social and emotional competence (Carter & Van Norman, 2010; Flower et al., 2016; Reinke et al., 2012). The three stories illustrate that the simple strategies taught in TOGETHER are easy to implement in everyday classroom practices. Over the two 120-minute workshops, teachers and educators are able to change their practices to grow children's social and emotional skills. And in our final story, we began to see how teachers and educators could be empowered to pass on the strategies to other parents, families, and colleagues who were unable to attend the TOGETHER workshops.

Empowering early childhood teachers and educators to pass on the skills learnt in the TOGETHER programme is one of the next steps in the continuing TOGETHER research project. While this book, together with the training manual, may be of assistance in empowering teachers and educators, strong partnerships with other early childhood professionals also need to be developed (Sheridan &

Kratochwill, 2007). The reason for developing partnerships with professionals is that families and children who are receiving early intervention are often assisted by other early childhood professionals who are not teachers or educators. Specifically, in Australian early childhood settings, children are often visited by preschool field officers, psychologists, speech therapists, occupational therapists, and maternal health care nurses, who may have not been previously trained in positive behaviour support strategies. Therefore, it is important that teachers and educators are also empowered to pass on strategies from the TOGETHER programme to other professionals to ensure consistency. By teachers and educators sharing their knowledge of the strategies they have learnt from the TOGETHER workshops with other professionals consistency between home and preschool may be consolidated even further.

While the third workshop revealed that the teachers and educators were beginning to think of ways to implement the strategies of TOGETHER with other families (such as one-on-one interviews with parents), further research is needed. Future research needs to explore how best the teachers and educators can pass on the TOGETHER knowledge to others, including other families, colleagues, and early childhood professionals. As we have discussed, the partnerships teachers and educators develop with parents and families are invaluable. As are the partnerships with other professionals. We need to be tapping into the connections that early childhood teachers and educators already have with parents, families, and the community. Therefore, as we move forward in improving the TOGETHER programme, it is important that we address the following question: How can the experience and knowledge of the teachers and the educators be used to prevent the need for higher-level intervention? We also need to widen the TOGETHER research, which brings us to the next section.

Widening the TOGETHER research

The case study approach we adopted to understand the effects of the TOGETHER programme meant that the number of children, parents, teachers, and educators involved in the programme was relatively small. Such an approach is warranted when trying to understand the effects of early intervention on children's social and emotional competence. This approach is also important in helping us understand the changes in parents', teachers', and educators' beliefs, practices, and relationships. The case study approach allows us to be flexible and adaptable, not only in the delivery of the TOGETHER programme but also in how we investigate and tell the stories of TOGETHER. The early childhood communities in which the TOGETHER training took place were contextually unique from each other. First, the case study approach provided a range of different ways that the information could be collected in order to show how the TOGETHER programme works in each community. Second, it enabled us to investigate the effects of TOGETHER in far more detail than might have been possible if we had been working with a larger population.

However, it is important to remember that the three stories are not generalisable to the wider population. The three stories were specific to three distinctly different contexts. In saying this, the three stories show how TOGETHER is adaptable across settings. Each story shows how the programme can be used for parents, teachers, and educators to build their skills in developing children's social and emotional competence. The stories also indicate how TOGETHER can deepen the parent–educator partnership. Therefore, the next challenge in exploring the effects of the TOGETHER programme is to continue the implementation of the programme in various other settings. You, the reader, can be part of this research. Through this book we have provided a variety of tools that you can use to explore the effects of TOGETHER in your own setting. Such tools include the Social Development Rating Scale (SDRS; Church et al., 2006) and the Beliefs, Practices, and Relationships Questionnaire (BPRQ). Observing the behaviours of the children, parents, teachers, and educators also revealed so much to us about the behaviour changes. Finally, important voices from the parents, teachers, and educators through the recordings of the workshops and interviews provided colourful illustrations of the effects of the TOGETHER programme. Such voices are important for future reflections.

Final conclusions

Let us return to the initial chapter where we placed the importance on you, the reader. That is, you being the early childhood teacher, educator, parent, or family member. This book has been written to empower some of the most important people in children's lives, and you are one of them. With your dedication to children's development, many of them will experience valuable interactions that will enhance their social and emotional skills. The role you play in a child's life is vital for them to develop skills in forming friendships, participating positively in social settings, regulating their emotions, and engaging in meaningful play and learning.

However, as Samuel's mum, Charlotte, eloquently said, "It's not all puppies and rainbows." As authors, we understand the struggles that early childhood teachers, educators, and parents often face in developing children's social and emotional skills. That is precisely why we developed the TOGETHER programme. From our own experience and the findings from many other evidence-based programmes (Fox & Hemmeter, 2009; Sheridan et al., 2012; Webster-Stratton et al., 2001), we know that there are practices that work in growing children's social and emotional skills. It is ensuring that consistency is maintained in such practices between the home and preschool settings that can be difficult. Therefore, TOGETHER is a programme that provides a platform to train parents, teachers, and educators in how to improve children's social and emotional skills and develop consistency in practices between the home and preschool settings. In the three stories, working through the easy-to-follow manual in the two, 120-minute workshops resulted in positive changes for all the children, teachers, educators, and parents who participated in the TOGETHER programme.

Furthermore, for each of the children, there had been an increase in both their social skills and emotional regulation. For example, Tamati was able to regulate his emotions when he became angry or frustrated and was able to verbalise how he was feeling. For Isabella, a significant improvement in her confidence when interacting with peers was observed in the period following the TOGETHER workshops. For Benjamin, he was engaging in more prosocial behaviours. Such behaviours included joining in with group activities, following group instructions, and taking on board the ideas of other children.

For the parents, teachers, and educators, there was a marked increase in the amount of positive attention they were giving to children's prosocial behaviours, including a rise in the level of descriptive praise and encouragement. These improvements in practices had not only been learnt in the TOGETHER workshops but also through the collaborative parent–educator partnerships. Providing opportunities to develop these partnerships during the workshops had built a strong foundation from which to help support their children in their social and emotional development. In each story, the TOGETHER programme had provided consistent opportunities for explicit, practical parent–educator interaction. As a result, a strengthening in the relationships between the parents, teachers, and educators had developed.

While there is still a long way to go in the journey and development of the TOGETHER programme, the three stories have signalled a promising way forward in the world of early intervention in children's behaviour. First, the stories have proved that social and emotional training programmes for parents, teachers, or educators do not need to be lengthy. There is the possibility that by taking a whole preschool community approach that more children will experience the benefits of such programmes, thereby reducing the need for higher-level interventions. Finally, through the three stories we found that growing children's social and emotional skills is enhanced when there are ample opportunities for the parent–educator partnership to flourish. As the title of our programme explicitly states, it is by being together and not apart that we will grow the social and emotional competence of young children.

Notes

1 The trust that teachers and educators have with parents may also be the key to reaching other families, too. Therefore, the approach of teachers and educators passing knowledge to all families is explained further in the fourth lesson of this final chapter 'Bringing TOGETHER to your preschool community'. In that lesson we explain the approach the TOGETHER programme takes to empower teachers and educators to pass on their newly acquired knowledge in the hope that it will break down barriers.

2 During the TOGETHER training remembering the shy/invisible child is emphasised – sometimes children miss out on praise because they are cooperative, shy, or nondemanding.

REFERENCES

Adams, K. S., & Christenson, S. L. (1998). Differences in parent and teacher trust levels: Implications for creating collaborative family–school relationships. *Special Services in the Schools, 14*(1–2), 1–22. https://doi.org/10.1300/J008v14n01_01

Allen, R., & Steed, E. A. (2016). Culturally responsive pyramid model practices: Program-wide positive behavior support for young children. *Topics in Early Childhood Special Education, 36*(3), 165–175. https://doi.org/10.1177/0271121416651164

Australian Government, Department of Education and Training. (2019). *Australian early development census national report 2018: A snapshot of early childhood development in Australia.* www.aedc.gov.au/resources/detail/2018-aedc-national-report

Bandura, A. (1977). *Social learning theory.* Prentice Hall.

Barnett, M. A., Shanahan, L., Deng, M., Haskett, M. E., & Cox, M. J. (2010). Independent and interactive contributions of parenting behaviors and beliefs in the prediction of early childhood behavior problems. *Parenting, 10*(1), 43–59. https://doi.org/10.1080/15295190903014604

Bellinger, S. A., Lee, S. W., Jamison, T. R., & Reese, R. M. (2016). Conjoint behavioral consultation: Community–school collaboration and behavioral outcomes using multiple baseline. *Journal of Educational & Psychological Consultation, 26*(2), 139–165. http://dx.doi.org/10.1080/10474412.2015.1089405

Bermudez, J. M., Zak-Hunter, L. M., & Silva, L. (2011). Experiences of parenting classes for Mexican American mothers parenting alone: Offering culturally responsive approaches. *American Journal of Family Therapy, 39*(4), 360–374. https://doi.org/10.1080/01926187.2010.539477

Bongers, I. L., Koot, H. M., van der Ende, J., & Verhulst, F. C. (2004). Developmental trajectories of externalizing behaviors in childhood and adolescence. *Child Development, 75*(5), 1523–1537. https://doi.org/10.1111/j.1467-8624.2004.00755.x

Bornstein, M. H., Hahn, C.-S., & Haynes, O. M. (2010). Social competence, externalizing, and internalizing behavioral adjustment from early childhood through early adolescence: Developmental cascades. *Development and Psychopathology, 22*(4), 717–735. https://doi.org/10.1017/S0954579410000416

Bronfenbrenner, U. (1986). Ecology of the family as a context for human development: Research perspectives. *Developmental Psychology, 22*(6), 723–742. https://doi.org/10.1037/0012-1649.22.6.723

Bronfenbrenner, U. (Ed.). (2005). *Making human beings human: Bioecological perspectives on human development.* Sage.

Bronfenbrenner, U., & Morris, P. A. (2006). The bioecological model of human development. In R. M. Lerner & W. E. Damon (Eds.), *Handbook of child psychology: Vol 1, Theoretical models of human development* (pp. 793–828). Wiley.

Campbell, S. B., Denham, S. A., Howarth, G. Z., Jones, S. M., Whittaker, J. V., Williford, A. P., Willoughby, M.T., Yudron, M., & Darling-Churchill, K. (2016). Commentary on the review of measures of early childhood social and emotional development: Conceptualization, critique, and recommendations. *Journal of Applied Developmental Psychology, 45*, 19–41. http://dx.doi.org/10.1016/j.appdev.2016.01.008

Carter, D. R. & Van Norman, R. K. (2010). Class-wide positive behavior support in preschool: Improving teacher implementation through consultation. *Early Childhood Education Journal, 38*, 279–288. https://doi.org/10.1007/s10643-010-0409-x

Chan, S. M., Bowes, J., & Wyver, S. (2009). Parenting style as a context for emotion socialization. *Early Education and Development, 20*(4), 631–656. https://doi.org/10.1080/10409280802541973

Church, R. J., Tyler-Merrick, G., & Hayward, H. (2006). Identifying antisocial development in New Zealand children. Phase 1: Development of the screening procedure. Unpublished final report prepared for the Ministry of Education.

Claessens, A., & Chen, J.-H. (2013). Multiple child care arrangements and child well being: Early care experiences in Australia. *Early Childhood Research Quarterly, 28*(1), 49–61. https://doi.org/10.1016/j.ecresq.2012.06.003

Coleman, J. C., Crosby, M. G., Irwin, H. K., Dennis, L. R., Simpson, C. G., & Rose, C.A. (2013). Preventing challenging behaviors in preschool: Effective strategies for classroom teachers. *Young Exceptional Children, 16*(3), 3–10. https://doi.org/10.1177/1096250612464641

Darling-Churchill, K. E., & Lippman, L. (2016). Early childhood social and emotional development: Advancing the field of measurement. *Journal of Applied Developmental Psychology, 45*, 1–7. https://doi.org/10.1016/j.appdev.2016.02.002

Dempsey, I., & Dunst, C. J. (2004). Helpgiving styles and parent empowerment in families with a young child with a disability. *Journal of Intellectual and Developmental Disability, 29*, 40–51. https://doi.org/10.1080/13668250410001662874

Denham, S. A. (2006). Social-emotional competence as support for school readiness: What is it and how do we assess it? *Early Education and Development, 17*(1), 57–89. https://doi.org/10.1207/s15566935eed1701_4

Denham, S. A., Bassett, H. H., & Zinsser, K. (2012). Early childhood teachers as socializers of young children's emotional competence. *Early Childhood Education Journal, 40*(3), 137–143. https://doi.org/10.1007/s10643-012-0504-2

Denham, S. A., Blair, K. A., Demulder, E., Levitas, J., Sawyer, K., Auerbach-Major, S., & Queenan, P. (2003). Preschool emotional competence: Pathway to social competence? *Child Development, 74*(1), 238–256.

Denham, S. A., Kalb, S., Way, E., Warren-Khot, H., Rhoades, B. L., & Bassett, H. H. (2013). Social and emotional information processing in preschoolers: Indicator of early school success? *Early Child Development and Care, 183*(5), 667–688. https://doi.org/10.1080/03004430.2012.682728

Department of Education, Employment and Workplace Relations. (2009). *Belonging, being and becoming: The early years learning framework for Australia.* Produced for the Council of Australian Governments. www.acecqa.gov.au/sites/default/files/2018-02/belonging_being_and_becoming_the_early_years_learning_framework_for_australia.pdf

Domenech-Rodríguez, M., & Wieling, E. (2004). Developing culturally appropriate, evidence-based treatments for interventions with ethnic minority populations. In M. Rastogi & E. Wieling (Eds.), *Voices of color: First person accounts of ethnic minority therapists* (pp. 313–333). Sage.

Dunst, C. J. (1997). Conceptual and empirical foundations of family-centered practice. In R. J. Illback, C. T. Cobb, & H. M. Joseph, Jr. (Eds.), *Integrated services for children and families: Opportunities for psychological practice* (pp. 75–91). American Psychological Association.

Dunst, C. J. (2002). Family-centered practices: Birth through high school. *The Journal of Special Education, 36*(3), 139–147. https://doi.org/10.1177/00224669020360030401

Dunst, C. J., & Dempsey, I. (2007). Family–professional partnerships and parenting competence, confidence, and enjoyment. *International Journal of Disability, Development and Education, 54*(3), 305–318. https://doi.org/10.1080/10349120701488772

Dunst, C. J., & Trivette, C. M. (1996). Empowerment, effective helpgiving practices and family-centered care. *Pediatric Nursing, 22*(4), 334–337.

Dunst, C. J., & Trivette, C. M. (2009). Capacity-building family-systems intervention practices. *Journal of Family Social Work, 12*(2), 119–143. https://doi.org/10.1080/10522150802713322

Fallon, L. M., O'Keeffe, B. V., & Sugai, G. (2012). Consideration of culture and context in school-wide positive behavior support: A review of current literature. *Journal of Positive Behavior Interventions, 14*(4), 209–219. https://doi.org/10.1177/1098300712442242

Fergusson, D., Stanley, L., & Horwood, L. J. (2009). Preliminary data on the efficacy of the Incredible Years basic parent programme in New Zealand. *Australian & New Zealand Journal of Psychiatry, 43*(1), 76–79. https://doi.org/10.1080/00048670802534382

Flick, U., Garms-Homolová, V., Herrmann, W. J., Kuck, J., & Röhnsch, G. (2012). "I can't prescribe something just because someone asks for it…": Using mixed methods in the framework of triangulation. *Journal of Mixed Methods Research, 6*(2), 97–110. https://doi.org/10.1177/1558689812437183

Flower, A., McKenna, J. W., & Haring, C. D. (2016). Behavior and classroom management: Are teacher preparation programs really preparing our teachers? *Preventing School Failure: Alternative Education for Children and Youth, 61*(2), 163–169. https://doi.org/10.1080/1045988X.2016.1231109

Forgatch, M. S., Bullock, B. M., & Patterson, G. R. (2004). From theory to practice: Increasing effective parenting through role-play: The Oregon model of parent management training (PMTO). In H. Steiner (Ed.), *Handbook of mental health interventions in children and adolescents: An integrated developmental approach* (pp. 782–814). Jossey-Bass.

Fox, L., Carta, J., Strain, P. S., Dunlap, G., and Hemmeter, M. L. (2010). Response to intervention and the Pyramid Model. *Infants and Young Children, 23*(1), 3–13. https://doi.org/10.1097/IYC.0b013e3181c816e2

Fox, L., Dunlap, G., Hemmeter, M. L., Joseph, G. E., & Strain, P. S. (2003). The teaching pyramid: A model for supporting social competence and preventing challenging behavior in young children. *Young Children, 58*(4), 48–52.

Fox, L., & Hemmeter, M. L. (2009). A programme-wide model for supporting social emotional development and addressing challenging behavior in early childhood settings. In W. Sailor, G. Dunlap, G. Sugai, & R. Horner (Eds.), *Handbook of positive behavior support* (pp. 177–202). Springer.

Fox, L., & Lentini, R. H. (2006). "You got it!" Teaching social and emotional skills. *Young Children, 61*, 36–42. https://challengingbehavior.cbcs.usf.edu/docs/YouGotIt_Teaching-Social-Emotional-Skills.pdf

Gaete, A., Gómez, V., & Benavides, P. (2017). The overuse of self-report in the study of beliefs in education: Epistemological considerations. *International Journal of Research & Method in Education, 41*(3), 241–256. https://doi.org/10.1080/1743727X.2017.1288205

Garvis, S., Phillipson, S., Rosunee, N., Kewalramani, S., McMahon, K., & Meyer, C. (2016). Time for reflection on maternal child health assessments in Australia: Making a case for a three-way partnership. *Journal of Nursing and Patient Care, 1*(1). https://doi.org/10.4172/2573-4571.1000104

Hadaway, S. M., & Brue, A. W. (2016). *Practitioner's guide to functional behavioral assessment: Process, purpose, planning, and prevention.* Springer.

Harris, P., & Manatakis, H. (2013). Children's voices: A principled framework for children and young people's participation as valued citizens and learners. Government of South Australia. www.education.sa.gov.au/sites/default/files/childrens-voices-framework.pdf?v=1476666418

Hemmeter, M. L., Ostrosky, M., & Fox, L. (2006). Social and emotional foundations for early learning: A conceptual model for intervention. *School Psychology Review, 35*(4), 583–601. https://doi.org/10.1080/02796015.2006.12087963

Hemmeter, M. L., Snyder, P., Fox, L., & Algina, J. (2016). Evaluating the implementation of the Pyramid Model for Promoting Social-Emotional Competence in early childhood classrooms. *Topics in Early Childhood Special Education, 36*(3), 133–136. https://doi.org/10.1177/0271121416653386

Henderlong, J., & Lepper, M. R. (2002). The effects of praise on children's intrinsic motivation: A review and synthesis. *Psychological Bulletin, 128*(5), 774–795. https://doi.org/10.1037/0033-2909.128.5.774

Hieneman, M., & Fefer, S. A. (2017). Employing the principles of positive behavior support to enhance family education and intervention. *Journal of Child and Family Studies, 26*(10), 2655–2668. https://doi.org/10.1007/s10826-017-0813-6

Houle, A. A., Besnard, T., Bérubé, A., & Dagenais, C. (2018). Factors that influence parent recruitment into prevention programs in early childhood: A concept map of parents', practitioners', and administrators' points of view. *Children and Youth Services Review, 85*, 127–136. https://doi.org/10.1016/j.childyouth.2017.12.014

Housman, D. K. (2017). The importance of emotional competence and self-regulation from birth: A case for the evidence-based emotional cognitive social early learning approach. *International Journal of Child Care and Education Policy, 11*(1), Article 13. https://doi.org/10.1186/s40723-017-0038-6

Kazdin, A. E. (1996). Developing effective treatments for children and adolescents. In E. D. Hibbs & P. S. Jensen (Eds.), *Psychosocial treatments for child and adolescent disorders: Empirically based strategies for clinical practice* (pp. 9–18). American Psychological Association.

Kazdin, A. E. (2000). Treatments for aggressive and antisocial children. *Child and Adolescent Psychiatric Clinics of North America, 9*(4), 841–858. https://doi.org/10.1016/S1056-4993(18)30095-6

Koerting, J., Smith, E., Knowles, M. M., Latter, S., Elsey, H., McCann, D. C., Thompson, M., & Sonuga-Barke, E. J. (2013). Barriers to, and facilitators of, parenting programmes for childhood behaviour problems: A qualitative synthesis of studies of parents' and professionals' perceptions. *European Child & Adolescent Psychiatry, 22*(11), 653–670. http://doi.org/10.1007/s00787-013-0401-2

Lim, S. M., Rodger, S., & Brown, T. (2013). Model of social competence in an early childhood environment. *Occupational Therapy in Mental Health*, 29(2), 114–133. https://doi.org/10.1080/0164212X.2013.788975

Lustick, H. (2016). Making discipline relevant: Toward a theory of culturally responsive positive schoolwide discipline. *Race Ethnicity and Education, 20*(5), 681–695. https://doi.org/10.1080/13613324.2016.1150828

Mac Naughton, G. (2003). *Shaping early childhood: Learners, curriculum and contexts.* Open University Press.

Mac Naughton, G., Rolfe, S. A., & Siraj-Blatchford, I. (2001). *Doing early childhood research: International perspectives on theory and practice*. Taylor & Francis.

Mathison, S. (1988). Why triangulate? *Educational Researcher, 17*(2), 13–17. https://doi.org/10.3102/0013189X017002013

Ministry of Education – Te Tāhuhu o te Mātauranga. (2017). *Te whāriki: He whāriki mātauranga mō ngā mokopuna o Aotearoa: Early childhood curriculum*. https://education.govt.nz/assets/Documents/Early-Childhood/ELS-Te-Whariki-Early-Childhood-Curriculum-ENG-Web.pdf

Murray, J., & Farrington, D. P. (2010). Risk factors for conduct disorder and delinquency: Key findings from longitudinal studies. *The Canadian Journal of Psychiatry, 55*(10), 633–642. https://doi.org/10.1177/070674371005501003

Neuhauser, A., Ramseier, E., Schaub, S., Burkhardt, S. C. A., Templer, F., & Lanfranchi, A. (2015). Hard to reach families: A methodological approach to early recognition, recruitment, and randomization in an intervention study. *Mental Health & Prevention, 3*(3), 79–88. https://doi.org/10.1016/j.mhp.2015.07.002

Nowell, L. S., Norris, J. M., White, D. E., & Moules, N. J. (2017). Thematic analysis: Striving to meet the trustworthiness criteria. *International Journal of Qualitative Methods, 16*(1), 1–13. https://doi.org/10.1177/1609406917733847

Ogden, T., & Hagan, K. A. (2008). Treatment effectiveness of parent management training in Norway: A randomized controlled trial of children with conduct problems. *Journal of Consulting and Clinical Psychology, 76*(4), 607–621. https://doi.org/10.1037/0022-006X.76.4.607

Park, J. L., Johnston, C., Colalillo, S., & Williamson, D. (2016). Parents' attributions for negative and positive child behavior in relation to parenting and child problems. *Journal of Clinical Child & Adolescent Psychology, 47*(1), 563–575. https://doi.org/10.1080/15374416.2016.1144191

Patterson, G. R., Chamberlain, P., & Reid, J. B. (2016). A comparative evaluation of a parent-training program – Republished article. *Behavior Therapy, 47*(6), 804–811. https://doi.org/10.1016/j.beth.2016.11.004

Patton, M. Q. (1999). Enhancing the quality and credibility of qualitative analysis. *Health Sciences Research, 34*(5), 1189–1208.

Phillips, J. G. (2014). *The effects of a brief in-service course on teacher's skill in building cooperation in three- to five-year-old children* [Master's thesis, University of Canterbury]. https://ir.canterbury.ac.nz/handle/10092/9585

Phillips, J. G., Phillipson, S., & Tyler-Merrick, G. (2017). *TOGETHER: Growing children's social and emotional skills: In-service teacher, educator and parent training program* [Unpublished manual]. Swinburne University of Technology.

Phillips, J. G., Tyler-Merrick, G., & Church, J. (2013). *Building cooperation in three- to five-year-old children* [Unpublished teacher training manual and workbook. https://ir.canterbury.ac.nz/handle/10092/9585].

Phillips, J. G., Tyler-Merrick, G., & Phillipson, S. (2021). Measurement of parents' and educators' beliefs, practices, and relationships using Rasch analysis: Towards advancing children's social and emotional competence. *Emotional and Behavioural Difficulties*. Under Review

Phillips, J. G., Tyler-Merrick, G., & Phillipson, S. (in press). The feasibility of TOGETHER: A collaborative educator–parent programme for teaching social and emotional competence in young children. *Emotional and Behavioural Difficulties*.

Reinke, W. M., Herman, K. C., & Stormont, M. (2012). Classroom-level positive behavior supports in schools implementing SW-PBIS: Identifying areas for enhancement. *Journal of Positive Behavior Interventions, 15*(1), 39–50. https://doi.org/10.1177/1098300712459079

Riojas-Cortez, M., Alanís, I., & Flores, B. B. (2013). Early childhood teachers reconstruct beliefs and practices through reflexive action. *Journal of Early Childhood Teacher Education, 34*(1), 36–45. https://doi.org/10.1080/10901027.2013.758536

Rouse, E., & O'Brien, D. (2017). Mutuality and reciprocity in parent–teacher relationships: Understanding the nature of partnerships in early childhood education and care provision. *Australasian Journal of Early Childhood, 42*(2), 45–52. https://doi.org/10.23965/AJEC.42.2.06

Sailor, W., Dunlap, G., Sugai, G., & Horner, R. (Eds.). (2009). *Handbook of positive behavior support*. Springer.

Santiago, R. T., Garbacz, S. A., Beattie, T., & Moore, C. L. (2016). Parent–teacher relationships in elementary school: An examination of parent–teacher trust. *Psychology in the Schools, 53*(10), 1003–1017. https://doi.org/10.1002/pits.21971

Sanders, M. R., Markie-Dadds, C., & Turner, K. M. T. (2002). *Theoretical, scientific and clinical foundations of the Triple P-positive parenting program: A population approach to the promotion of parenting competence.* Parent Research and Practice Monograph *No.* 1. https://csds.qld.edu.au/sdc/Provectus/GAPP/Understanding%20behaviours/files/Sander%20triple%20P%202003.pdf

Sheridan, S. M., Bovaird, J. A., Glover, T. A., Garbacz, A. S., Witte, A., & Kwon, K. (2012). A randomized trial examining the effects of conjoint behavioral consultation and the mediating role of the parent–teacher relationship. *School Psychology Review, 41*(1), 23–46.

Sheridan, S. M., Clarke, B. L., Marti, D. C., Burt, J. D., & Rohlk, A. M. (2005). *Conjoint behavioral consultation: A model to facilitate meaningful partnerships for families and schools*. Harvard Graduate School of Education. https://archive.globalfrp.org/publications-resources/publications-series/family-involvement-research-digests/conjoint-behavioral-consultation-a-model-to-facilitate-meaningful-partnerships-for-families-and-schools#:~:text=Conjoint%20behavioral%20consultation%20(CBC)%20is,competencies%20of%20all%20parties%20(Sheridan%2C

Sheridan, S. M. & Kratochwill, T. R. (2007). *Conjoint behavioral consultation: Promoting family–school connections and interventions* (2nd ed.). Springer.

Shonkoff, J. P., Radner, J. M., & Foote, N. (2017). Expanding the evidence base to drive more productive early childhood investment. *The Lancet, 389*(10064), 14–16. https://doi.org/10.1016/S0140-6736(16)31702-0

Stern, S. B., Walsh, M., Mercado, M., Levene, K., Pepler, D. J., Carr, A., Heppell, A., & Lowe, E. (2015). When they call, will they come? A contextually responsive approach for engaging multistressed families in an urban child mental health center: A randomized clinical trial. *Research on Social Work Practice, 25*(5), 549–563. https://doi.org/10.1177/1049731514548038

Trillingsgaard, T., Trillingsgaard, A., & Webster-Stratton, C. (2014). Assessing the effectiveness of the "Incredible Years® parent training" to parents of young children with ADHD symptoms: A preliminary report. *Scandinavian Journal of Psychology, 55*(6), 538–545. https://doi.org/10.1111/sjop.12155

Tyler-Merrick, G. M. (2015). *Screening for Antisocial Development*. [Doctoral thesis, University of Canterbury]. https://ir.canterbury.ac.nz/handle/10092/10263

Vartuli, S. (2005). Beliefs: The heart of teaching. *Young Children, 60*(5), 76–86.

Victorian Government, Department of Education and Training. (2016). *Victorian early years learning and development framework: For all children from birth to eight years*. www.education.vic.gov.au/Documents/childhood/providers/edcare/veyldframework.pdf

Vincent, C. G., Randall, C., Cartledge, G., Tobin, T. J., & Swain-Bradway, J. (2011). Toward a conceptual integration of cultural responsiveness and schoolwide positive behavior support. *Journal of Positive Behavior Interventions, 13*(4), 219–229. https://doi.org/10.1177/1098300711399765

Walker, J. M. T. (2008). Looking at teacher practices through the lens of parenting style. *The Journal of Experimental Education, 76*(2), 218–240. https://doi.org/10.3200/JEXE.76.2.218-240

Webster-Stratton, C. (1990). *The incredible years: A trouble-shooting guide for parents of children ages 3–8 years*. Umbrella Press.

Webster-Stratton, C. (2000). *How to promote social and academic competence in young children*. Sage.

Webster-Stratton, C., Reid, M. J., & Hammond, M. (2001). Preventing conduct problems, promoting social competence: A parent and teacher training partnership in Head Start. *Journal of Clinical Child & Adolescent Psychology, 30*(3), 283–302. https://doi.org/10.1207/S15374424JCCP3003_2

Webster-Stratton, C., Reid, M. J., & Stoolmiller, M. (2008). Preventing conduct problems and improving school readiness: Evaluation of the Incredible Years teacher and child training programs in high-risk schools. *Journal of Child Psychology and Psychiatry, 49*(5), 471–488. https://doi.org/10.1111/j.1469-7610.2007.01861.x

Webster-Stratton, C., & Taylor, T. (2001). Nipping early risk factors in the bud: Preventing substance abuse, delinquency, and violence in adolescence through interventions targeted at young children (0–8 years). *Prevention Science, 2*(3), 165–192. https://doi.org/10.1023/A:1011510923900

Whitted, K. S. (2011). Understanding how social and emotional skill deficits contribute to school failure. *Preventing School Failure: Alternative Education for Children and Youth, 55*(1), 10–16. https://doi.org/10.1080/10459880903286755

Wigelsworth, M., Humphrey, N., Kalambouka, A., & Lendrum, A. (2010). A review of key issues in the measurement of children's social and emotional skills. *Educational Psychology in Practice, 26*(2), 173–186. https://doi.org/10.1080/02667361003768526

Woodruff, K., & Lee, B. (2011). Identifying and predicting problem behavior trajectories among pre-school children investigated for child abuse and neglect. *Child Abuse & Neglect, 35*(7), 491–503. https://doi.org/10.1016/j.chiabu.2011.03.007

Wyatt, T. R. (2014). Teaching across the lines: Adapting scripted programmes with culturally relevant/responsive teaching. *Pedagogy, Culture & Society, 22*(3), 447–469. https://doi.org/10.1080/14681366.2014.919957

APPENDIX A

Part 1: Communication styles and demographics

TABLE AA.1 Communication Styles and Demographics (CSD) Questionnaire: Parent version

Please take time to think about how you like to communicate when working with your child's educators. **There is no right or wrong answer** – simply record your response on each statement that best reflects your family situation. If you wish, please add comments to elaborate further.
1. My home language is____________________ My cultural background is __________________ At preschool, I prefer to communicate in my home language. Yes/No (please circle) At preschool, a translator would help me in my communication. Yes/No (please circle) At preschool, I prefer to communicate in English. Yes/No (please circle)
2. The times that suit me for parent–educator meetings or preschool gatherings are … (tick as many as you like) o Before kindergarten starts o Mornings o After kindergarten finishes o Evenings o During the kindergarten session o After dinner o Other__________________

TABLE AA.1 Cont.

<table>
<tr><td>3. a) The days that suits me the best for parent–educator meetings or preschool gatherings are … (please circle as many as you like): Monday/Tuesday/Wednesday/Thursday/Friday/Saturday/Sunday
b) Are there any barriers that may stop you attending preschool meetings? Yes/No.
If yes, please specify_______________________________</td></tr>
<tr><td>4. I prefer to communicate through … (tick as many as you like)
o Face-to-face meetings   o Smart phone applications
o Email   o Phone calls
o Text message   o Other ______________</td></tr>
<tr><td>5. My family comes to the preschool by (tick as many as you like)
o Walking
o Car
o Bike
o Other ___________________</td></tr>
<tr><td>6. I need to bring my child to parent–educator meetings as we don't have a babysitter. Yes/No (please circle)</td></tr>
<tr><td><u>Group size</u>
7. I enjoy working with large groups of people. Yes/No (please circle)
8. I prefer to be working with small groups of people. Yes/No (please circle)</td></tr>
<tr><td><u>Cultural practice</u>
9. When working with a parent–educator group I follow particular cultural practices. Yes/No (please circle)
If yes, please write down the cultural practices that are important to you.</td></tr>
<tr><td>Do you have other views on communication?

Yes/No (please circle)

If yes, what are your additional views on communication?</td></tr>
</table>

Part 2: Beliefs, Practices, and Relationships Questionnaire (BPRQ)

TABLE AA.2 Your beliefs on guiding children's behaviour

Please take some time to think about your beliefs on guiding children's behaviour and circle the number that applies best. **There is no right or wrong answer** – simply record your response to each statement that best reflects your beliefs. If you wish, please add comments at the end to elaborate further.

	Completely Disagree	Disagree	Agree	Completely Agree
1. I believe that my child's good behaviour needs to be praised/ encouraged frequently	1	2	3	4
2. I believe that giving affection to my child is important	1	2	3	4
3. I believe that when my child tries hard (even at the small things) I should give praise and encouragement	1	2	3	4
4. I believe that it is important to talk to my child about the bad behaviour when they misbehave	1	2	3	4
5. I believe that children need to be spoken to calmly when they are misbehaving	1	2	3	4
6. I believe that children must always do what I say	1	2	3	4
7. I believe that punishment is important when a child is misbehaving	1	2	3	4
8. I believe that children need to be told when they do not meet my expectations	1	2	3	4
9. I believe that there are times when I need to use an angry voice when my child is misbehaving	1	2	3	4

TABLE AA.2 Cont.

	Completely Disagree	Disagree	Agree	Completely Agree
10. I believe that parents should always be in control of their children	1	2	3	4
11. I believe that the child should always get what they want	1	2	3	4
12. I believe that bribes are OK in helping children be good	1	2	3	4
13. I believe I am confident in my parenting	1	2	3	4
14. I worry if I discipline my child they may not like me	1	2	3	4
15. I believe that bad behaviour needs to be ignored	1	2	3	4
16. I believe that parents take the main responsibility for raising a child	1	2	3	4
17. I believe that it takes many people to raise a child	1	2	3	4
18. I believe that eye contact is important when communicating	1	2	3	4
19. I believe that children's opinions are important	1	2	3	4
20. I believe that children should work hard to achieve success at kindergarten and school	1	2	3	4
21. I believe in a consistent routine for my child (e.g. bedtime routines, dinner routines, classroom routines)	1	2	3	4

(*continued*)

TABLE AA.2 Cont.

	Completely Disagree	Disagree	Agree	Completely Agree
22. I believe that my child should be encouraged to do things on their own	1	2	3	4
23. I believe that my child needs help with most things	1	2	3	4
24. I believe that children need to sit quietly at school	1	2	3	4
25. I believe that children should be able to voice their opinions at school	1	2	3	4
Do you have other views on guiding children's behaviour? Yes/No (please circle) **If yes, what are the additional views?**				

TABLE AA.3 Your parenting practice in guiding children's behaviour

Please take some time to think about your parenting practice in guiding children's behaviour and circle the number that applies best. **There is no right or wrong answer** – simply your response for each statement that best reflects your parenting practice. If you wish, please add comments at the end to elaborate further.

	Completely Disagree	**Disagree**	**Agree**	**Completely Agree**
1. I give more attention to good behaviours rather to than bad behaviours	**1**	**2**	**3**	**4**
2. I let my child know when they are doing a good job	**1**	**2**	**3**	**4**
3. I like to give frequent compliments to my child for good behaviour	**1**	**2**	**3**	**4**
4. I single out the good behaviours I want my child to do	**1**	**2**	**3**	**4**
5. I share how happy I feel with my child when they do things well	**1**	**2**	**3**	**4**
6. When my child has been naughty, has calmed down, and is being good again I immediately return my attention to the good behaviour	**1**	**2**	**3**	**4**
7. I make my praise and encouragement genuine when my child is playing well	**1**	**2**	**3**	**4**
8. I frequently let my child know that I believe that they can succeed	**1**	**2**	**3**	**4**
9. I encourage children to talk about themselves in positive ways	**1**	**2**	**3**	**4**

(*continued*)

TABLE AA.3 Cont.

	Completely Disagree	Disagree	Agree	Completely Agree
10. I share my child's good behaviour with my family and friends	1	2	3	4
11. I calmly explain to my child why his/her bad behaviour was wrong	1	2	3	4
12. I am consistent with how I address bad behaviour	1	2	3	4
13. I have a clear set of rules for my child	1	2	3	4
14. I involve my child in making up the rules	1	2	3	4
Are there any areas of behaviour guidance you would like more assistance with? Yes/No (please circle) **If yes, what are they?** **Do you have other views on behaviour guidance?** Yes/No (please circle) **If yes, what are they?**				

TABLE AA.4 Your relationship with your child's educators

Please take some time to think about your relationship with your child's educators and circle the number that applies best. **There is no right or wrong answer** – simply your opinion and perception on each statement that best reflects your family situation. If you wish, please add comments to elaborate further.

	Completely Disagree	**Disagree**	**Agree**	**Completely Agree**
1. I have clear communication with my child's educators	1	2	3	4
2. My child's educators are responsive to my child's needs	1	2	3	4
3. My child's educators are responsive to my family's needs	1	2	3	4
4. My child' educators value my child's and family's strengths	1	2	3	4
5. My child's educators are approachable	1	2	3	4
6. My child's educators are caring	1	2	3	4
7. My child's educators honour our cultural beliefs	1	2	3	4
8. My child's educators treat my family with dignity				
9. I feel that my child's educators view me as a partner in my child's development at kindergarten or school	1	2	3	4
10. I view my child's educators as partners in my child's development	1	2	3	4

Do you have anything else that you feel is important to mention about your relationship with your child's educators? Yes/No (please circle)

If yes, please elaborate below.

APPENDIX B

Adapted from: Tyler-Merrick, G. M. (2015). *Screening for Antisocial Development*. [Doctoral thesis, University of Canterbury]. https://ir.canterbury.ac.nz/handle/10092/10263.

Part 1: Children with behavioural difficulties

Instructions for teachers

1. Read the definition of "children with behaviour difficulties" in Table AB.1 and write down the names of any children in your kindergarten who qualify as "children with behavioural difficulties."
2. When completed, pass this form to the Head Teacher.

TABLE AB.1 Children with behavioural difficulties

Teacher Nomination Form

(Kindergarten 3–6-year-olds)

Kindergarten: ___________________________ **Session:**___________

Teacher's initials:____________________ **Today's date:** __/ __/ __

Children with behaviour difficulties

Please list any children in your kindergarten who (a) comply with teacher instructions much less frequently than other children of the same age and any children who (b) engage in antisocial behaviour much more frequently than other children of the same age.

	Child who meets definition above	***Child who does not meet the definition above and is of the same age and gender***
1		
2		
3		
4		
5		
6		

Part 2: Social Development Rating Scale

Instructions for teachers

The scale that follows in Tables AB.3 and 4 consists of descriptions of 30 different social behaviours.

1 Decide whether each of these behaviours is one that the child identified in Table AB.2 engages in "very frequently," "often," "about half the time," occasionally," or "not at all" and *place a circle* around the appropriate number.
2 When making these decisions, please take into account only the behaviour that you yourself have seen. It is most important that you do not allow your judgement to be influenced by what other people have told you.
3 When making these decisions, please take into account only the behaviour that you have seen during the past four weeks. It is most important that you do not allow your judgement to be affected by earlier events.
4 When making these decisions, please record your immediate or first impression. Do not spend time pondering over individual behaviours.
5 Please complete every item. An incomplete scale cannot be used.
6 Each scale takes about ten minutes to complete. Please select a period of time when you know that you will be free from interruptions to complete the scale.
7 After completion, please return your scale(s) to the Head Teacher.

Thank you for your assistance.

TABLE AB.2 Social Development Rating Scale: Child's details

Social Development Rating Scale

To be completed by the teacher. Use this Scale for 3- to6-year-old children

(Please select where necessary)

Kindergarten:	Child's initials:	**Gender**	
		Girl	Boy
DOB:	Age: yrs months	Ethnicity:	
Does this child have a disability?		Yes	No
If yes, name the disability			
Has the kindergarten received extra assistance for this child within the past 12 months? e.g. from early intervention, etc.		Yes	No
Does the kindergarten currently receive extra assistance for this child? e.g. from early intervention, etc.		Yes	No
Is this child on the early intervention/other waiting list?		Yes	No
Does this child currently receive 2 or more hours per day of teacher aide assistance?		Yes	No
For how long have you had day-to-day contact with this child?	Weeks		
This scale completed by: *(initials only)*	Date:		

For Office Use Only	Part 1	
	Part 2	
	Total	

TABLE AB.3 Social Development Rating Scale Part 1

Part 1	(Please select one number for each item)				
	Very frequently	*Often*	*About half the time*	*Occasionally*	*Never*
1. Knows and complies with centre limits and boundaries.	**5**	**4**	**3**	**2**	**1**
2. Complies promptly with teacher instructions.	**5**	**4**	**3**	**2**	**1**
3. Joins adult directed activities (e.g. coming to the mat) as soon as this is signalled or requested.	**5**	**4**	**3**	**2**	**1**
4. Persists with (continues to work on) tasks when left unsupervised.	**5**	**4**	**3**	**2**	**1**
5. Uses polite remarks/requests to gain the attention of peers.	**5**	**4**	**3**	**2**	**1**
6. Responds appropriately when other children try to interact socially with him/her.	**5**	**4**	**3**	**2**	**1**
7. Shows interest in what others are saying during conversations, e.g. by nodding, smiling, commenting, etc.	**5**	**4**	**3**	**2**	**1**
8. Shows appreciation when others offer to help, e.g. by smiling, saying "thank you", etc.	**5**	**4**	**3**	**2**	**1**
9. Takes his/her turn when others are waiting.	**5**	**4**	**3**	**2**	**1**
10. Eats, drinks, and behaves appropriately during break/snack time.	**5**	**4**	**3**	**2**	**1**
11. Compromises with others when conflicts or disagreements arise.	**5**	**4**	**3**	**2**	**1**

(*continued*)

TABLE AB.3 Cont.

Part 1	(Please select one number for each item)				
	Very frequently	*Often*	*About half the time*	*Occasionally*	*Never*
12. Offers toys to, and shares toys with, others.	**5**	**4**	**3**	**2**	**1**
13. Approaches peer groups in a way thatresults in acceptance into the current group activity or conversation.	**5**	**4**	**3**	**2**	**1**
14. Associates with a range of typically developing peers.	**5**	**4**	**3**	**2**	**1**
15. Expresses anger appropriately (without becoming destructive or violent).	**5**	**4**	**3**	**2**	**1**

TABLE AB.4 Social Development Rating Scale Part 2

Part 2	(Please select one number for each item)				
	Very frequently	*Often*	*About half the time*	*Occasionally*	*Never*
16. Ignores initial requests and directions even though he/she has heard them.	**1**	**2**	**3**	**4**	**5**
17. Reacts in a cheeky or impertinent way to requests or directions from adults.	**1**	**2**	**3**	**4**	**5**
18. Continues talking after others have indicated that they would like to comment or that they would like to get on with something else.	**1**	**2**	**3**	**4**	**5**
19. Interrupts or annoys others when they are working or relaxing on their own.	**1**	**2**	**3**	**4**	**5**
20. Disrupts the play or the activities of the other children.	**1**	**2**	**3**	**4**	**5**

TABLE AB.4 Cont.

Part 2	(Please select one number for each item)				
	Very frequently	*Often*	*About half the time*	*Occasionally*	*Never*
21. Uses demands where others would use requests.	1	2	3	4	5
22. Continues to plead, nag, or whine after his/her initial request or demand has been refused.	1	2	3	4	5
23. Tries to get own way by throwing tantrums e.g. by sulking or shouting, or swearing and refusing to cooperate.	1	2	3	4	5
24. Continues to behave inappropriately after being reprimanded, warned, or asked to stop.	1	2	3	4	5
25. Says things that indicate that he/she doesn't care about the consequences of his/her inappropriate behaviour.	1	2	3	4	5
26. Shouts others down when he/she disagrees with them.	1	2	3	4	5
27. Blames others when reprimanded for behaving inappropriately.	1	2	3	4	5
28. Acts violently towards others, e.g. shoves, hits, punches, or kicks others.	1	2	3	4	5
29. Does things that put the safety of other children at risk (e.g. throws hard objects or hits with objects).	1	2	3	4	5
30. Behaves in ways that result in other students actively avoiding having to talk or play with him/her.	1	2	3	4	5

APPENDIX C

TABLE AC.1 Child observation

The TOGETHER programme: Child observation sheet			Page:
Preschool name:	Session no:	Date: / /	
Setting: preschool/home (circle)	Educator name/code:		
Child's name/code:	Parent name/code:		
BL / PI / FU (circle) 0b 1 / Ob 2 / Ob 3	Start time:	Finish time:	

Note: *If no interaction between an adult/peer is occurring still record if child is being appropriate or inappropriate every minute and place line though columns 2, 3, 4, and 6 (for target/control child observations only).*

R = request; S = signal; Q = question; PP = positive praise; CP = contingent praise; D = discouragements; Xt = planned ignoring; X = no response

1. Observation	2. Educator/ parent	3. Other child	4. Educator/ parent compliance request			5. Child behaviour		6. Educator/parent/child response to appropriate or inappropriate behaviour					7. Notes
1			R	S	Q	App	InApp	PP	CP	D	Xt	X	
2			R	S	Q	App	InApp	PP	CP	D	Xt	X	
3			R	S	Q	App	InApp	PP	CP	D	Xt	X	
4			R	S	Q	App	InApp	PP	CP	D	Xt	X	
5			R	S	Q	App	InApp	PP	CP	D	Xt	X	
6			R	S	Q	App	InApp	PP	CP	D	Xt	X	

7			R	S	Q	App	InApp	PP	CP	D	Xt	X	
8			R	S	Q	App	InApp	PP	CP	D	Xt	X	
9			R	S	Q	App	InApp	PP	CP	D	Xt	X	
10			R	S	Q	App	InApp	PP	CP	D	Xt	X	
11			R	S	Q	App	InApp	PP	CP	D	Xt	X	
12			R	S	Q	App	InApp	PP	CP	D	Xt	X	
13			R	S	Q	App	InApp	PP	CP	D	Xt	X	
14			R	S	Q	App	InApp	PP	CP	D	Xt	X	
15			R	S	Q	App	InApp	PP	CP	D	Xt	X	
16			R	S	Q	App	InApp	PP	CP	D	Xt	X	
17			R	S	Q	App	InApp	PP	CP	D	Xt	X	
18			R	S	Q	App	InApp	PP	CP	D	Xt	X	
19			R	S	Q	App	InApp	PP	CP	D	Xt	X	
20			R	S	Q	App	InApp	PP	CP	D	Xt	X	
			R	S	Q	App	InApp	PP	CP	D	Xt	X	
Sheet totals													
All sheet totals													

TABLE AC.2 Teacher observation

The TOGETHER programme: Teacher observation sheet | Page:

Preschool name:	Session no:	Date: / /	
Setting: preschool/home (circle)	Educator name/code:		
Child's name/code:	Parent name/code:		
BL / PI / FU (circle) 0b 1 / Ob 2 / Ob 3	Start time:	Finish Time	

Note: *If no interaction between an adult/peer is occurring still record if child is being appropriate or inappropriate every minute and place line though columns 2, 3, 4, and 6 (for target/control child observations only).*

R = request; S = signal; Q = question; PP = positive praise; CP = contingent praise; D = discouragements; Xt = planned ignoring; X = no response

1. Observation	2. Notes on requests	3. Educator/ parent compliance request			4. Child behaviour		5. Educator/parent/child response to appropriate or inappropriate behaviour					6. Notes
1		R	S	Q	App	InApp	PP	CP	D	Xt	X	
2		R	S	Q	App	InApp	PP	CP	D	Xt	X	
3		R	S	Q	App	InApp	PP	CP	D	Xt	X	
4		R	S	Q	App	InApp	PP	CP	D	Xt	X	
5		R	S	Q	App	InApp	PP	CP	D	Xt	X	
6		R	S	Q	App	InApp	PP	CP	D	Xt	X	

7		R	S	Q	App	InApp	PP	CP	D	Xt	X	
8		R	S	Q	App	InApp	PP	CP	D	Xt	X	
9		R	S	Q	App	InApp	PP	CP	D	Xt	X	
10		R	S	Q	App	InApp	PP	CP	D	Xt	X	
11		R	S	Q	App	InApp	PP	CP	D	Xt	X	
12		R	S	Q	App	InApp	PP	CP	D	Xt	X	
13		R	S	Q	App	InApp	PP	CP	D	Xt	X	
14		R	S	Q	App	InApp	PP	CP	D	Xt	X	
15		R	S	Q	App	InApp	PP	CP	D	Xt	X	
16		R	S	Q	App	InApp	PP	CP	D	Xt	X	
17		R	S	Q	App	InApp	PP	CP	D	Xt	X	
18		R	S	Q	App	InApp	PP	CP	D	Xt	X	
19		R	S	Q	App	InApp	PP	CP	D	Xt	X	
20		R	S	Q	App	InApp	PP	CP	D	Xt	X	
		R	S	Q	App	InApp	PP	CP	D	Xt	X	
Sheet totals												
All sheet totals												

INDEX

Lightning Source UK Ltd.
Milton Keynes UK
UKHW022211091122
411944UK00008B/49

9 781032 045979